Edwin Abbott Abbott

Bible Lessons

Edwin Abbott Abbott

Bible Lessons

ISBN/EAN: 9783337095840

Printed in Europe, USA, Canada, Australia, Japan

Cover: Foto ©Lupo / pixelio.de

More available books at **www.hansebooks.com**

BY THE

REV. EDWIN A. ABBOTT, M.A.

HEAD MASTER OF THE CITY OF LONDON SCHOOL.

London:

MACMILLAN AND CO.

1871

[*The Right of Translation and Reproduction is reserved.*]

LONDON:
R. CLAY, SONS, AND TAYLOR, PRINTERS,
BREAD STREET HILL.

PREFACE.

THESE Bible Lessons exhibit, with some compressions and alterations, the nature of the religious instruction which I have been for the last four or five years in the habit of giving to the two highest classes in the City of London School. My object has been twofold. In the first place, I have endeavoured to avoid all mention or question about incidents of Sacred History which do not illustrate morality. The length and breadth of Palestine, the names and dates of all the Kings of Judah and Israel; the enumeration of all the miracles of Elijah and Elisha; the number and names of the wives of Herod—these and similar facts have been studiously avoided, except where they throw light on other facts of greater importance. The staple of my teaching has been truths of a different kind—truths that bear more directly upon the gradual development of Divine revelation and human morality, by which the Supreme Being is shown to us in the Bible as training, guiding, rewarding, punishing, and judging nations and individuals, that He may bring them nearer to Himself, teaching them line upon line and precept upon precept until they were prepared for that complete Revelation of God as a Father which is given in Christ Jesus our Lord. In brief, the spirit, not the statistics of the Bible, is the subject of these dialogues. I have found that it is possible for boys to leave school (and, I may add, for men to give up reading and believing in the Bible) without ever having had explained to them, or ever having understood, the meaning of such terms as prophecy, forgiveness, resentment, vindictiveness, prayer, sacrifice, priest, mercy, faith, miracle, sign, and many others that may be called technical terms of the Old and New Testament. One object of this treatise is to furnish a kind of dictionary of such technical terms. Only, as it is extremely important that boys should thoroughly understand and not merely repeat the correct explanation, I have preferred, where time allowed, to let them find out the truth for themselves in the course of a dialogue instead of setting the truth before them in a lecture. In practice the dialogue would be no doubt more lengthy than it is in this book, but though it has been absolutely necessary to omit and compress much, I have inserted many erroneous answers that are very commonly given, and that illustrate the ordinary difficulties which present themselves to boys.

It may be thought that difficulties are unnecessarily brought forward and dwelt upon in these pages. My reply must be, first, that the difficulties are introduced in order that they may be at least partially solved; and, secondly, that the teaching is intended for boys old enough to think for themselves, who have begun to think, and are not likely to cease thinking. Sooner or later these difficulties must be faced, and, as far as I know anything of Cambridge and Oxford, it is much better that a youth should go from school prepared with some explanation of difficulties than in the expectation of finding the explanation at the Universities. It is a painful and a common experience to meet with men of high culture and training (as far as the Universities give culture and training) who have ceased to believe in Christ. When asked for the reason of their disbelief, they have often alleged reasons so slight, difficulties so trivial (in comparison with the real difficulties and obstacles to belief), that the replies at once show they have never thoroughly studied either the Old or New Testament. In these circumstances, it must surely be the duty of every teacher to endeavour so to arm his pupils that they may not fall before the first slight missile—as old, may be, as Juvenal and older, but now furbished up to look like new—that may assail the utility and reality of prayer, or the general morality of the Bible.

My second object is negative. It has been to avoid giving offence. The Act of Parliament upon which the City of London School is founded enacts simply that "the Authorized Version of the Scriptures shall be read and taught." No restrictions are laid upon the teacher, except such as may be implied by the letter and spirit of these words. But at least a third of the sixth form are Nonconformists. I need hardly say, therefore, that any teacher would feel bound in honour—and all the more because of the absence of definitive restriction, which leaves the pupils comparatively unprotected—to abstain from anything that may injure the feelings or insidiously change the peculiar denominational opinions of any of his Christian pupils. I conceive that a teacher is more worthy, not less, of the honour of being called a minister of the Church of England, because he does not forget that he is a Christian also, and must do to the children of others as he would that others should do to a child of his.

Different views may be taken of the disadvantage under which this self-imposed restriction places the teacher. I can only say that I am scarcely sensible of any disadvantage. The mass of Biblical truth on which all Protestant scholars are agreed is so vast, and the ignorance of boys is so great, that I have never yet had leisure to turn my attention to any of the points of difference between the Church of England and Nonconformist Protestants. The only exception to this statement is the desirableness of Infant Baptism. The remarks on this point (on which I feel somewhat strongly) have not been delivered in the class-room.

The questions annexed to each chapter and placed at the end of the book may serve as useful exercises whether answered orally or on paper. I am not without a hope that this book may help to make the Bible more intelligible in private families as well as in schools. At present, I say it with shame, a careful and thorough study is bestowed by English boys on the letter and spirit of Thucydides and Plato that is not yet deigned to the Holy Scriptures.

CITY OF LONDON SCHOOL,
  July, 1870.
                    E. A. A.

PREFACE TO PART II.

THE purpose of the following pages has been already explained in the Preface to the First Part, which treats of the Old Testament. Were it not for the remarkable ambiguities and varieties of interpretation attending the word "unsectarian," I would briefly describe these Lessons as "an attempt to teach unsectarian theology." There are passages—as, for example, those which touch on Transubstantiation and Infant Baptism—which are added for completeness, and have not formed a part of my actual teaching in the class-room. These are exceptional passages; and there may be other expressions scattered here and there which I should modify if I were teaching a class of pupils of whose religious opinions I knew nothing more than that they profess the Christian faith. But the great bulk of the dialogues represents in the spirit, and often in the words, the religious instruction which I have been in the habit of giving to the Fifth and Sixth Forms of the City of London School.

It need scarcely be said to any who have practical experience in teaching, that the dialogues in the class-room would be longer and less condensed than they appear in this book. For the sake of economizing space and increasing the interest, I have assumed for my *Pupil* in the dialogues somewhat—not, I think, much, more than the average of ability and quickness. In practice, a teacher would select those who were rather below than above the average for his interlocutors, in order to draw out as distinctly as possible his pupils' ignorance before he attempted to teach. I may add, that though the dialogues often represent the actual words of my teaching, it does not follow that the Lessons were given *continuously* in the form in which they are here set down. On the contrary, the dialogues on the Life and Times of Christ, the Technical Terms of St. Paul, and Christian Casuistry, would be scattered over the work of several terms, or even years, according as the portion of the Bible that happened to be studied suggested this or that remark. In a word, the dialogues which here appear independent have been practically a dependent commentary upon the portions of Scripture read from time to time.

These remarks are intended to answer the inquiries of several able and experienced teachers as to the exact way in which it is hoped that the book may be useful in schools. Certainly not as a book to be got up by pupils and to be reproduced verbatim, nor as a book that will *pay* in examinations. But I do venture to hope that in the Sixth Forms of our principal Public Schools there may be some pupils in whose hands this specimen of Sixth Form teaching may be placed with advantage, and with the result of inducing them to think a little about phrases which are far more often repeated than understood. If I could believe that still older readers, and in some cases teachers themselves, might think it worth while to consult my book, my wishes would be amply gratified. The Questions in the Appendix are intended to increase the utility of the work for Schools and Teachers.

I must own one other object. For the State Schools, which may hereafter be supported by the rates, it is enacted that "no religious catechism or religious formulary which is *distinctive of any particular denomination* shall be taught in the school." There appears to be at present some confusion as to the meaning of these words. It would seem that they do not exclude any religious formulary which is already adopted, or may hereafter be adopted, by two or more denominations. But whatever may be the meaning ultimately attached to these words, it is surely a desirable object to show, if possible, that without catechism, creed, or formulary, a Christian schoolmaster, if he is allowed to explain the Bible in a Christian spirit, can teach a mixed class of Christian pupils something of their duty toward God, their duty toward individuals, and their duty toward their country.

If this cannot be done, and if the privilege of thus using the Bible is to be taken from schoolmasters in rate-aided schools, then we may shortly expect to find the moral tone of a profession in which much depends upon moral tone, seriously lowered; for who can wonder if many schoolmasters, who have hitherto enjoyed the privilege of giving direct moral instruction through the medium of the Bible, are unable to accept without some sense of degradation their new position, in which they are to be told that this privilege is forfeited? If this cannot be done, it will also follow that great masses of English children will depend for their religious instruction, supposing them to receive any, entirely upon the professed Ministers of Religion, who will be forced to monopolize the interpretation of the Bible—a result, in the opinion of many laymen, not to be desired, and not likely to diminish our present sectarian differences.

But if, on the other hand, this can be done with a class of boys, some of whom are verging upon manhood and old enough fully to appreciate the force of denominational differences, may it not far more easily be done in the case of elementary instruction given to little children, for whom the most appropriate "Bible Lessons" will be the stories of the Good Samaritan and the Prodigal Son?

CITY OF LONDON SCHOOL,   E. A. A.
   November, 1870.

TABLE OF CONTENTS.

PART I.—*OLD TESTAMENT.*

CHAPTER I.
GOD'S PURPOSE AS REVEALED IN THE BIBLE 11–16

CHAPTER II.
GOD'S TRAINING OF THE PATRIARCHS 17–28

CHAPTER III.
GOD'S TRAINING OF THE NATION OF ISRAEL 29–50

CHAPTER IV.
SACRIFICES AND PRIESTS 51–59

CHAPTER V.
PROPHETS 60–78

QUESTIONS 79–88

PART II.—*NEW TESTAMENT.*

CHAPTER I.
THE TIMES OF CHRIST 91–105

CHAPTER II.
THE LIFE OF CHRIST 106–138

CHAPTER III.
CHRIST'S MIRACLES 139–152

CHAPTER IV.
CHRIST'S SACRIFICE 153–159

CHAPTER V.
LOVE 160–166

CHAPTER VI.
FORGIVENESS 167–181

CHAPTER VII.
FAITH 182–195

CHAPTER VIII.
PRAYER 196–207

CHAPTER IX.
THE SACRAMENTS 208–222

CHAPTER X.
THE HOLY SPIRIT 223–237

CHAPTER XI.
THE TECHNICAL TERMS OF ST. PAUL 238–248

CHAPTER XII.
CHRISTIAN CASUISTRY, OR THE APPLICATION OF CHRIST'S TEACHING TO MODERN TIMES 249–260

QUESTIONS 261–272

BIBLE LESSONS.

PART I.—*OLD TESTAMENT.*

CHAPTER I.

GOD'S PURPOSE AS SHEWN IN THE BIBLE.

Teacher.[1]—Who made man?
Pupil.—God.
Teacher.—God created many other things before man. Can you tell me why?
Pupil.—Man could not have existed until the world had been prepared and replenished for his support.
Teacher.—True. Of course it might be called in one sense possible for God (though it was not really possible for Him to go against His own will and order) to create man at once, while the earth was still "without form, and void." But it pleased Him to plan His works upon a scheme of progress, from the lower to the higher. Millions of years (for the six days of creation do not represent the literal truth) passed away, while creation rose higher and higher in the scale of vital development, till at last man was created. Thus at the very outset the Bible reminds us that the processes of God's operations are often slow and gradual; and that His highest works are sometimes preceded by a very long course of preparation. How is God said to have created man different from other animals?

---

[1] Critical questions concerning the interpretation of this and other passages of the Bible are not discussed in these Dialogues.

Pupil.—God made man in His own image.

Teacher.—What do you mean by that? In what respects was man made in the image of God?

Pupil.—In wisdom and power.

Teacher.—These are attributes of God. But no author in the Holy Scriptures says "God is Wisdom" or "Power;" whereas St. John says——?

Pupil.—God is Love.

Teacher.—Then man is most like God when he can love most perfectly, and man is more like God than other animals are because he is able to do this to a greater degree than they are, and because his love is combined with reason and will, and not dictated by instinct. Now tell me whether men have completely lost the image of God?

Pupil.—No; for they still retain some power of loving one another.

Teacher.—Has God given up His intention of making men exactly like Himself?

Pupil.—That seems impossible.

Teacher.—It is impossible. God cannot fail. Though we may have to wait as many millions of years for the fulfilment of the perfect creation, as the world had to wait for the first creation of man, God is bent on making us like Himself. For that purpose, ever since the creation of the world, He has been unveiling His nature to us, inviting us to know Him, to respect Him, to trust in Him, and to love Him; because, if we can only love Him, we shall become (such is the spiritual law) like Him, and conformed to His image. This unveiling of God's nature is called——?

Pupil.—Revelation.

Teacher.—What other Revelation has God given of Himself beside the Bible?

Pupil.—Nature.

Teacher.—Yes; God has revealed Himself to men partly through inanimate nature, shewing that He is a God of Order, in the orderly motions of the planets and the regular recurrence of the seasons. His power and love are partially revealed by the beauty and grandeur of His works, and by the care with which the world appears to have been adapted to the support and development of its tenants. But has God revealed himself in no other natural way beside the Bible? You, when you were a child, how did you gain your first notion of goodness and kindness?

Pupil.—I suppose from my parents.

Teacher.—Well then, God has also revealed Himself through animate nature, especially through human beings. From the love which binds together father and child, husband and wife, brother and sister; from the affection which unites together friends, acquaintances, and fellow-countrymen, He has led men onwards in an ever-widening circle of love, which is intended at last to include all those who are made in God's image—that is, all men; and thus at the same time He has led men through recognizing His image to recognize Himself, the Supreme Love. But has this "natural revelation," as it may be called, proved sufficient? If not, why not?

Pupil.—Because men misunderstood God.

Teacher.—True. Men reversed God's process, and made gods in their own image, instead of suffering Him to conform them to His. They thought more highly of the power, wisdom, and skill which they perceived in the world and in themselves, than of love, and therefore they made unto themselves a god of Power, and another of Wisdom, and another of Skill, and another of mere sensual Love; and they worshipped their false gods, and missed the meaning of the true God. Besides, there is a special difficulty in nature which prevents men from trusting in God.

Pupil.—I suppose you mean death?

Teacher.—Yes, death. The fact that the life of one half of the creation is being perpetually supported by the death of the other half; and again the fear that there may be nothing after death—no meeting of friends, no power of loving, no presence of God—but that the soul dies with the body, so that men need do no more than "eat and drink, for to-morrow they die." How then did God further reveal Himself?

Pupil.—He revealed Himself to the Patriarchs and Prophets, and through them to the Children of Israel and to other nations. But above all He sent His own Son, who lived and died, upon earth. He was perfectly good, and had power to draw men to Himself, and to make men like Himself, and therefore like God.

Teacher.—But why did not God send His Son before, in order to reveal Himself, instead of suffering the world to live on for so many hundreds of years in darkness and ignorance?

Pupil.—I do not know.

Teacher.—Nor do I *know*. But I think it can be illustrated by other actions of God. Have we not inferred from the Bible, and does not geology teach us, that the world went on for millions of years tenanted by animals of a very low order in vital organization before man was created; and by analogy may we not expect a considerable interval to elapse from the creation of the first man to the birth of the perfect Man? And as in the former case creation rose not at once, but gradually in the scale of development till the way was prepared as it were for man, so may we not expect a gradual training and progress in morality as a preparation for the coming of the perfect Man? Let me make this clear. Tell me; is it possible for a boy to begin Long Division as soon as he begins Arithmetic?

Pupil.—No. He must learn the four simple rules first.

Teacher.—And in the same way, I take it, it was necessary for the human race to learn the simple rules of morality before they could reach the highest of all knowledge—the knowledge of God. And the history of the world, and above all that part of it which contains the history of the Jewish people and their ancestors, tells us how God gradually taught men the rules or laws of morality, and prepared them to learn the highest lesson of all, which Christ came at last to teach. You told me that St. John speaks of God as being "Love." How did Christ speak of God, and by what title did he exhort us to pray to God?

Pupil.—He taught us to call God "Our Father."

Teacher.—Now what do you learn from that title about God and His dealings with us?

Pupil.—We learn, I suppose, that if we want to know anything about God, we ought to consider the conduct of the best possible human father toward his children.

Teacher.—Well, and how does a good father act towards his children? Does he give them all that they ask? Does he always reward, or sometimes also punish? Does he tell his children everything beforehand, or, while he warns them of some dangers, does he allow them to find out others by painful and impressive experience? Does he keep them out of all temptations, or suffer them to undergo some temptations in order that they may grow strong by trial and resistance? Does he, in a word, do everything for them, or train them to do much for themselves?

Pupil.—He trains them to act for themselves.

Teacher.—And does such a father encourage his children to express their desires to him, or to suppress them? Does he laugh at their wishes when they happen to be childish or foolish, or does he explain to them, either by word or deed, either at once or in course of time, why their desires cannot be granted?

Pupil.—He will never laugh at them, because they could not feel trust in him if they hid anything from him, and they would hide their wishes from him if he laughed at them.

Teacher.—Well, in the same way, we may believe that God the Father punishes and rewards, teaches by warnings and by experience, and listens to the prayers of His children; and we are now going to trace how He did all these things in His dealings with the Patriarchs and the people of Israel, and how He gradually prepared men to recognize Him as a Father. But, before we pass on to the History of the Old Testament, let me ask you one final question or two. We have agreed, have we not, that the purpose of God as manifested in the Bible is to reveal Himself to men as the Father, and to conform men perfectly to His own image?

Pupil.—Yes.

Teacher.—But do you not remember who is said to be, not, like ordinary men, "made in God's image," but "the express image of God?"

Pupil.—Yes, in the Epistle to the Hebrews this title is given to Christ.

Teacher.—It follows then, does it not, that the purpose of God through the whole of the history of the world has been to conform men to the pattern of Christ, and that all His dealings with the heathen, the Patriarchs, and the people of Israel, as well as with us in modern times, have this object: and when this object is attained and men are conformed to Christ, the "express image" of God, then, and not till then, the purpose of God will have been perfectly fulfilled, "Let us make man in our own image." One last question. When is a man most like Christ? What was the sign of obedience and discipleship which Christ Himself gave us?

Pupil.—"By this shall all men know that ye are my disciples, if ye have love one to another."[1] .

Teacher.—Thus then we come round again through the precepts of Christ to the earliest teaching in the Bible, that man is most like God in his power of loving his fellow men, and we see the connection between theology and morality, between our relations with God and our relations with men. Conversely we shall see in Chapter ix. that it is not possible to love men without loving the Supreme Goodness in the image of which men are made.

[1] St. John xiii. 35.

CHAPTER II.

GOD'S TRAINING OF THE PATRIARCHS.[1]

Teacher.—Let us now consider how God is said to have revealed Himself to individuals in the History of the Old Testament. Abraham, Isaac, Jacob, Joseph, Moses,—were the lives of these men comfortable and full of pleasure, or did they have trials?

Pupil.—They had their trials.

Teacher.—Mention some of the trials of Abraham.

Pupil.—Abraham was tempted by God, and——

Teacher.—Stop. What do you mean when you say that Abraham was "tempted by God"? Does not St. James[2] say that God does not tempt any man? How do you explain this?

Pupil.—I cannot explain it.

Teacher.—Well, the word "tempt" is the same in many passages of the original text of the Bible as the word "try." God "tries" men for their good; the devil tempts men to their harm. Do you understand the difference?

Pupil.—Yes; but why does God suffer men to be tempted to their harm?

Teacher.—I am glad you asked that question, though it is one that I cannot answer. We cannot understand how it is that the all-loving and all-powerful God suffers men to be tempted to their harm, any more than we can understand why He permits sin. There are some mysteries in life that we shall never understand in this

---

[1] The plan adopted in this chapter is to take the Bible narrative just as it stands, without entering into any critical questions.

[2] St. James, Epist. i. 13.

world. If we could understand everything we should have no need of faith. We have need of faith, that we may trust in God in spite of appearances. While we are upon this subject I will ask you whether you know a case in which God is said to have tempted man to his harm? Turn to 2 Sam. xxiv. 1. Read it.

Pupil.—"And again the anger of the Lord was kindled against Israel, and he moved David against them to say, Go, number Israel and Judah."

Teacher.—Now the tenth verse.

Pupil.—"And David said unto the Lord, I have sinned greatly in that which I have done."

Teacher.—Yes, the sin is thought by some to have consisted in his ambitious purposes of foreign conquest. Now read 1 Chron. xxi. 1.

Pupil.—"And Satan stood up against Israel, and provoked David to number Israel."

Teacher.—Now then, who tempted David?

Pupil.—I do not know what to say. One place speaks of "the anger of the Lord," the other of "Satan."[1]

Teacher.—This is a very deep question, as I told you, and neither I nor anybody else will ever fathom it in this life. But it seems that Satan is regarded as intending to do his own will, but actually forced to execute the punishments of the Supreme—a mere tool to work "the anger of the Lord." We are taught by Milton similarly to believe that to God

"All things ill
Are but as slavish ministers of vengeance."

But now let us return to the temptations and trials of Abraham. What were they?

Pupil.—He was called upon to leave his home, friends, and country, and to exchange present certainties for the promise of future greatness. Then for many years he had no child to be his

---

[1] It seems probable that the later book, the Book of Chronicles, used the less difficult expression designedly.

heir, and when at last he had an heir, he felt bound to obey a voice from God which bade him offer up his only child as a sacrifice. His son was saved : but he had other trials. For though he felt assured by Divine promises that his descendants should become a great nation, and should dwell permanently in the very land in which he was wandering, yet he himself was a mere wanderer all his life.

Teacher.—What name do you give to that virtue which enabled Abraham to put trust in God's promises, which he could not hope himself to see fulfilled ?

Pupil.—Faith.

Teacher.—Yes ; faith in God. Well then, all these trials of Abraham successfully undergone strengthened his faith ; just as the continual trial to lift heavy weights, if they are not too heavy, and if they can be lifted without straining, strengthens the arm to lift weights still heavier.

Pupil.—But did Abraham's faith want strengthening ?

Teacher.—I think his conduct in Egypt[1] and in Gerar[2] showed that his faith did want strengthening, for he condescended to equivocation in order to avoid risk. But now let me ask you how far God revealed Himself to Abraham by means of promises, as distinct from the life-training which is afforded by trials and troubles, or by prosperity ? What is God recorded to have *said* to Abraham about Himself ?

Pupil.—I do not remember that He said anything, except that He would bless Abraham and be his shield and reward. He promised also that all the nations of the world should share in the blessing through him.

Teacher.—How many gods did Abraham worship ?

Pupil.—One only.

Teacher.—But almost all the rest of the world worshipped more than one. And even in the family of Laban, the son of Isaac's

---

[1] Gen. xii. 13.   [2] Ib. xx. 2.

cousin, there were "images"[1] which were called "gods."[2] But is it said that Abraham worshipped "gods" or thought that he was called by "gods"?

Pupil.—No; and therefore I suppose God must have revealed to Abraham that He was One.

Teacher.—What is the good of knowing that God is one? What was the mischief of believing in one god of Power, and another of Love, and another of Skill, as the heathens did?

Pupil.—They came to think that, since there were many gods, the will of one god might be different from the will of another; and so they believed the gods quarrelled among themselves and acted wickedly; and hence they might infer that men might do the same without much harm.

Teacher.—And by believing that God is One and infinitely Wise and Good, we are more likely to believe that He can never change His mind, and that His promises may be trusted, though the fulfilment may be deferred for thousands of years.

Pupil.—Yes, and I suppose the revelation that God is One helped Abraham to believe in God's promises.

Teacher.—Now did God reveal anything else about Himself to Abraham?

Pupil.—I do not know that He said anything else about Himself.

Teacher.—But God might reveal Himself, might He not, without the sound of uttered words or even without those sudden unaccountable thoughts which are often referred to the direct inspiration of God? A human father does not *say* to his child "I am wise" or "I am good," but he convinces his child of his wisdom and goodness by his actions. How then did God reveal Himself to Abraham?

Pupil.—He shewed that He could perform seeming impossibilities,

---

[1] Gen. xxxi. 19.

[2] Ib. xxxi. 30. See *Dict. Bible*, "Teraphim:" but compare Josh. xxiv. 2, which is less doubtful.

in giving him a son when Abraham seemed, humanly speaking, destined to be childless, and He also shewed Himself a present Guide and Protector as well as a Promiser of future blessings that should never fail.

Teacher.—Did God never appear to Abraham in the light of one who punishes?

Pupil.—No; not that I know of.

Teacher.—I can quite understand your saying so. Abraham is called "the friend of God," and there is scarcely any character in the whole of the Bible whose life contains so little reference to the trials and chastisements of God. But I dare say that word "chastisement" reminds you of a saying in the Epistle to the Hebrews about "chastening."

Pupil.—"Whom the Lord loveth He chasteneth."[1]

Teacher.—Yes, and therefore we cannot doubt that the long-continued childlessness of Abraham, his unsettled wanderings without end, the discord which obliged him to banish his first-born son Ishmael with the mother Hagar, the incredulous character of Sarah, the dissension between him and his nephew Lot,—all these troubles must have appeared to him sometimes as "chastening" that "for the present seemeth not to be joyous,"[2] while at other times he must have felt that he was being purified and taught by them, and that it was good for him to be afflicted. But all these punishments or chastenings were reformative, not destructive. Can you mention any passage in the life of Abraham where God sends destructive punishment?

Pupil.—He utterly destroyed the men of Sodom and Gomorrah in a single night.

Teacher.—Yes, with no further teaching or training for them, after they had rejected the teaching of Lot's example, no further leisure for repentance. He destroyed them in the midst of their sins. This is again one more of the many mysteries in the operations of Him who is called by Moses the God of the spirits of all flesh. We

---

[1] Heb. xii. 6.   [2] Ib. xii. 11.

cannot indeed tell whether the most sudden death may not leave some brief space for purifying pain. It may possibly be that even these kinds of death called instantaneous may, by the very suddenness of the shock, bring home to a sinner's soul feelings which a lingering death by disease might never have taught. About this we can never know the certainty. Thus much God has revealed, that sometimes when men are gone to certain lengths in sin, He destroys. He takes the sinners from this world into another. As Abraham believed, so are we with much better reason bound to believe, that He does all things rightly, and that, whatever is the ultimate fate of sinners, such destruction from the face of the earth is the best thing both for them and for their fellow-men. But now, did God reveal Himself to Abraham in any other way not yet mentioned?

Pupil.—Yes. God revealed Himself by a vision.[1] "When the sun went down and it was dark, behold a smoking furnace and a burning lamp that passed between the pieces" of the victim that he had sacrificed.

Teacher.—What did this mean?

Pupil.—I do not understand your question. It was a vision, a mystery.

Teacher.—What is the meaning of the word "vision?"

Pupil.—Something seen.

Teacher.—Is a landscape a vision?

Pupil.—A vision means something divine seen by a prophet or seer, not visible to ordinary men.

Teacher.—Something divine. I suppose then something true not false? Some truth of the Divine nature? And a "seer" is one who sees more than common men see of the Divine nature?

Pupil.—Yes.

Teacher.—What truth about the Divine nature did this vision reveal? Must it not be that the spiritual operations of God in some way resemble the material operations of fire?

Pupil.—Yes.

[1] Gen. xv. 17.

Teacher.—What are the operations of fire?

Pupil.—To consume, to enlighten, and to warm.

Teacher.—What passage in the Bible attributes this first operation to God?

Pupil.—The words in Heb. xii. 29: "For our God is a consuming fire."

Teacher.—Do we use fire to consume the metal or the dross? And therefore (if the analogy is to hold), does God consume what is good, or what is bad?

Pupil.—What is bad.

Teacher.—When we by means of fire separate the dross from the gold or silver, what process do we say the metal has passed through?

Pupil.—We say it has been tried or purified in the fire.

Teacher.—Do you remember any passage in the Bible where the "furnace" is used metaphorically for a place of "trial" or "purification?"

Pupil.—Egypt is called "the fiery furnace" because I suppose it tried the people of Israel.

Teacher.—Now I think you can understand part of the meaning of this vision.[1] God revealed Himself through fire as the Trier and Purifier, and also as the Giver of light and of the warmth of spiritual life. We shall see hereafter in what respects this vision resembles others that follow it; now, however, let me ask you to sum up the different ways in which God reveals Himself to Abraham?

Pupil.—God revealed Himself by blessings and trials from which Abraham could infer God's nature, by speaking sometimes more directly to his heart, and by visions.

Teacher.—Well, in the same way we can trace this triple revelation of God as it was given to others besides Abraham. Tell me something of the revelation by "trial" to Jacob, for instance. What was Jacob's great fault, and how was he purified from it?

---

[1] It should be added that it was customary for the contracting parties of a *covenant* to pass between the fragments of a sacrifice.

Pupil.—Jacob deceived his father Isaac. As a consequence of this deceit, he was forced to leave his home through fear of Esau, and to go to a foreign land where he lived as a servant under a deceitful master. Here he was deceived in receiving Leah for Rachel.

Teacher.—Yes, and after all his precautions he was forced to meet Esau and to humble himself before the brother whom he had injured. Thus by trials and patience he was trained from being Jacob, a "supplanter," to become Israel the "Prince of God." But even after that high title had been bestowed upon him, his trials were not yet ended. He was deceived by his wife Rachel, who stole the "gods" of her father Laban without her husband's knowledge; and finally, as he had deceived his father, so in turn he was outraged, deceived, and made miserable by his sons. Similarly Joseph, Gideon, Moses, and David, did not merely learn to acknowledge God as the Giver of joy and happiness. They were tried and trained both by many trials and adversity, and in particular by long periods of patient waiting that might have daunted any ambition that was not based upon unselfish confidence in God. In a word, the lives of the patriarchs and heroes of Israel (as well as the lives of the great men of all times in all nations) shew that "whom the Lord loveth He chasteneth," and that He often reveals Himself and blesses through trials. This was the first mode of revelation. Now for the second or more direct revelation. Tell me, what direct message about Himself is God said to have given to Jacob?

Pupil.—He repeated the blessing of Abraham, and further revealed Himself to Jacob by the name of God Almighty.[1]

Teacher.—Yes; and the whole course of Jacob's life and the wonderful manner in which he had been protected and guided in his exile might well have prepared him for this revelation. But can you mention any incident which seems to shew that the pure worship of the one God was not yet established even in the household of Jacob?

Pupil.—Jacob himself told his household to put away their strange gods.[2]

---

[1] Gen. xxxv. 11   [2] Ib. xxxv. 2.

Teacher.—Is the revelation of God as Almighty a perfect revelation?

Pupil.—No, not unless God's infinite goodness is revealed also. For men might believe that the world was governed by an Almighty evil spirit.

Teacher.—True, and in Exod. vi. 3, it is implied that the revelation to Jacob by the name of God Almighty was inferior to the revelation expressed to Moses by the name of Jehovah. It is generally thought that Jehovah implies the eternal oneness of God. By what other name did God reveal Himself to Moses?

Pupil.—As "I AM."

Teacher.—And what is implied in One who can always describe Himself as "I AM"?

Pupil.—Perpetual existence.

Teacher.—But if a mind is one mind at one time and another at another, can it describe itself as "I am" without incorrectness? What therefore is implied by this title besides eternity?

Pupil.—The unchangeableness of God's nature.

Teacher.—Still, an evil spirit may be all-powerful and always the same. Once more, therefore, what other revelation was given to Moses?

Pupil.—God proclaimed Himself as being "merciful and gracious, long-suffering and abundant in goodness and truth, keeping mercy for thousands, forgiving iniquity and transgression, and that will by no means clear the guilty: visiting the iniquity of the fathers upon the children and upon the children's children unto the third and fourth generation."[1]

Teacher.—Here again is one of the knots that cannot be loosed, though they may be cut. God is said to visit on children the sins of their fathers. And we see every day that it is so. The children of thieves or drunkards are frequently made thieves or drunkards themselves by the example of their parents. And besides, physical Nature is equally severe. Intemperance and vice in one generation often produce disease and melancholy in the second, and insanity or idiotcy

---
[1] Exod. xxxiv. 6, 7.

in the third or fourth. But supposing the melancholy or disease turns the hearts of the second generation to God, or suppose disgust and pity for the vices of their fathers deter the children from vice and guide them to virtue, then we may say, may we not, that though the punishment of the father's sin falls on the son, yet the punishment is really a blessing, and that the severity of Nature is but a tool in the hand of Mercy?

Pupil.—Yes.

Teacher.—This was felt to be a difficulty even by the Israelites, who sometimes excused their faults by saying that the faults of their fathers were visited upon them. But Ezekiel explained the meaning, and said that only the sinful children inherited the father's sins. I do not say this or any other explanation completely destroys the difficulty; but at least we can remember that those who find fault with it in the Bible are bound also to find fault with it in Nature, and that in some cases the visitation is a blessing and not a curse. Now, did Moses consider the revelation just now mentioned to be complete?

Pupil.—I do not know.

Teacher.—Well, in describing the promise of this same revelation, the Bible says that Moses could not see the "face," but only the "back parts" of God. Now we believe that God has no corporeal parts, and, therefore, that this is not literally true. How is it true then?

Pupil.—Metaphorically.

Teacher.—Expand the metaphor.

Pupil.—As by seeing the back of a man we cannot see much that will enable us to recognise him, and can only see the size and figure, but not the expression and features which are the most important parts of a man, so Moses could only receive the revelation of some few, and those not the most important, attributes of God.

Teacher.—Did Moses then look forward to a more complete revelation. Quote Deut. xviii. 15.

Pupil.—"The Lord thy God will raise up unto thee a Prophet from the midst of thee, of thy brethren, like unto me; unto him ye shall hearken."

Teacher.—Tell me briefly how did God reveal Himself to the Prophets in a manner different from the revelation of Moses.

Pupil.—I cannot express it briefly.

Teacher.—Justice, mercy, goodness and truth, inflexibility in punishing injustice combined with willingness to forgive those who repent—these were the attributes of God revealed to Moses, over and above His eternal nature and omnipotence. What more do we want in a revelation of God?

Pupil.—Perhaps we want nothing more, if we really can believe that God is perfectly good and merciful as well as just.

Teacher.—But why do we find it hard to believe that?

Pupil.—We sometimes see good men miserable and bad men happy, and that makes men doubt whether God can be perfectly just, or, if perfectly just, whether He can be perfectly powerful.[1] I suppose, too, since we ourselves are not perfectly good, we find it hard to believe that any one is.

Teacher.—Well then, how did the Prophets fill up this gap? They admitted, as you say, that there is much wrong in the world. Whom did they speak of as the Person who was to set it right? And to what new state of changed circumstances did they look forward?

Pupil.—They spoke of a Deliverer and King who was to rule in righteousness and destroy sin, and they looked forward to a time when there should be no more oppression and injustice, when the just should flourish and the unjust perish, and there should be no more war, famine, or poverty.

Teacher.—Did the blessings of this promised period extend to other nations beside Israel? What, for example, about the promise to Abraham?

Pupil.—It was said that in the seed of Abraham all the nations of the world should be blessed.

Teacher.—This part of the promise is repeated in different forms by the Prophets. We shall see this hereafter. Meanwhile I must

[1] Job.

ask you to remember that this expectation of a Deliverer or Redeemer, and the prophecies of His coming, run through the whole of the Old Testament. Men were expressly taught to be dissatisfied with the imperfect present, and to look forward not merely to a better but to a perfect future. What virtue is that which helps men to expect good and not evil as the ultimate result?

Pupil.—Faith.

Teacher.—Faith or Hope. Faith when the expectation is based on definite promises; Hope perhaps in other cases. It is well for us to remember that hopefulness is a virtue, one of the three Christian virtues. We now come to the third source of revelation, Visions; but it will be more convenient to discuss this in the chapter on the Prophets.

CHAPTER III.

GOD'S TRAINING OF THE NATION.

Teacher.—Let us now consider how God trained the people of Israel and made it a great nation. To do that I must first ask what constitutes a great nation?

Pupil.—I should have thought a great nation was one that was very powerful and wealthy, or one that had a very large population.

Teacher.—Why then, if wealth is that which constitutes greatness, Tyre might be considered the greatest of ancient cities; for Tyre had the carrying-trade of all the world, and her merchants were called princes. Yet Tyre is little more than a fishing-village now, and the name of Tyre is scarcely known in comparison with that of Jerusalem or Athens or Rome. And again, if numbers constitute a great nation, then I suppose at the present moment China is the greatest nation in the world.

Pupil.—Well then, power makes a great nation.

Teacher.—What sort of power? If you mean power to conquer, the Assyrians and Babylonians, or, in later times, the Tartars and Huns, were far greater than the nation of Israel.

Pupil.—But no one knows anything, or at least much, about them.

Teacher.—Why not?

Pupil.—Because they did little worth remembering except that they were conquerors.

Teacher.—What is worth remembering in the history of great nations; for example, in the history of Greece or Rome?

Pupil.—Their poems and laws, their investigations into truth, their skill in administration and organization, their patriotism, bravery, and perseverance—all these have influenced us.

Teacher.—Then a nation is great in proportion as it influences others, and all the commerce and carrying-trade in the world will not give greatness to a selfish, isolated, and uninfluential nation. Measured by this standard of greatness, is the nation of Israel great?

Pupil.—Yes, for we read the books of men of Israel more than those of any other nation. Their thoughts have become ours. We call English children by Jewish names. Our churches and cathedrals are consecrated to the memory of Jewish peasants; and, lastly, our blessed Lord himself was of that nation.

Teacher.—Your answer makes it clear that the greatness of Israel sprang from their knowledge of the one true God. For it was by this knowledge that they influenced us. How then did God prepare them for the reception of this knowledge? What do you think was the effect upon the people of Israel of their long bondage in Egypt?

Pupil.—I suppose they were "tried" by it, as Abraham and Jacob were tried.

Teacher.—Their bondage in Egypt gave them a protection under which they gradually increased, and from being a collection of nomadic families became a nation. This they could not have done, perhaps, had they still wandered like Abraham in Canaan. This was an advantage. But if you were enslaved for thirty or forty years, would that have a good effect upon your character? Your servitude might make you long for liberty. Might it not also make you cowardly, cringing and deceitful?

Pupil.—I suppose it might.

Teacher.—And if your master were wiser and better educated than you, and yet an idolater, would not you be in danger of falling into idolatry?

Pupil.—Yes. But did the people of Israel become idolaters, and were they made cowardly by their bondage?

Teacher.—As to idolatry, Joshua [1] tells them to put away the gods which their fathers served in Egypt; and Ezekiel [2] alludes to the

[1] Josh. xxiv. 14.   [2] Ezek. xx. 7, 8.

same fault. And then, as to their becoming cowardly, did they not lose heart repeatedly in moments of danger under Moses their deliverer? Did they not at times long after the old servitude and plenty which they had enjoyed in Egypt, and murmur against their leader? And because they were so demoralized, so unfit to undertake the conquest of Canaan, were they not forced to wander for forty years in Arabia till a new and bolder generation had sprung up?

Pupil.—Yes.

Teacher.—During these forty years, how did God reveal Himself to the nation?

Pupil.—By delivering, guiding, and punishing them, and by giving them a Law.

Teacher.—We will speak of the Law presently. What did the people of Israel learn of God from their deliverance and subsequent guidance through the desert?

Pupil.—I suppose they learned to regard Him as a God of Righteousness who would not tolerate oppression, but would judge the cause of the weak against the strong. They must also have learned that He would punish rebellion and discontent, and that though He would deliver them from slavery, He would not deliver them from labour and hardship.

Teacher.—And from the Law, what direct revelation did they obtain?

Pupil.—They learned that God was just and holy, requiring justice and holiness in His worshippers, and extending His claim upon their allegiance even to the unfulfilled desires, for they were forbidden to "covet" as well as to "steal." It was also impressed upon them in the new name of Jehovah that God was one and unchangeable.

Teacher.—There was perhaps less temptation to polytheism in a monotonous desert like Arabia than in a land of cornfields or pastures with woods, hills and streams. Can you tell why? Who were the Oreads, Dryads, and Naiads among the Greeks?

Pupil.—They were the Deities of the mountains, the trees and the springs. I suppose polytheists worship God's separate works instead of God: and wherever His works strike the mind as being various and separate, men would be in most danger of polytheism. But where all Nature seemed the same, they might be in less danger of forgetting that God is one.

Teacher.—True; and yet even in the desert the men of Israel were drawn into the worship of other gods beside Jehovah. Can you mention any instances? Turn to the speech of Stephen in Acts vii. 43.

Pupil.—They worshipped a golden calf and the gods, Moloch and Remphan.

Teacher.—Well, it is thought that the fire-god Moloch may be connected with the planet Saturn, and observe, he speaks of the "star of Remphan, figures which ye made to worship them:" and perhaps it is natural that in a great level desert those who are ready to worship things created instead of the Creator should bow down before stars as the most conspicuous objects for admiration. But we do not know for certain the exact natures of these gods or of the worship of the golden calf. I will now only ask you whether you can explain this relapse into idolatry after the revelation of the one true God, and if you can point out the connection between idolatry and polytheism. What tempts men to idolatry, and what is the harm of it?

Pupil.—Surely idolatry is wrong and forbidden by the second commandment.

Teacher.—But why is it wrong, and why is it forbidden?

Pupil.—Because an idol is not worthy of worship.

Teacher.—But supposing the idolater said, "I do not worship the idol. But I want something to remind me of the One above who rules me. You like to have images and portraits of your friends; so I like to have a visible memorial of the perpetual presence of Him who though present is invisible." What would you say to such an idolater as this?

Pupil.—I should not know what to say.

Teacher.—Could you not reply that, though you like to have a portrait of your friend, it is because the portrait is like him; but that if the portrait were no portrait, but a caricature, or if it represented only one or two unimportant parts of your friend's figure, or merely his clothes, you would not care for it? And could you not apply the same argument to the idolater?

Pupil.—You mean that no sculpture or painting could represent the Supreme Being?

Teacher.—I mean more than that. I mean that any sculpture or painting purporting to represent God must misrepresent Him, for it would only represent one or two of His attributes, and those not perfectly. The nearest approximation to the Supreme God is, as Plato says, "a man who is as just as possible;" but each man has individual characteristics which God has given him. It does us good and gives us an insight into God's goodness to see the correct portrait expressive of the justice or goodness of a good man as long as we remember "this is a man," "this is one of God's noblest works." But if we take away all that is peculiar to the individual, and leave only what seems to us the essence of goodness, and then say, "this portrait represents God," we learn less instead of more of the Supreme Goodness.

Pupil.—But did the ancient heathens do this?

Teacher.—Did they not? They began perhaps by heaping up stones or piling unhewn monuments to be memorials of God. Then, as they craved to know more about Him, they were not content with any memorial that was not something like Him, an image of Him. And now I think you will be able to tell me how idolatry brought in polytheism. Imagine the Egyptian mason, chisel in hand, being ordered by the Priests to execute a figure of the Supreme God, and what will the Priest say?

Pupil.—I suppose the Priest might say that the mason is to represent a Being perfectly strong, and swift, and beautiful, all-seeing and all-wise, just and merciful.

Teacher.—Well, that is enough for our present purpose. What will the mason say to this?

Pupil.—He would be obliged to answer that he could not represent the same human figure perfectly strong and swift and beautiful, for the muscles of a Hercules are too ponderous to allow of the swiftness of an Atalanta.

Teacher.—Well, that's what he would say if he were a Greek artist. But, if he were an Assyrian artist—you have seen the Assyrian marbles, and can tell me how he would get out of the difficulty.

Pupil.—Yes. He will give the god the strength of a bull, and the head and crown and majesty of a king, with the wings of an eagle.

Teacher.—And now what is there that this mason's god has not, that very attribute of God which St. John dignifies so highly as to think that single name a sufficient revelation of Him?

Pupil.—Love.

Teacher.—True. And now I think you see that idolatry or image worship must in the end lead to polytheism or worship of many gods in many images, and you will better understand why the mere manufacture of emblems of God was so rigidly forbidden by Moses.

Pupil.—Yes I do ; but still I cannot quite see how or why the people of Israel so easily fell into idolatry after the revelation of Jehovah.

Teacher.—For one thing, in those times men (like children now-a-days) found it hard to realize what we call abstractions, such as strength, unless they were expressed in concrete forms, as a strong man, or bull, or lion ; and they had not yet received the revelation of Jesus Christ, which has taught us that the most divine attributes are those which cannot be expressed in shape or colour. Besides, the quiet and orderly worship of an invisible Jehovah may perhaps have seemed dull and spiritless compared with the service of Ashtaroth or Moloch, in whose temple there were not only sacrifices but also visible statues, paintings, feasts, dances, processions, self-torturing priests, and sensual indulgences made lawful under the name of worship. But the great attraction must have been the prospect of escaping from the tedious and painful restrictions of the pure law of Jehovah to a god of the Gentiles, who could be propitiated by mere sacrifices if they were but costly enough.

Pupil.—But was not Jehovah propitiated by sacrifices too?

Teacher.—We shall answer that question presently. Meantime, having touched upon the training which the nation received from their servitude in Egypt and their hardships and wanderings in the wilderness, let us pass on to the period of their settlement in Canaan, and instead of examining the law of Moses as it was given from Sinai, let us endeavour to understand how the law worked in Canaan. Let us put ourselves in the position of a man of Israel during the times of the Judges, and try to imagine what kind of life we should have led under the law. Suppose you were a tradesman or a professional man of the present time, what would be (I do not say what ought to be) one of your first thoughts on entering upon your business?

Pupil.—I suppose one of the first things I should think of would be how I could get on.

Teacher.—What do you mean by "getting on?"

Pupil.—Earning my living and improving my business, or rising in my profession.

Teacher.—Well, now, suppose you were a man of Israel, how could you improve your business or rise in your profession? Tell me, though, first, what business or profession you would choose.

Pupil.—Suppose I am a tradesman?

Teacher.—I do not know what kind of tradesman you could be. The sale of the native products of Palestine could not employ a class of retailers. Then, commerce is out of the question. It is only perhaps twice that we read of Jewish fleets, and these are royal monopolies, and even these are discouraged. For it is recorded with evident satisfaction that the ships of Jehoshaphat "were broken at Ezion-Geber."[1] Neither do I know to what kind of manufacture you could turn your hand. All necessary clothing would probably be home-made.

Pupil.—But I do not know what kind of professions existed in Israel.

Teacher.—Nor do I, except those of Priest, Levite, or Prophet

---

[1] 1 Kings xxii. 48.

and those not lucrative professions. There was no painting, no sculpture, no poetry considered as a profession, no literary class, no science, no lawyers or schoolmasters, and we hear very little of any medical profession.

Pupil.—I suppose I must be an agriculturist.

Teacher.—I think so. And being an agriculturist, how will you "get on"?

Pupil.—By careful farming and economy I would save enough to increase my land.

Teacher.—But you cannot do that. The land returns to its original owners after fifty years at the utmost, in the jubilee year. At least, if you regard the law, the evident intention of the law is to prevent the accumulation of large estates. Isaiah distinctly protests against those who "join house to house and lay field to field."[1] And you must not lay too much stress on economical or careful farming. Every seventh year the law commands you to let your ground lie fallow: you are also to take care that in collecting your harvests you do not altogether disregard the claims of the poor, who are allowed by law the right of gleaning in your fields.

Pupil.—Then I might lend my money upon interest.

Teacher.—No, you might not: not at least to your countrymen.[2] On the contrary, it is your duty to lend your money without interest to your poorer neighbours, and to assist them without recompense.

Pupil.—Then I do not see how I could get on.

Teacher.—Nor do I, if "getting on" means accumulating wealth. But there is more contained in the Law than these restrictions. Tell me what is there?

Pupil.—I do not know where to begin.

Teacher.—I should adopt our modern division. There is the civil law regulating the relations of masters and servants, the ties of the family, the tenure of land and other property, and a few brief regulations as to taxation; then the criminal law, the judicial law, and, if it can be so called, the constitutional law, consisting in a few

---

[1] Isaiah v. 8.　　[2] Exod. xxii. 25; Levit. xxv. 36; Deut. xxiii. 19.

remarks about royal power. Now, what have you to say about this law, as compared with ours, for instance?

Pupil.—It was given by God.

Teacher.—True, but do not forget that all law that is based on equity and righteousness comes to us from God. But was the Law of Israel a perfect law?

Pupil.—Must it not have been, since it was given by God?

Teacher.—You may infer from its having been given by God that it was the best possible law for Israel. But are we to infer that it was such a law as would be the best now for us or any modern nation? Take, for instance, the law which relates to the Avenger of blood.[1] What is provided by that law?

Pupil.—That a man who has killed another by mistake must for a time take refuge in some one of certain cities appointed for the purpose. Else, though he might be known to be quite innocent of any evil intent, he could be lawfully killed by the nearest relative of the deceased.

Teacher.—Does that seem to you just in itself?

Pupil.—I suppose not.

Teacher.—Nor to me. But we must remember that in ancient times (as in the Highlands till a comparatively recent period) the nearest relative of any one who was killed conceived himself bound to kill the killer. The death might, perhaps, be the result of accident, but it was not always easy to distinguish between accident and purpose, and, besides, an act and the motive of an act were not so easily separated then as now. The blood spilt seemed so much loss to the relations, who were entitled to the compensation of blood in return, and the unsettled state of society and deficiency of law gave to the next of kin the right of exacting blood for blood. Moses, therefore, adopting the imperfect custom of the times, limited it as far as possible by forbidding the ancient right of blood compensation, provided that the accidental homicide went into exile for a certain time. We may apply to this the words which Our Lord uttered with reference to another enactment of Moses. Quote them.

[1] Numb. xxxv. 12; Deut. xix. 6.

Pupil.—" Moses, because of the hardness of your hearts, suffered you to put away your wives."[1]

Teacher.—But do you suppose that Moses went against the will of God in sanctioning this?

Pupil.—We are not told so.

Teacher.—And we have no right to think so. Take another case. What was the punishment inflicted on the man who broke the law by collecting firewood on the Sabbath?

Pupil.—Death.

Teacher.—Yes; and note that in this case Moses is said to have expressly consulted the Lord : " And the Lord said unto Moses, The man shall surely be put to death." Death was also the penalty for blasphemy, idolatry, and false prophecy. There were no prisons in the Arabian desert, and a fine did not seem an appropriate penalty for an offence against Jehovah. Some visible and terrible punishment was needed to move the stubborn hearts of Israel. And therefore " for the hardness of men's hearts" the penalty of death was inflicted even for the most trifling infringement of the sanctity of the Sabbath.

Pupil.—But does not death seem a too severe punishment for picking up a few sticks on the Sabbath?

Teacher.—In what cases do we inflict the severest punishments?

Pupil.—When the crime to be punished is most injurious to society.

Teacher.—Well, and think what a help to society the Sabbath was intended to be. It was intended to force men out of worldliness and the weekly-beaten path of worldly work, and to compel them if possible to rise up above thoughts of fig-trees and vineyards, corn-fields and olive-presses, to some thought of the Lord God who had brought out Israel from the land of Egypt, the Infinite, the Supreme, the perfectly righteous Jehovah. The Sabbath, to a nation where there were no synagogues and no books, no painting or sculpture, must have been one of the most painful, though salutary, of all the restraints of the law. A nation that gave up one entire day to an invisible God, whom they acknowledged to be One and

---

[1] St. Matthew xix. 8.   [2] Numb. xv. 32.

Supreme, could not but by degrees rise to a higher state of spiritual feeling than other nations that made no such sacrifice. The Mosaic Sabbath was therefore a great national institution, intended to raise a whole people from a carnal to a spiritual state. But everything depended upon its rigid observance. If one man transgressed it with impunity, others would soon follow his example, either willingly or in self-defence. Was not the man who, to pick up a few sticks for firewood, violated a great national institution like this, guilty of a great injury against society?

Pupil.—Yes, I suppose he was. But the man may not have thought of this.

Teacher.—I do not suppose he did. I imagine he thought less about society than about Jehovah. And this leads us to the mention of that which is the key-note of the whole law. Tell me how, in the motive for punishment, the law of Moses differs from that of other nations, as for example the legislation of Solon, or what you know of the Roman law; or, if you like, take our own law. We punish crime, do we not?

Pupil.—Yes.

Teacher.—The word "crime" is not mentioned in the Old Testament. What is the Old Testament word for punishable offences?

Pupil.—Sin.

Teacher.—What is the distinction between sin and crime?

Pupil.—Crime is an offence against the State, sin against God.

Teacher.—Well, we punish crimes; the men of Israel punished sins. We punish in the name of the State; the men of Israel punished in the name of Jehovah. My remarks about the *utility* of the Sabbath were merely intended to explain why God inspired Moses to enact its observance with special emphasis in the ten commandments. But when once enacted, the utility of it or inutility was not the question. It was to be observed, not as useful, but as the will of Jehovah, and an offence against it was punished, not as harmful to Israel, but as a sin against Jehovah. Can you mention, say with respect to usury, any motive that is constantly set before the

Israelites for the performance of the law? Take for instance Lev. xxv. 37.

Pupil.—"Thou shalt not give him (thy brother) thy money upon usury, nor lend him thy victuals for increase. I am the Lord your God, which brought you forth out of the land of Canaan."

Teacher.—Hence we see that what patriotism was to the Greeks and Romans, that the love and fear of Jehovah were to the people of Israel. We find, it is true, in Greek and Roman authors occasional recognitions that injustice, oppression, and cruelty are visited by the wrath of the gods; but the will of God is not made by other nations, as by the Israelites, the one guide and law of life. There is no notion among the Greeks of *sin* as being something internal, impure, and loathsome, like a disease of the soul. It is rather treated as something external, like a slip or false step or mistake. Read the Psalmist's lamentation over his sin: Psalm li., and in particular the 10th verse.

Pupil.—"Create in me a clean heart, O God; and renew a right spirit within me."

Teacher.—You will not find, I think, anything in Greek or Latin that quite comes up to that, though in the name of "Healer" applied to Apollo there is something like it. Then again, where among heathen authors can we find the longing for God's purifying presence expressed in the words of the Psalmist: "O God, thou art my God; early will I seek Thee: my soul thirsteth for Thee; my flesh longeth for Thee in a dry and thirsty land where no water is; Thy loving-kindness is better than life."[1] I think, therefore, that we may fairly say that the law brought out the idea of sin, purity, and holiness (without regard to punishment or immunity) with a clearness that is not to be found in heathen nations. But we said just now that Jehovah stood to the people of Israel in the relation of the country to the Greeks and Romans. Were there no patriots in Israel? Mention some.

Pupil.—Gideon, Barak, Deborah, Ehud, and others.

Teacher.—What were the circumstances that called their patriotism into action?

[1] Psalm lxiii. 1, 2.

Pupil.—The people of Israel were oppressed by the surrounding nations.

Teacher.—And what was one great cause of discord between Israel and the neighbouring nations?

Pupil.—The difference of religion.

Teacher.—This then is one incidental way in which the patriotism and the religion of Israel were connected together. Tell me, is patriotism a virtue?

Pupil.—Yes.

Teacher.—Why?

Pupil.—Because it makes men noble and unselfish.

Teacher.—But what if it makes men neglectful or even contemptuous of other nations, unjust and oppressive to all but their own people, as among the Spartans?

Pupil.—Then it is not a virtue.

Teacher.—Patriotism is love of country. I suppose you mean love of one's countrymen. But why should one love one's countrymen?

Pupil.—I suppose because one knows them better than foreigners.

Teacher.—I believe you must be right (at all events as a rule), and the more you really know any one the more you will like him, though you may dislike his faults. But whom does one know best?

Pupil.—The members of one's own family; one's brothers.

Teacher.—What is the name which throughout the law is given to the collective people of Israel to denote their relation to one another?

Pupil.—Brethren.

Teacher.—The old proverb about charity says that "Charity begins at home;" and so, I suppose it may be said that love begins with the family, then passes to the country, and lastly to all one's fellow men. Whom are we as Christians taught to love as brethren?

Pupil.—All men.

Teacher.—Well then, you see, we in Christian times have come to the third development of the word "brethren," while the people of Israel were in the second. But now turn to Isaiah xix. and there see whether you can find any trace of the development of the patriotism of Israel into the third stage.

Pupil.—In the twenty-fourth verse there is, "In that day shall Israel be the third with Egypt and Assyria, even a blessing in the midst of the land: whom the Lord of Hosts shall bless, saying, Blessed be Egypt my people and Assyria the work of my hands and Israel my inheritance."

Teacher.—And you will also remember the terms of the original promise to Abraham.

Pupil.—In Abraham's seed all the nations of the world were to be blessed.

Teacher.—We see, then, God trained Israel as he trained Greece and Rome, through the simple rules of the love of the family and country, leading them up to the higher golden rule of Christ. But Patriotism, as we have seen, is often combined with hatred and contempt for foreigners. Did the people of Israel hate foreigners?

Pupil.—I suppose they did, the Midianites, the Amalekites, the Ammonites, and the Moabites; the Canaanites also. At all events they acted cruelly toward them.

Teacher.—They did act cruelly, and if you have ever seen the Assyrian marbles in the British Museum, you will understand why. War did not then mean, as it does now mostly, battle between regular soldiers and, as far as possible, gentleness towards civilians. It meant devastation with fire and sword, your house burnt down, your wells stopped up, your fruit-trees felled, your family and friends dragged away in a long file of captives, beneath the lash of the slave-driver. For the prisoners it often meant not mere imprisonment, but immediate death by impalement, or a life prolonged in blindness, with the loss of hand or ear, or still more hateful mutilation. After a nation had been groaning under twenty years of oppression such as this, can you wonder if they hated their oppressors, all the more because their enemies were enemies of Jehovah and the Law? Hence we find David saying, with a consciousness that he is right,

"Do not I hate them, O Lord, that hate Thee? And am not I grieved with those that rise up against Thee? I hate them with perfect hatred: I count them mine enemies."[1] Is it right for us to hate any one?

Pupil.—I scarcely know. Our Lord says we are to love them that hate us: but may we not hate a person who does us personally no harm, but who is a monster of iniquity like Nero?

Teacher.—Can we pray for a person whom we hate?

Pupil.—No.

Teacher.—Is there any sinner so far gone in sin that Christ did not die for him, and would not gladly save him and receive our prayers for him?

Pupil.—I suppose not.

Teacher.—Then if Christ would desire us to pray for a man however sinful, we ought to hate no one however sinful.

Pupil.—It seems so: but it also seems impossible.

Teacher.—Remember that there is a difference between punishing and hating, between resentment and vindictiveness, and that it is quite possible to punish a man without hating him, and to feel an intense hatred for the crime and at the same time an intense pity for the criminal.

Pupil.—Then surely the people of Israel were wrong in hating as they did. How can you justify the words in the 109th Psalm: "Set thou a wicked man over him: and let Satan stand at his right hand. When he shall be judged, let him be condemned, and let his prayer become sin. Let his children be fatherless and his wife a widow. Let his children be continually vagabonds and beg"?

Teacher.—I do not profess to justify "hatred." I think it wrong, just as I think the law of the avenger of blood wrong. "For the hardness of their hearts," Our Lord teaches us, many things were then allowed in the infancy of the nation that are not allowed now. But the particular passage which you quoted is perhaps capable of

---

[1] Psalm cxxxix. 21, 22.

explanation. It is thought by some that the execration is not intended to be the expression of the Psalmist, but of the "wicked man" who is previously mentioned. I cannot enter into that now. But I wish to elicit from you the nature of the training which this stage of "hating" conferred on the people of Israel. How does a child attain to the idea of goodness or of wickedness?

Pupil.—Of course by seeing people who, though differing in other respects, have goodness or wickedness in common.

Teacher.—Then, I ask, what would be the natural result developed by this intense hatred of the heathen not merely as oppressors, but also as idolaters and offenders against Jehovah, and, in one word, as *sinners?*

Pupil.—From hating sinners they would learn to hate sin.

Teacher.—Now, quitting this subject, let us briefly consider the changes of government through which Israel passed, and their effect upon the national character and history. What were the advantages and what the disadvantages of the government under the Judges?

Pupil.—It was a disadvantage to have no defined successor to fill the seat of power when vacated: and the uncertainty of succession and election might give rise to different rulers in different parts of the kingdom, thus causing disunion and weakness. On the other hand, it must have been an advantage to have only such rulers as were brought forward by trial and danger, men who had proved their capacity for ruling. And the occasional absence of any visible head of the people may have led them to look more earnestly to the invisible head—Jehovah.

Teacher.—Now what were the advantages of a monarchy? As manifested under the first king, for example?

Pupil.—The power of the nation was more easily concentrated for military purposes. Injustice was more easily checked or punished, and the whole nation was united by having a visible centre of power.

Teacher.—True. The military power of Israel was greatly increased by the establishment of royalty, as can be seen by comparing the condition of the nation before or during the time of Saul with the times of David, Solomon, and subsequent kings. Conversely, but similarly, the military power of Rome was at first weakened by the expulsion of the kings. Such were the advantages. Now what were the disadvantages?

Pupil.—I do not know.

Teacher.—What is said with respect to the influence of some of the kings upon the nation either for good or for evil?

Pupil.—Some are said to have "made Israel to sin" by bad example, and by leading their subjects to the worship of false gods; others to have kept the nation in the worship of the true God.

Teacher.—That seems to shew, does it not, that the people, many of them, believed, as we may express it, at second-hand in Jehovah, and were ready to adopt the worship of the reigning king as being most in fashion? And thus the vicegerent and representative of the invisible King attracted the worship that should have been paid to none but Jehovah himself.

Pupil.—But did not the kings pay special attention to the worship of Jehovah, and was it not by them that the Temple was built and the Temple ritual elaborated?

Teacher.—Yes; but what if that very Temple and its ritual, like the kings themselves, did harm as well as good, by diverting the worship of the thoughtless and shallow from the invisible to the visible? Can you not quote some passages in the beginning of Isaiah which show that in his time many people *idolized* the Temple and its worship? I mean that they regarded it as a reality in itself, instead of a mere emblem to remind them of the supremely Righteous God. Read Isaiah i. 11.

Pupil.—" To what purpose is the multitude of your sacrifices unto me? saith the Lord. I am full of the burnt-offerings of rams and the fat of fed beasts; and I delight not in the blood of bullocks or of lambs. . . . . . Wash you, make you clean: put away the evil of your doings from before mine eyes: cease to do evil: learn to do well: seek judgment, relieve the oppressed, judge the fatherless, plead the cause of the widow." Then it would seem that the Monarchy and the Temple-worship did more harm than good, and did not "train" the people.

Teacher.—Well, I think all must admit that both the Monarchy and the Temple concentrated the nation, and that but for these institutions the twelve tribes might have separated before they had ever become a nation, or might have been overpowered and assimilated to surrounding nations before they had done their work in developing theology and morality. You will remember that Jeroboam thought a common worship so necessary to the nationality of the ten tribes that he erected national temples at Dan and Bethel. But besides, does not a father sometimes think it the best kind of training for his children to give them what they want though it may be somewhat hurtful at the time? If he does, why does he?

Pupil.—To show them by experience that what they want is not good for them.

Teacher.—Or not so good as something else: not good enough to satisfy them. And so the people of Israel, who were always looking forward to a great King that should conquer the Gentiles and raise their nation to the highest point of glory and honour, were taught by the history of a long line of monarchs that neither a David, nor a Jehoshaphat, nor a Hezekiah could fulfil their aspirations, but they must still look forward to a future King. And similarly the Temple, with all its gorgeous buildings, its armies of priests and choristers, the perpetual sound of psalms and instruments of music, the cries of slaughtered victims and all the stir and smoke of sacrifice, might by its very splendour teach a thoughtful worshipper, more impressively than any prophet, that the worship of God requires something more than earthly pomp and ceremony, and that "the sacrifices of God are a broken spirit: a broken and a contrite heart, O God, thou wilt not despise." Can you tell me what influence arose, some time after the establishment of the Monarchy, as a counterpoise to the influence of the Monarch and the Temple?

Pupil.—The Prophets.

Teacher.—Yes. They had existed apparently from very early times. We find schools of the prophets in the time of Samuel. They appear as reprovers of sin in the reigns of David and Ahab. But it was not till the reign of Uzziah that the full duties of the Prophetic office come out prominently. What was the duty of a Prophet?

Pupil.—To predict future events that could not be known to ordinary men.

Teacher.—But surely the books of the Prophets do not consist wholly or for the most part of predictions; for example, the first chapters of Isaiah?

Pupil.—No. They consist mostly of moral precepts.

Teacher.—You know, perhaps, that the original meaning of "prophet," as derived from the Greek, is "spokesman" or "interpreter." Let me also say that the Hebrew words which we render "prophet" mean "one who bubbles over," or "one who sees." And now, what is that which the Prophets "interpreted," "spoke," "saw," that with which their hearts were said to "bubble over?"

Pupil.—The will of God.

Teacher.—Yes; God's will in the present and past as well as in the future. It was to bring home to the hearts of the people the will of God when it was obscured or parodied by worldly idols, that the Prophets arose. We shall hereafter describe the Prophetic mission more in detail. Now let me return to the political history of Israel and its effect upon the nation. What were the two great misfortunes which befel the nation under the Kings?

Pupil.—The secession that divided the ten tribes of Israel from Judah and Benjamin, and then the captivity of Israel followed by that of Judah. Surely the secession was no "training," but a positive mischief and injury to the people.

Teacher.—Perhaps it was, at least to the ten tribes. But we have now come to a point in the history of the chosen people where it will be necessary to bear in mind that God often trains both individuals and nations for special purposes by means that are not always pleasant or even harmless. Thus a lawyer, a physician, an explorer, an astronomer, may become great and useful at the expense of health or culture; a dramatist or minister of religion may learn to sympathize with and help human nature through much trouble—nay, through much sin and remorse. And so God, training a nation for a special purpose, may fulfil His purpose by means of the calamities or even the destruction of part, perhaps a great part, of the nation. In what special way did the Jews influence the world?

Pupil.—By proclaiming the unity and holiness of God, and preparing the way for Christianity.

Teacher.—Did the secession in any way tend to the retention of the true religion?

Pupil.—I should have thought not, unless perhaps the people of Judah were in some degree incited to remain in the true faith, out of a sense of superiority to their benighted brethren in Israel. But that surely must have been an unworthy feeling.

Teacher.—I do not think it need have been an unworthy feeling. To see the Kings of Israel pulled down and set up at the mere will of the army, the priesthood filled by "the lowest of the people," the ten tribes sinking deeper and deeper into idolatry, the land teeming with disorder and anarchy, and, to close the prospect, the captivity and deportation of their brethren,—this might surely have taught the men of Judah, without any unworthy exultation on their part, to ask themselves in the words of Deuteronomy, "Wherefore hath the Lord done this unto this land?" and to reply in the words of the same book, "Because they have forsaken the covenant of the Lord God of their fathers, which he made with them when he brought them forth out of the land of Egypt."[1] Besides, the ten tribes must have served, against the Assyrian influence, as a kind of breakwater, unsound indeed, and insufficient and tottering to its fall but still a temporary and partial protection against the coming wave. Now, what was the result of the captivity upon the Jewish mind?

Deut. xxix. 25.

Pupil.—I suppose there can be no doubt that it had the effect of utterly destroying in the Jews all inclination towards idolatry.

Teacher.—Yes; and yet it had not that effect upon the ten tribes. And possibly one reason for this difference of result may have been that Israel had not yet grasped like Judah the truth of the unity of God with sufficient firmness to withstand the powerful influence of surrounding idolatry. We are now passing out of the period of Old Testament history; but I will ask you whether you know of anything that in the second century before Christ increased the attachment of the Jews to the law and intensified their hatred of idolatry?

Pupil.—The attempt of Antiochus Epiphanes to set up the worship of images in Jerusalem and the successful resistance of the Maccabees.

Teacher.—Right. We have now to sum up the result of more than nineteen centuries of training, commencing with the call of Abraham in 1921 B.C.: and we find a people diminished in population and territory, weak in military power, deprived of independence, not remarkable for wealth, and singularly destitute of such culture as is derived from the fine arts, but trained by prosperity and adversity, by their law and by their prophets, by traditions of martyrdom and successful resistance, to abhor idolatry, to believe in the unity, eternity and righteousness of God, and to reverence the very letter of the written records that revealed His will. These may be called passive qualities. What other belief and hope had the Jews which might incite them to action, to aggressive action.?

Pupil.—The hope of a Deliverer.

Teacher.—Are there any descriptions of the Deliverer that might point to aggression?

Pupil.—Yes. Such passages as that in the Psalms (ii. 9), which said that the Deliverer should "rule the nations with a rod of iron, and break them in pieces like a potter's vessel."

Teacher.—Can you tell me of another hope that sprang up in the later history of the Jews, a hope not entertained by all the nation, not by the Sadducees, for example, but held by the Pharisees and the majority of the people, a hope that is not clearly mentioned in the Old Testament?

Pupil.—The hope of the immortality of the soul.

Teacher.—What is there in misfortune and trouble that might prepare a nation to welcome this hope?

Pupil.—Finding things wrong here on earth, and believing that the world is governed by Righteousness, a disappointed and humiliated nation might gradually come to hope and then to believe that there must be some future state, where the wrong shall be made right or shall be shown to have tended towards right.

Teacher.—So much for the advantages of their training. Now, what was the most striking fault of the people during this period, between the return and the birth of Christ?

Pupil.—I do not know. Were they not better, more religious?

Teacher.—That depends on the sense in which you use the word "religious." Who were their teachers during this period?

Pupil.—The Priests and Scribes.

Teacher.—Where were the Prophets?

Pupil.—There were none.

Teacher.—What was the difference between a Prophet and a Scribe?

Pupil.—The Prophet developed while the Scribe merely explained. The Prophet professed to teach "with authority;" the Scribe merely gave his opinion.

Teacher.—That is right. Isaiah interpreted the will of the Divine Spirit which he felt breathing and living within him; the Scribes interpreted the letter of the written law. We can describe the difference between the times by the difference between these representative offices. Let us express it in a proportion. As the Scribe is to the Prophet, as the letter is to the spirit, so was the period just before Christ to the period of Isaiah. But what does St. Paul say about the difference between the spirit and the letter?

Pupil.—"The letter killeth, but the spirit giveth life."[1]

[1] 2 Cor. iii. 6.

CHAPTER IV.

SACRIFICES AND PRIESTS.

Teacher.—What is the meaning of a sacrifice?
Pupil.—The offering up of some animal.
Teacher.—Could the slaughter of an animal, except for the purpose of supporting human life, be acceptable to God in *itself?*
Pupil.—Yes: for He ordered it.
Teacher.—Then you mean to say that if a man of Israel offered up a bullock to Jehovah, that was acceptable to Him?
Pupil.—Yes: if it was done because Jehovah ordered it.
Teacher.—But suppose the man reasoned thus with himself: "I have kept back the wages of my labourers; I have shed innocent blood; I have oppressed the fatherless and widow; I have sat in the seat of judges and delivered unjust decisions. Thereby I have made powerful friends and have accumulated a fortune; but I fear Jehovah will punish me, and unless I propitiate Him by offering the sacrifice which He has ordered, I shall not be able to go on, as I intend to do, making money by fraud and oppression. I will therefore purchase His favour with this bullock." Would such a sacrifice be acceptable to Jehovah?
Pupil.—Surely, it could not be.
Teacher.—If not, why not?
Pupil.—I suppose because the sacrifice was wicked.
Teacher.—Are we not all wicked, more or less? Besides, I thought "sin offerings" were expressly intended to be offered up by those who had sinned, by the wicked in fact.
Pupil.—Yes, but this man intends to go on being wicked.

Teacher.—Then, in order that a sacrifice may be acceptable to God, a man must intend not to go on being wicked; in other words he must do what?

Pupil.—Repent.

Teacher.—What definition is given of sacrifice in the Psalms?

Pupil.—"The sacrifices of God are a broken spirit: a broken and a contrite heart, O God, wilt thou not despise."

Teacher.—Then if the sacrifices of God are a "broken spirit," what need of the death of an animal?

Pupil.—I do not know.

Teacher.—Why do we often pray aloud to God, sometimes in churches, sometimes by ourselves? Cannot God understand, even though we think the words without uttering them?

Pupil.—Yes, but by speaking we remind ourselves and others of what we are praying for. The words keep us wakeful and attentive, and are the signs of our thoughts.

Teacher.—So, I suppose the offering up of an animal was the sign of something invisible, some spiritual offering. Of what? Expand the metaphor above mentioned: "The sacrifice (*i.e.* victim) of God is a broken spirit."

Pupil.—As an animal is offered up, flesh, blood, and life, so a man is dedicated with all his powers and faculties to the service of God.

Teacher.—But the animal dies. Expand that.

Pupil.—As the animal passes out of its present state of existence, when offered to God, so man is to pass out of his present degraded life of bondage and service to sin, and is hereafter to be dead to sin and alive to God.

Teacher.—If a man were already dead to sin and alive to God, he would not, I imagine, require sacrifice. What is it that forces upon him the necessity of sacrifice, "thank offering" as well as "sin offering?"

Pupil.—I suppose his consciousness of imperfection and ingratitude might oblige him to remind himself by a "thank offering" of his duty of thankfulness and devotion; and his sense of sin and alienation from God might drive him to express in some way that he desired to give himself up to God, and to say "Thy will be done."

Teacher.—Why did not the ancient Patriarchs say as you have suggested—"Thy will, not mine, be done?" Surely that would have been shorter, simpler, and clearer than to slay a bullock or a sheep?

Pupil.—I cannot explain that.

Teacher.—What is the "will?"

Pupil.—I scarcely know how to express it.

Teacher.—If you do not, certainly the Patriarchs did not, who were much more accustomed to action than to speech. Besides, their words would have failed them. After many thousands of years we have accumulated a large store of words to express different aspects and actions of human nature, such as "will," "sin," "righteousness," "purity," "forgiveness," and the like. The Patriarchs felt no less, perhaps more, than we feel, but they had no words to express their feelings glibly, and therefore they talked through the medium of "signs," strange ceremonies, piled-up stones, huge monuments, music and dances, and sacred rites. Hence, when a man in the old times felt that he had not lived in harmony with the Supreme Lord, that he had sinned against His will by doing his own will, that he had not only injured his neighbour, whom he could compensate, but also One above whom he could not compensate, the thought might naturally arise, "How can I unite myself to God and merge my will in His? How can I express my complete submission to Him? I must not kill myself since He has sent me here, and He will summon me hence, and until His angel of Death calls me I must not go. Yet I desire to die, and to give up my life to God." And the answer came with Divine authority that the death of one out of his flock or herd might best express the spiritual sacrifice which he could not put into definite words. And as the smoke of the victim rose in the air, the heart of the man rose upward with it, forswearing the life of sin, and consecrating himself to a new life in the service of God. With such sacrifices God was well pleased: for they expressed the very words of our prayer, "Thy will be done."

Pupil.—I do not quite see why death should be a necessary part of a sin-offering; why, for instance, it might not have been sufficient to offer up some simpler offering of the fruits of the earth as an emblem of the offering of one's own life.

Teacher.—But is there not a natural connection between sin and death?

Pupil.—Yes. We are taught that it was sin that brought death into the world.

Teacher.—And, setting that aside, do we not continually see that sin brings upon us death and disease and sorrow, which are akin to death? If it be true that

> "'Tis the eternal law that where guilt is
> Sorrow shall answer it."

it would be a most insufficient expression of the sense of guilt and repentance to offer up wheat-ears or fruits. We have a feeling that it is good and right for us to be pained and chastened for our sins, that law demands some pain from us as acknowledgment and purification of our sin, and that we ought not to expect to avoid all punishment, although we hope to be delivered entirely from the sin. You may say, "But where is your pain in putting to death a harmless sheep?" I reply, that if the sacrifice is a real one, the pain is considerable. It is not merely the feeling of one's own shame and repentance, but also the consciousness of the mischief that one has done, not only to one's self but to others, to all created things; the deadly nature of the offence against all life and happiness, so deadly that it cannot be expiated but by the agony and blood of a poor innocent beast. Is there anything more that requires explanation?

Pupil.—Why were the sacrificers sprinkled with the blood of the victim?

Teacher.—What is said about the "blood" of animals in the Bible?

Pupil.—It is said to be "the life" of the animal.

Teacher.—I imagine then that by being sprinkled with the blood of the slaughtered victim the sacrificers were emblematically identified with the life of the victim, and it was implied that their life was offered up to God in its life, and thereby purified and sanctified. Thus the blood (emblematically) purified them from sin, and, so far as their hearts realized the meaning of the sacrifice, so far there was a real and not merely emblematic purification. It was a common expression that "the sins" of the sacrificers were "laid upon the head" of the victim. What was meant by that?

Pupil.—That the punishment which the sacrificer had deserved was laid upon the victim.

Teacher.—Indeed? I thought we had agreed that a man who came merely wishing to escape punishment and not to escape sin could not offer up a pleasing sacrifice to God. Why do you here substitute "punishment" for "sins"?

Pupil.—I had forgotten. I suppose the meaning was that the sinful life of the sacrificer became identified with the victim, and was purified by being sacrificed to God. But was not the notion of propitiation and escaping punishment also closely connected with the notion of sacrifice?

Teacher.—Which do you mean, propitiation or escaping from punishment?

Pupil.—Are they not the same?

Teacher.—May not a repentant child have, as you call it, propitiated his father and obtained his forgiveness, and yet be punished because punishment may be for the child's good?

Pupil.—Yes; and it follows that to propitiate and escape from punishment are not the same. But I thought they were often closely connected?

Teacher.—So they are in all heathen notions of sacrifice. What is the meaning of a hecatomb? And how came a man to offer up hecatombs?

Pupil.—A hecatomb meant a hundred oxen: and men used to offer up a hundred oxen instead of one because they thought the offering would be more likely to gain the favour of the gods.

Teacher.—Is it worthy of the Divine nature to be more pleased with a hecatomb than an ox?

Pupil.—No.

Teacher.—Could a man consecrate himself to a being whom he thought covetous and grasping?

Pupil.—No.

Teacher.—Put into your own words the feelings of such a heathen sacrificer.

Pupil.—" If I offer up one ox the gods will not forgive me. I will persuade them to forgive me by offering a hundred oxen."

Teacher.—That is not saying " Thy will be done," is it?

Pupil.—No; rather " My will be done." [1]

Teacher.—True: and that is just the difference between true and false sacrifice. The true says "Thy will be done," conforming man to the image of God; the false says: " My will be done," striving to make God in the image of man. The former tends to the worship of the one true God and to make men one with God, or in other words tends to the atonement between God and man; the latter to idolatry and superstition. Did you never hear of the ring of Polycrates of Samos?

Pupil.—No.

Teacher.—The story goes that Polycrates was King of Samos, and more prosperous and powerful than all the neighbouring kings. In the midst of his prosperity he was warned by a wise man that the gods regarded with aversion the excessive prosperity of mortals, and that it would be well for him to propitiate them by some sacrifice, the more costly the more likely to be acceptable. He accordingly cast a precious ring into the sea; but the gods would not be propitiated: the ring returned to the King's palace in the belly of a fish; and the King himself soon afterwards perished miserably. That was the common heathen notion of sacrifice—a costly bribe to buy the favour of the gods—and hence sprang the terrible custom

---

[1] Yet, where the *spirit* of the sacrifice is right, it is also right to feel " neither will I offer burnt offerings unto the Lord my God of that which doth cost me nothing."—2 Sam. xxiv. 24.

of sacrificing human beings and even one's own children. But this heathen parody of sacrifice is frequently rebuked in the Old Testament. Can you tell me of any such passages?

Pupil.—1 Sam. xv. 22 : "Behold, to obey is better than sacrifice, and to hearken than the fat of rams;" and Isaiah says, i. 11-13, "Bring no more vain oblations; incense is an abomination to me. I delight not in the blood of bullocks, or of lambs, or of he-goats."

Teacher.—How could Isaiah say that God "delighted not in the blood of bullocks," since in the law He had ordered that it should be shed?

Pupil.—He meant that God delighted not in the outward sign of the sacrifice without the inward reality.

Teacher.—But does not the Epistle to the Hebrews add something about the inefficacy of the blood of bulls and of goats?[1]

Pupil.—It says the blood of bulls and of goats could never take away sin.

Teacher.—Then what was the use of the sacrifice?

Pupil.—We said just now that it was like the words of a prayer, intended, besides reminding us of the penalty of sin, to help us to offer our hearts to God, and so to let Him purify us from sin. It was intended to remind us of the sacrifice which we are all bound to strive to make, though we cannot make it perfectly.

Teacher.—What epithet do you give to that which men strive to attain to but never reach, which exists only in the form of an "idea?"

Pupil.—Ideal.

Teacher.—Did any man among the Patriarchs, or before the Christian era, attain to this ideal sacrifice; and, if not, why not?

Pupil.—No man did, for though Abraham so trusted in God that he could be called the friend of God, yet no man could attain to perfect sinlessness or union with God so that he could say "I am one with God, and my will is one with God's."

Teacher.—Then were the sacrifices of the Patriarchs and others utterly useless?

---

[1] Heb. x. 4.

Pupil.—No, not utterly. They were useless so far as they were imperfect, but useful in so far as they partook of the ideal and perfect sacrifice.

Teacher.—What is the ideal and perfect sacrifice?

Pupil.—That of Christ.

Teacher.—And therefore all the previous sacrifices, since they pointed the attention towards the ideal, pointed to——?

Pupil.—The sacrifice of Christ.

Teacher.—And since they were only useful in so far as they partook of the ideal sacrifice, they were only so far useful in so far as by anticipation and in spirit they partook of——?

Pupil.—The sacrifice of Christ.

Teacher.—Who offered up these sacrifices?

Pupil.—Priests.

Teacher.—Why?

Pupil.—They were ordained for that purpose by Jehovah.

Teacher.—Can you give any reason why Jehovah may have ordained them? Do they in any way add to the lesson taught by sacrifice?

Pupil.—I suppose the presence and officiation of a Priest taught the sacrificers that they themselves could not offer up the perfect sacrifice of will to God, that they themselves required to be brought nearer to God by one who knew Him, and through whom He must be addressed.

Teacher.—Yes. In other nations, as well as in Israel, it was believed that sacrifices must be offered up by chosen persons set apart for the purpose, often anointed, Priests or Kings, persons of pure and spotless lives, who knew the will of God and the kind of sacrifice that was acceptable to Him. But did the Priests always know best the kind of sacrifice that best pleased God?

Pupil.—I suppose they did: they would know best the details of the natures of the animals to be killed, and the manner in which they were to be offered.

Teacher.—But let me recall to your mind the kind of sacrifice that best pleases God.

Pupil.—The sacrifice of the spirit or heart.

Teacher.—And did the appointed Priests, the sons of Eli, for instance, know this always better than others, better than the most untaught and simple worshipper?

Pupil.—No. The Priests did not always fulfil the intention of their appointment, in fact never, except so far as they approximated to the "ideal" Priest.

Teacher.—What is the duty of the "ideal" Priest?

Pupil.—To know the nature of the "ideal" sacrifice.

Teacher.—That is to say, the perfect sacrifice of one's own will to God's will. Can any one know that without offering it?

Pupil.—I should say not.

Teacher.—So should I. And hence the perfect or ideal Priest will be the Priest who has perfectly offered up his own will to God, whose whole life has been a sacrifice. Who has offered up this ideal sacrifice?

Pupil.—Christ.

Teacher.—Then Christ is the ideal Priest as well as the ideal sacrifice; and just as all previous and imperfect sacrifices pointed to the perfect sacrifice of Christ, so all previous and imperfect Priests pointed to Christ's perfect Priesthood.

CHAPTER V.

THE PROPHETS.

Teacher.—We have found that the business of the Prophets was to declare the will of God, that they were called "seers" because they could see God's purpose more clearly than others, and we have also found that another of their titles implied that their hearts were filled and, as it were, fermenting with God's Holy Word. Can you give me a brief description of the general tenor of the "Word of the Lord" which they proclaimed?

Pupil.—They predicted what God would hereafter bring to pass.

Teacher.—I thought we had agreed that only a small part of the Prophecies consisted of predictions. Take the first chapters of Isaiah and tell me what is their purport.

Pupil.—In the first chapter Isaiah warns his countrymen that sacrifice and worship without righteousness are useless. He prophesies the destruction of sinners and the purification from sin. Then in the next three chapters he prophesies a time of trial and humiliation to end in universal peace; and in the fifth chapter he compares Judah in her past history to a barren though cultivated vine, and he predicts punishment from a foreign nation.

Teacher.—That is enough. You see there is not so much prediction here as precept, a proclamation of the moral laws of God. Now tell me what is the moral law which the Prophets are continually proclaiming as the will or word of God?

Pupil.—That the righteous shall be prosperous, and the unrighteous shall be destroyed.

Teacher.—Yes; that right shall be might, and not might right.

Why was there a special necessity of proclaiming this in a country like Judah encompassed by powerful enemies?

Pupil.—I suppose because some of the surrounding nations, such as Egypt and Assyria, were much more powerful than Judah, and it might seem, according to the modern proverb, that God must be "on the side of the large battalion."

Teacher.—Do you remember what it was in the royal period which, we said, especially called for the proclamation that right is might?

Pupil.—Sometimes the King with his nobles deserted the worship of Jehovah and acted unjustly and oppressively. Thus the people might be tempted to think that high rank and a splendid position could excuse sin.

Teacher.—Again, in the magnificent ritual of the Temple, what was there that required, as we said, the counterpoise of the prophetic precepts?

Pupil.—Men were tempted to set rites above righteousness, and to degenerate into the heathen superstition that God could be propitiated or bribed by sacrifices of bulls and goats without the sacrifice of the heart.

Teacher.—Give me some of the figurative expressions by which the Prophets used to describe God as punishing.

Pupil.—Sometimes the punishment was compared to a fire refining ore and separating the useless dross from the useful metal; sometimes to an axe felling down the tall trees, *i.e.* the princes of the offending people, and leaving nothing but brushwood, *i.e.* the poor and humble, sometimes to a deluge or a storm sweeping the evil away sometimes; to a winnowing fan[1] separating the chaff from the wheat. But most frequently the sinners are said to be destroyed by fire.

Teacher.—And how were these punishments fulfilled in many cases, Take, for example, Isaiah vii. 20, where it is said that the Lord shall "shave (the land) with a razor that is hired." What is said in the same verse to be meant by the "razor?" Illustrate by x. 5.

Pupil.—The King of Assyria is meant: and in x. 5 he is called by God "the rod of mine anger."

[1] Jer. xv. 7; li 2.

Teacher.—Then you see that sometimes the fulfilments of the prophecies took place in a natural way and soon after the utterance of the prophecies. Can you mention any prophecy that was not fulfilled till long after the prophecy was uttered?

Pupil.—Isaiah mentions Cyrus by name long before his birth [1] and he also prophesies the birth of Christ from the Virgin.

Teacher.—Both of these are cases in point. The first is unique in the Prophets.[2] I do not think you will find another instance in the whole of sacred Prophecy where such a detail as a name is mentioned hundreds of years before the birth of the person named. But let us take the second case in detail. How does St. Matthew refer to it?

Pupil.—"That it might be fulfilled which was spoken of the Lord by the prophet, saying, 'Behold a virgin shall be with child, and shall bring forth a son, and they shall call his name Emmanuel.'"

Teacher.—But now turn to Isaiah (chap. vii.)[3] You will there find that Isaiah prophesies to Ahaz the defeat of his enemies, the Kings of Israel and Samaria, and offers to give a sign that the prophecy will be fulfilled. On the refusal of Ahaz to ask for a sign, the Prophet replies: "Behold a virgin shall conceive and bear a son, and shall call his name Immanuel (God with us). Butter and honey shall he eat, that he may know to refuse the evil and choose the good. For before the child shall know to refuse the evil and choose the good, the land that thou abhorrest shall be forsaken of both her kings." He goes on to say that the land shall be devastated as with a razor, and that the cornfields and vineyards shall be destroyed, so that the people will have to live on butter and honey. Then in the next chapter it is recorded that Isaiah now married a wife, and that he had a son who was called not Immanuel, but Maher-shalal-hash-baz (Speed-to-the-spoil-hasten-to-the-prey); and it is added, "Before the child shall have knowledge to cry 'My father and my mother,' the riches of Damascus and the spoil of Samaria shall be taken away

---

[1] Isaiah xlv. 1.
[2] See, however, 1 Kings xiii. 2; and the *Dictionary of the Bible*, vol. i. p. 886.
[3] For the view here adopted see *Dictionary of the Bible*, "Immanuel."

before the King of Assyria." Here then a primary and partial fulfilment of the prophecy seems to be found in the deliverance of Judah under Ahaz from the Kings of Syria and Samaria, of which deliverance the birth of Isaiah's child was a "sign."[1] In the same way it may be shown that as a rule the other prophecies of the Scriptures have their primary fulfilment in contemporary history. But it has been well said[2] of the Hebrew Psalms, and applies with equal force to the prophecies, "You will always find the language too large for the special event, the terms too magnificent, the consequences too vast and enduring: in short, you will find it to include and enclose the particulars of that special event as the heavens do surround and encompass the earth." Thus in the present instance, the Prophet seems to look forward to another and more remote deliverance which will be given by Immanuel (viii. 18); and so of other prophecies. For example, the magnificent proclamation, "Prepare ye the way of the Lord, make straight in the desert a highway for our God. Every valley shall be exalted, and every hill shall be made low;"[3] together with the similar prophecy "And a highway shall be there . . . and the ransomed of the Lord shall return, and come to Zion with songs and everlasting joy upon their heads: they shall obtain joy and gladness, and sorrow and sighing shall flee away,"[4] may have originally referred to the return from the captivity, but the language is "too large for the special event." Again, when Isaiah prophesies that God "will swallow up death in victory, and the Lord God will wipe away tears from off all faces, and the rebuke of His people shall be taken away from off all the earth," the Prophet may have looked forward primarily and immediately to the peace and prosperity of Judah described in the following verses: "For in this mountain shall the hand of the Lord rest, and Moab shall be trodden down under Him;" or when the same Prophet declares the promise of God to Jerusalem as follows: "Behold, I will

[1] Compare "Behold I and the children whom the Lord hath given me are for signs." (Isaiah viii. 18.)
[2] Edward Irving.   [3] Isaiah xl. 3, 4.   [4] Ib. xxxv. 8, 10.

lay thy stones with fair colours, and lay thy foundations with sapphires, and I will make thy windows of agate, and thy gates of carbuncles, and all thy borders of pleasant stones. And all thy children shall be taught of the Lord, and great shall be the peace of thy children," he may have been primarily looking forward to a glorious period of prosperity in store for his native land; but once more the language is "too vast for the special event," and the complete fulfilment of the prophecy is still expected by the author of the book of Revelation, who saw "the heavenly city, New Jerusalem, coming down from God out of heaven, prepared as a bride adorned for her husband." Now I wish to ask you why did the Prophet use this "vast language:" why for instance, in describing the future restoration and prosperity of Jerusalem, might not the Prophet content himself with saying that there should be peace, prosperity, justice, and concord? That would have been more correct, would it not?

Pupil.—But I thought the Prophet was not looking forward to one isolated and partial restoration and blessing of God's people, but to all such acts of restoration culminating in a final and perfect act.

Teacher.—Where do we look for finality and perfection?

Pupil.—In heaven.

Teacher.—Where did the Prophets?

Pupil.—They speak as though they looked for it on earth.

Teacher.—Yes. The Prophets make a marked distinction between the present where God's will is not done, and the future where it shall be done, but none of that distinction between a place called earth and another place called heaven, which is so common with us. They do not, as some modern Christians do, say that upon earth there must be evil, sin, wrong and oppression, but there shall be amends in heaven. On the contrary, the Prophets prophesied that sin should be destroyed on earth, sorrow driven away, death swallowed up in victory, the nations should beat their swords into ploughshares, the lion should cease to devour, the cockatrice to sting, and the righteous should shine out like stars. Some of these predictions are obviously hyperbolical, if literally taken: for instance, the lion's eating straw like an ox, and the city of Jerusalem being founded on sapphires. Such expressions pass the rules of ordinary language. If therefore they correctly express the meaning of the Prophet, what must we infer about that meaning?

Pupil.—I suppose that the Prophet's meaning passes the bounds of ordinary thought.

Teacher.—I think so. The Prophets felt sure that the will of Jehovah must at last, far off, be perfectly wrought out, and His triumph must be complete. When that time should come and His will should be done perfectly on earth, the joy and happiness of righteous and holiness of all men would be so great that words were incapable of expressing the greatness. Now can you tell why the Prophets do not make that marked distinction which we make between this life and the next—between earth and heaven?

Pupil.—Did they know anything about heaven? I thought it was doubted whether the early Israelites recognized the life of the soul after death.

Teacher.—That is true: and Warburton, in his Divine Legation of Moses, dwells with great force on the absence of the mention or recognition of a future life in the Books of the Law. But what is heaven?

Pupil.—A place above, where there is perfect happiness and eternal life.

Teacher.—I suppose you will admit that perfect happiness consists in doing the will of God; and as for eternal life, I dare say you remember the only definition of eternal life given by Our Lord?

Pupil.—" And this is eternal life, to know Thee the only true God, and Jesus Christ whom Thou hast sent."

Teacher.—Then heaven is a place above where the will of God is willingly done and perfectly known by men. You say "a place above." If it is "above" to you, what must it be to the antipodes: must it not be "below" to them?

Pupil.—Yes. Perhaps I had better say ' a place " merely.

Teacher.—Yes, a place or a state. Now how does the Prophet's conception of heaven differ from ours? Take Isaiah's description[1] of the Holy Mountain, from which all that is bad or harmful shall be banished. He gives "the knowledge of the Lord" as the sign and cause of the future blessed state. "They shall not hurt nor destroy in all my holy mountain: for the earth shall be full of the knowledge of the Lord, as the waters cover the sea."

Pupil.—It does not differ at all, I suppose, for they too looked forward to a place where God's will should be perfectly known and done.

Teacher.—Well, there were points of difference in the details of the manner in which they supposed God's will should be done. For example, they did not dwell on the fact, if indeed it was revealed to them as yet, that they themselves should witness or share in the future perfection. All that they insisted upon was that the remnant of Israel, Judah, should not wholly be deserted or destroyed, but should attain unto the future kingdom. About themselves they said nothing. We are given to look at one aspect of heaven, to the exclusion of the rest, as a place where we individually shall be perfectly happy. The Prophets spoke of heaven as a place where their nation should be perfectly happy. Neither aspect is complete, but which is the worthier, the more unselfish of the two?

Pupil.—I suppose that of the Prophets.

Teacher.—I think so: and now it is not difficult to see that, when revelation had gone so far, the people were not far off the complete revelation of the future state which includes the immortality of the individual soul. Can you tell me how a lamentable calamity like the lasting captivity and disappearance (as a separate nation) of the Ten Tribes may have led on to a belief in a second state of heavenly, as distinct from earthly, existence?

Pupil.—We agreed before, did we not, that disappointment with the imperfect present naturally led to the expectation of a perfect future?

---

[1] Isaiah xi. 9.

Teacher.—Yes. It must have been felt by many that it could not be that the descendants of Abraham should perish in captivity and dishonour, but Jehovah must raise them up again. It could not be that so many promises, so many gifts, so many years of guidance and training, had all been wasted. And even to the men of Judah, confidently anticipating return, yet meanwhile, during that long captivity, seeing two generations of men dying off, generations that had never trodden the soil of the sacred land, or duly observed the sacrifices and feasts which could only be duly observed in the precincts of the Temple,—it might seem intolerable that some amends should not be made to the unhappy dead. To men thus circumstanced the prophecy, "Behold, O my people, I will open your graves, and cause you to come up out of your graves, and bring you into the land of Israel,"[1] might not only bring conviction as regards this special case, but it might also lead on to further inferences, that in other cases where life seemed wasted and misused, perhaps even in all cases, there might be a second life in a second perfect state.

Let us now consider further the subjects of the prophecies. Were the Prophets wholly intent upon the future of Israel and Judah, or did they find leisure for the contemplation of the history of other nations?

Pupil.—They spoke of other nations also : Moab, Ammon, Egypt, Assyria, Æthiopia, Babylon, and others.

Teacher.—And what was the general tenor of their prophecies?

Pupil.—That all these nations must be destroyed.

Teacher.—Why? Because they were enemies of Judah?

Pupil.—No; because they were ignorant and sinful, enemies of Jehovah and worshippers of idols.

Teacher.—Yes, "They shall go to confusion together that are makers of idols. But Israel shall be saved in the Lord with an everlasting salvation."[2] That is the language of Isaiah. But these nations conquered Judah and Israel sometimes, did they not? How did the

---

[1] Ezek. xxxvii. 12. [2] Isaiah xlv. 16.

Prophets explain that? Turn to the tenth chapter of Isaiah for your answer.

Pupil.—Isaiah there says that Assyria is "a rod" and "an axe" in the hand of Jehovah, which shall be destroyed as soon as it has served its purpose and begins to "boast itself against him that heweth therewith."

Teacher.—Then there is nothing capricious, you see, in the punishments and destructions prophesied upon foreign nations by the Prophets of Judah. The destruction is as inevitable as the melting of wax in the fire or the removal of chaff by the whirlwind. It is the necessary consequence of sin, and could only be quenched by relinquishing sin. Can you mention a case where such destruction was prophesied and yet averted?

Pupil.—Jonah prophesied that Nineveh would be destroyed in forty days; but upon the sincere repentance of the people destruction was averted.

Teacher.—Did the Prophets at all influence the relations between their country and others? If so, mention an instance.

Pupil.—Yes; they often influenced them. Isaiah deprecated a confederacy with foreign nations against Assyria[1] and an alliance with Egypt[2] and Æthiopia. The same prophet stimulated Hezekiah to resist Assyria, while on the other hand Jeremiah dissuaded resistance against Babylon.

Teacher.—It would appear then that the main subject of the Prophets was the internal condition of their own country, or its external relation with foreigners? In other words——

Pupil.—Politics.

Teacher.—Yes; but not politics based on finesse or craft, or letting things alone, or making temporary shifts, or patching up compromises—but upon what?

Pupil.—The will of God.

Teacher.—The Prophets recognized no other rule. No matter for all the carrying-trade and wealth and cultivation of Tyre. Tyre

---

[1] Isaiah viii. 12.   [2] Ib. xx. 5; xxxi. 1.

was idolatrous, and by her arts and culture incited other nations to idolatry—or, in the strong language of Isaiah, Tyre was adulterous, and caused other nations to commit adultery: therefore Tyre must perish. So of Egypt: spite of all its past conquests and its present power, its horses and its chariots, "the Egyptians are men and not God, and their horses flesh and not spirit: when the Lord shall stretch out his hand, both he that helpeth shall fall, and he that is holpen shall fall down, and they all shall fall together."[1] And even though Assyria should prevail over Egypt, yet he also should perish, for "the Lord of hosts hath purposed, and who shall disannul it? and his hand is stretched out, and who shall turn it back?"[2] All things else might fail, but God's righteousness could never fail. "The heavens shall vanish away like smoke, and the earth shall wax old like a garment, but my salvation shall be for ever, and my righteousness shall not be abolished."[3] Against all hope and appearances the Prophet prophesies, confident that though victory might be delayed for a thousand years, yet in the end right and truth must prosper. And further, he had a divine insight which frequently enabled him to predict a speedy retribution when to the eye of the world it seemed far distant Now, to pass from the destruction of evil to the establishment of righteousness. What was to be the future of Judah in the new kingdom of God as described by the Prophets?

Pupil.—They were to be a nation of Kings and Priests, called by other nations "the ministers of God."[4]

Teacher.—And how were they to attain this high position? Quote from Isaiah xi. 4, and lxiii. 6; also from the Psalms ii. 9.

Pupil.—I find it said by the Psalmist to the person whom he addresses as God's "King" and "Son:" "Ask of me, and I shall give thee the heathen for thine inheritance, and the uttermost parts of the earth for thy possession. Thou shalt break them with a rod of iron; thou shalt dash them in pieces like a potter's vessel." In Isaiah xi. 1, it is prophesied of "a rod out of the stem of Jesse" that "with

---

[1] Isaiah xxxi. 3.   [2] Ib. xiv. 27.   [3] Ib. li. 6.   [4] Ib. lxi. 6.

righteousness shall he judge the poor, and reprove with equity for the meek of the earth: and he shall smite the earth with the rod of his mouth, and with the breath of his lips shall he slay the wicked." In Isaiah lxiii. 6, the speaker says "I will tread down the people in mine anger and make them drunk in my fury," and in Isaiah xxxiv. 2, "The indignation of the Lord is upon all nations, and his fury upon all their armies."

Teacher.—Here then we have one aspect of the future kingdom; the Gentiles are to be subdued, utterly conquered and crushed. Now give me another from Isaiah ii. 3, xi. 10, xi. 14, xiv. 2, xxxii. 1, lx. 10—16, lxi. 5.

Pupil.—In these passages I find mention of a King who shall reign in righteousness, and it said that the Gentiles shall of their own accord flock towards the hill of the Lord and the Temple, seeking the light of the truth of Jehovah. They will willingly restore the captive children of Israel, and will bring their treasures to Zion, coming thither to the house of the rod of Jacob. Gentile kings and queens shall become the nurses and servants of the chosen people; the Temple and the Holy City shall be built by Gentile hands; Gentiles shall willingly become ploughmen and vine-dressers in the service of the chosen seed, who shall be Priests and Levites, the special ministers of God.

Teacher.—Here then is another aspect of the conquest of God's righteousness that was to establish His kingdom. Which is the worthier?

Pupil.—The latter.

Teacher.—Why?

Pupil.—Because the former is a conquest by force, the latter by righteousness and truth: the former is over the bodies of men, the latter over their hearts.

Teacher.—But perhaps both aspects are necessary for a full appreciation of the conquest of the kingdom. We said that God's trials were compared by the Prophets to fire acting upon ore. What is the double action of fire?

Pupil.—It destroys the dross and purifies the metal.

Teacher.—" Destroys the dross." That is a metaphor when applied to God's judgments. Expand it.

Pupil.—As the dross is separated from metal by fire and destroyed, so by God's trials sin is separated from righteousness and destroyed.

Teacher.—But the Prophets seldom, if ever, speak of sin being thus destroyed, but rather of sinners.

Pupil.—But I thought you told us the men of Israel had not yet been taught, as we have been by Christ, to separate the sin from the sinner, and that they were being led up to the abstract idea of sin by the concrete term "sinners."

Teacher.—I believe you are right. And hence we should be wrong in finding fault with the Prophets or Psalmists for exulting in the destruction of sinners. The Son of Man had not yet introduced on earth the new power of forgiving sins, that is of putting them away from the sinner. Therefore the same just resentment which we feel against sin, they felt against sinners. And, remember, their resentment did not extend to another world. We have seen that they had as yet no conception of a second individual existence. Read Psalm cxlix. 5—8.

Pupil.—" Let the saints be joyful in glory: let them sing aloud upon their beds. Let the high praises of God be in their mouth, and a two-edged sword in their hand; to execute vengeance upon the heathen, and punishments upon the people ; to bind their kings with chains, and their nobles with fetters of iron."

Teacher.—That may seem to us somewhat cruel. Slaughter and praise of God may seem inconsistent. But I must repeat that the Psalmist regarded the removal of sinners' guilt from the face of the earth as the best thing for them and for the inhabitants of the earth also ; and as a vindication of the glory of Jehovah. We shudder at the thought, partly because we dislike bloodshed and pain more than the ancients did, partly because we foresee punishment in store for sinners hereafter. But it was not so with the Psalmist. When we repeat this Psalm and other similar utterances, we ought to Christianize them by a kind of proportion. As Judaism is to Christianity, so is the Psalmist's meaning to our meaning. We know what the "two-edged sword" is in the Book of Revelation,[1] and every other term of the Psalmist ought to be Christianized in the same proportion, multiplied as it were by the Christian factor. We have found the Deliverer represented by the Prophets in two aspects, as conquering by force and as conquering by righteousness, as destroying and as purifying. Can you tell me of a third aspect in which the Prophets, and more especially Isaiah, regarded Him?

Pupil.—As a sufferer.

Teacher.—Here again we may perhaps trace the training of national calamity and its effects through God's grace on the mind of the Prophet. Isaiah looks back upon the history of Israel the Prince of God, the Chosen or Elect, and he finds a chronicle of disaster and suffering: yet he perceives that God's purpose has been and will be fulfilled to reveal Himself to the Gentiles through His servant Israel. Follow me while I pass rapidly through the ten chapters, beginning at the forty-first.[2] Isaiah begins by describing the call of a Deliverer raised up by the Lord from the East, before whose sword and bow kings would be as the dust or as driven stubble.[3] "But thou, Israel, art my servant, Jacob whom I have chosen, the seed of Abraham my friend."[4] "Behold my servant, whom I uphold; mine elect, in whom my soul delighteth; I have put my Spirit upon him; he shall bring forth judgment to the Gentiles."[5] "I the Lord have called thee in righteousness, and will hold thy hand, and will keep thee, and give thee for a covenant of the people, for a light of the Gentiles."[6] "Who gave Jacob for a spoil, and Israel to the robbers? Did not the Lord, He against whom we have sinned? *For they would not walk in His ways, neither were they obedient unto His law. Therefore He hath*

---

[1] Rev. i. 16.

[2] The question whether these chapters were written by the author of the previous chapters does not seem of vital importance. In any case it does not affect the argument, nor come within the scope of this work.

[3] Isaiah xli. 2.   [4] Ib. xli. 8.   [5] Ib. xlii. 1.   [6] Ib. xlii. 6.

poured on him the fury of His anger."[1] *"Ye are my witnesses,* saith the Lord, *and my servant whom I have chosen:* that ye may know and believe me, and understand that I am he."[2] "But thou hast not called upon me, O Jacob; but thou hast been weary of me, O Israel."[3] "Therefore I have profaned the princes of the sanctuary, and have given Jacob to the curse, and Israel to reproaches."[4] "Yet now hear, O Jacob, my servant, and Israel, whom I have chosen."[5] "I will pour my Spirit upon thy seed, and my blessing upon thine offspring."[6] *"Fear ye not, neither be afraid: have not I told thee* from that time, and have declared it? *ye are even my witnesses.* Is there a God beside me? Yea, there is no God; I know not any."[7] "Behold, I have refined thee, but not with silver; I have chosen thee in the furnace of affliction."[8] "Listen, O isles, unto me. The Lord hath called me from the womb, and said unto me, *Thou art my servant, O Israel,* in whom I will be glorified."[9] "And now, saith the Lord *that formed me from the womb to be his servant, to bring Jacob again to him."*[10] "I will also give thee for a light to the Gentiles, that thou mayest be my salvation unto the end of the earth."[11] "The Lord God hath given me the tongue of the learned, that I should know how to speak a word in season to him that is weary. . . . The Lord God hath opened mine ear, and I was not rebellious, neither turned away back. I gave my back to the smiters, and my cheeks to them that plucked off the hair: I hid not my face from shame and spitting."[12] "He is despised and rejected of men, a man of sorrows and acquainted with grief; and we hid as it were our faces from him."[13] "But he was wounded for our transgressions, he was bruised for our iniquities: the chastisement of our peace was upon him, and with his stripes we are healed."[14] You will see here that at one time the suffering servant seems identified with Israel, at another time with the Prophet, at

---

[1] Isaiah xlii. 24, 25.
[2] Ib. xliii. 10.
[3] Ib. xliii. 22.
[4] Ib. xliii. 28.
[5] Ib. xliv. 1.
[6] Ib. xliv. 3.
[7] Ib. xliv. 8.
[8] Ib. xlviii. 10.
[9] Ib. xlix. 1, 3.
[10] Ib. xlix. 5.
[11] Ib. xlix. 6.
[12] Ib. l. 4—6.
[13] Ib. liii. 3.
[14] Ib. liii. 5.

another with a Deliverer quite distinct from these. In the italicized passages you will perceive that different conceptions are blended together. Thus, in xlii. 24, 25, the ideal nation, or Jacob, on whom the fury of the Lord is poured, seems separated from the individual members of the nation who would not walk in God's ways. And so in xlix. 3, Israel is regarded as the servant in whom the Lord will be glorified, whereas in the fifth verse the same speaker speaks of himself as called " to bring Jacob again." It is probably now impossible for us to ascertain the exact meaning which the Prophet originally assigned to each utterance. An important lesson, however, may still be learnt from these mysterious prophecies. We catch glimpses of a quite new revelation that pain and suffering have a conquering power ; that the ideal nation and the ideal Deliverer live not for themselves but for others ; that the King must be a servant, the ·Conqueror must be a sufferer, and the Giver of Life to others must Himself die. Lastly, we have faint traces of a new spiritual law by which the righteous can bear the sins of the unrighteous, and a prediction that when the Deliverer comes He will vindicate His supremacy by bearing the iniquities of the world.

I should now be glad if you would mention one or two of the passages which most clearly bring out the inclusion of the Gentiles among the promised people. Take the nineteenth and fifty-sixth chapters of Isaiah.

Pupil.—In the former, Isaiah includes the nations of Egypt and Assyria in the blessing of Jehovah, and in the latter chapter he says, " Neither let the son of the stranger that hath joined himself to the Lord speak, saying, The Lord hath utterly separated me from his people, for thus saith the Lord, The sons of the stranger that join themselves to the Lord, to serve him, and to love the name of the Lord, to be his servants, every one that keepeth the Sabbath from polluting it, and taketh hold of my covenant : even them will I bring to my holy mountain and make them joyful in my house of prayer : their burnt-offerings and their sacrifices shall be accepted upon mine altar: for mine house shall be called an house of prayer for all people."[1]

Teacher.—We have now, I think, a fair notion of the work of a prophet. His business was to combine theology and politics; to bring the will of Jehovah to bear upon the internal and external relations of His people; to comfort the weak and faint-hearted; to rebuke the proud; to remind his countrymen that no amount of wealth, armies, or pomp could permanently uphold a lie; that the will of Jehovah was righteousness, not sacrifice or ritual; that righteousness would prevail in the end; that sin would be destroyed, and though all the world were on the one side and the faithful few of Israel on the other, God was on the side of the weak, and the weak would conquer; nor would God be contented with an imperfect fulfilment of His will; there would be a perfect kingdom hereafter, where there should be perfect truth, justice, and holiness; and this perfection was identified with a perfect King who should reign in righteousness and conquer in meekness. Now what was it that gave the Prophets especially the power to proclaim these truths?

Pupil.—I suppose it was their insight into these truths.

Teacher.—And upon what was this insight based?

Pupil.—On their insight into the nature of God.

Teacher.—And how did God give them this insight?

Pupil.—I do not know. I suppose by His Holy Spirit.

Teacher.—But the Holy Spirit works through means, teaching us by the ties of relationship, friendship, and patriotism, by the beauty and order of the universe, and in other ways. Can you not tell me of any special way in which God taught the Prophets?

Pupil.—They had visions.

Teacher.—True. We may not be able to comprehend the meaning of these visions entirely, but I think, as the sacred writers have thought it worth while to record them, it must be our duty to study them, in the belief that "all Scripture," as St. Paul says, "is profit-

[1] Isaiah lvi. 3—7.

able." Perhaps if we knew more of the personal history of the Prophets we might be able to trace how each vision was accommodated to the circumstances and character of the "seer." The "word of the Lord" is one and the same, but the language and illustrations by which the Prophets express it differ greatly. The royal Prophet Isaiah, the herdsman Amos, the priestly Ezekiel, proclaim the same principles in very different forms. A prophet was no automaton, nor even a lifeless harp vibrated by the finger of God, but a living man with all his individual characteristics quickened and consecrated to the prophetic work. Let us here set down briefly the principal visions mentioned in the Bible, and then I will ask you what they have in common, and whether any development can be traced in them.

First, then, there was the vision of Abraham, "a smoking furnace and a burning lamp;"[1] then that of Moses, "the angel of the Lord in a flame of fire out of the midst of a bush: and behold the bush burned with fire, and the bush was not consumed."[2] Then it is recorded that Moses and Aaron with the elders "saw the Lord God of Israel; and there was under his feet as it were a paved work of a sapphire stone, and as it were the body of heaven in his clearness;"[3] "and the sight of the Lord was like devouring fire on the top of the mount in the eyes of the children of Israel." Then to the royal Prophet Isaiah, living in the royal period of Judah, while the Temple and its worship were still intact, the "King" and "Lord of Hosts" revealed Himself, encompassed by attendant seraphim, crying, "Holy, holy, holy is the Lord of Hosts; and the house was filled with smoke."[4] To the priest Ezekiel, in the land of Babylon, whose sculptures have made the winged bull familiar to us, a more complicated vision appears. He sees four living creatures having the likeness of a man, yet each with four faces, mysteriously connected together with a system of "wheels" whose appearance was "like burning coals of fire, like the appearance of lamps:" the noise of their wings was "like the noise of great waters." Above them was

[1] Gen. xv. 17. [2] Exod. iii. 2. [3] Ib. xxiv. 10. [4] Isa. vi. 3.

"the likeness of a throne, as the appearance of a sapphire stone, and upon the likeness of the throne was the likeness as the appearance of a man above it." The whole vision is preceded by a whirlwind, a cloud, a fire, and a brightness as the colour of amber.[1]

Pupil.—Is it known what is meant by the vision of Ezekiel?

Teacher.—It is thought by some that the "wheels" represent inanimate nature revolving in its regular course, and the winged creatures mean the vital spirit that quickens created beings. In any case it seems probable that together they stand for the works of Jehovah— the Universe with all its subtle organization subordinate to the Creator. I will ask you here to pause and note how the visions, as they go on, reveal more and more the personal and what I may almost call social nature of God. I mean the impossibility of knowing Him apart from His relations with the beings that He has created. The earliest vision reveals God as fire, a revelation that you see pervades almost all subsequent visions; we then learn that He is a fire that sometimes devours but sometimes purifies without consuming; then that He is a King in splendour; then that He is a King attended by adoring seraphim; and lastly, that the Universe is His throne, and His figure is revealed as "the appearance of a man above it." Turn now to the seventh chapter of the book of Daniel, and this development is still more striking. The Ancient of Days is revealed sitting on a throne of flame, supported by wheels of fire. A fiery stream issues from before Him. So far we recognize the ancient visions. But God is now revealed for the first time in conjunction with men. "Thousand thousands ministered unto him, and ten thousand times ten thousand stood before him." Such were the visions of the Prophets of God, full of appalling splendour, causing the "seers" to fall on their faces at the unbearable revelation of God's righteousness. Now tell me what was the vision seen by Jesus when He went forth to be baptized and to preach the Kingdom of God?

[1] Ezekiel i.

Pupil.—"He saw the heavens opened, and the Spirit like a dove descending on him."

Teacher.—And did He fall to the ground like Daniel, or cry, "Woe is me," like Isaiah?

Pupil.—No. He heard "a voice from heaven saying, Thou art my beloved Son, in whom I am well pleased."

Teacher.—You may learn something by thinking more at leisure about this contrast.

QUESTIONS.

CHAPTER I. LESSON 1.

1. Shew the connection between Christianity, and the purpose of God as revealed in the creation of man.

2. How would you meet the objection that the Revelation of Christ cannot come from God, or it would not have been so long delayed?

3. By what means has God trained the heathen nations who were ignorant of the Bible? Illustrate from ancient history.

4. What does St. Paul say in the Epistle to the Romans about Natural Theology? What elsewhere?

CHAPTER I. LESSON 2.

1. What difficulties present themselves in Natural Theology, and how should a Christian meet them?

2. What is meant by analogy?

3. By what name does Our Lord generally speak of God, and what may we infer by analogy from that name concerning God's relation to men?

4. Shew the connection between Christian theology and morality.

CHAPTER I. LESSON 3.

1. What is Revelation? "God is Power": in what sense is this a Revelation of God, and in what sense is it not?

2. Mention any passages in the Old Testament which illustrate the Revelation of God to man through Nature.

3. Shew how the following Books in the Bible tend to reveal God to men:

(*a*) Exodus. (*b*) Judges. (*c*) Psalms. (*d*) Job. (*e*) Isaiah.

CHAPTER II. LESSON 1.

1. On what occasions is God said to have "tempted" men? Reconcile these statements with the statement of St. James, that God tempts no man.

2. What is meant by the prayer "lead us not into temptation?"

3. How is Satan regarded in the Book of Job, in the Book of Chronicles, and by Milton?

CHAPTER II. LESSON 2.

1. Shew how (*a*) Abraham, (*b*) Jacob, (*c*) Joseph, (*d*) Moses, (*e*) Gideon, (*f*) David were trained by the circumstances of the earlier part of their lives for the part which they were afterwards called on to play.

2. Mention instances derived from ancient history or modern times, where the effect of early training can be traced in the development of great men.

CHAPTER II. LESSON 3.

1. What traces of idolatry are found in the household of the Patriarchs?

2. What is the connection between morality and the belief in the unity of God?

3. Shew from the history of the followers of Mohammed the force of the belief in the unity of God.

Chapter II. Lesson 4.

1. What is the meaning and purpose of a "vision"? What was the meaning of Abraham's vision?

2. Trace the development of God's revelation of Himself from the time of Abraham to that of Moses.

3. What is the difficulty in the statement that God "visits the sins of the fathers upon the children"? Illustrate this by reference to the History of the Old Testament and to Nature.

Chapter II. Lesson 5.

1. How did Ezekiel explain the visitation of the sins of the fathers upon the children?

2. What was wanting in the Law and the Revelation of the Law that was supplied by the Prophets?

3. Shew how the promise to Abraham was repeated and illustrated by the Prophets.

Chapter III.[1] Lesson 1.

1. What constitutes the greatness of a nation? Illustrate your answer by reference to ancient and modern history.

2. What constituted the greatness (*a*) of the Greeks, (*b*) the Romans, (*c*) the Jews?

3. What were the effects of the sojourn in Egypt upon the people of Israel?

Chapter III. Lesson 2.

1. How did God reveal Himself to the people of Israel (*a*) at the time of the Exodus, (*b*) during the wandering in the wilderness?

2. How might the natural features of the desert have acted as an antidote against idolatry?

3. Trace the influence exerted by the physical geography of (*a*) Greece, (*b*) Rome, (*c*) Palestine, upon their respective inhabitants.

---

[1] See throughout the excellent article on the "Law of Moses" in the *Dictionary of the Bible*.

Chapter III. Lesson 3.

1. Explain the temptation to idolatry.
2. Why is idolatry wrong?
3. Compare the idolatry of Greece with the idolatry of Assyria, and shew the mischief of both.

Chapter III. Lesson 4.

1. Why are we less exposed than the ancients to the temptations of idolatry?
2. In what respects was the worship of Moloch more exacting, and in what respects less exacting, than that of Jehovah?
3. Illustrate by references to the Bible the temptations which drew the people of Israel to the worship of foreign gods.

Chapter III. Lesson 5.

1. How far was the law of Moses in accordance with the modern rules of political economy?
2. In what estimation were (*a*) the fine arts, (*b*) commerce, held under the law of Moses?
3. Collect the laws of Israel relating to the tenure of land mentioned in the Old Testament. Shew how they affected the people. Compare the feudal theory of land with that of Israel.

Chapter III. Lesson 6.

1. Collect the laws of Israel relating to (*a*) lending money upon interest, (*b*) the relief of the poor. Are they applicable to modern times?
2. State, explain, and, if you can, justify the law relating (*a*) to the Avenger of blood, (*b*) to divorce. Illustrate from the New Testament.
3. What effect was the Sabbath intended to produce upon Israel?

Chapter III. Lesson 7.

1. What is the distinction between *crime* and *sin*? Illustrate from the Old Testament the fact that the men of Israel punished *sin* as *sin*.

2. What motive is constantly urged throughout the law for obedience to the law? Compare the law of Moses in this respect with the so-called laws of Lycurgus.

3. What attempts have been made, and with what success, to revive the Mosaic Law, (*a*) in England, (*b*) on the Continent? (See *Life of Huss*.)

Chapter III. Lesson 8.

1. Shew by quotations from the Old Testament, and by reference to the words and works of Greek and Latin authors, that the ideas of *sin* and *holiness* were expressed by the people of Israel with a clearness not found in other nations. Trace this to the influence of the law.

2. When is Patriotism a virtue? When a vice? Illustrate by examples from the Old Testament and elsewhere.

3. Shew how from the time of Abraham the Patriotism of Israel contained the germs of a higher virtue which was developed by the Prophets.

Chapter III. Lesson 9.

1. Explain the cruelty of the men of Israel toward their enemies.

2. Shew by quotations that the conquest of Canaan was (*a*) gradual, (*b*) imperfect. Illustrate from the Dorian emigration and the Norman conquest of England. How did these characteristics of the conquest influence the character of the people?

3. Describe and comment upon the 109th Psalm.

4. Illustrate the answer to Question 1 by detailed reference to the Assyrian marbles in the British Museum.

Chapter III. Lesson 10.

1. Describe and explain the conduct of Jael towards Sisera. What unsatisfactory extenuations have been suggested by the Rabbis to account for her conduct? (See *Dictionary of the Bible*, "Jael.")

2. What moral benefit may have been ultimately derived from the perpetual hatred subsisting between Israel and the surrounding nations?

3. Mention any irregularities as regards religious rites that seem to have been allowed during the period of the Judges and the earlier Kings. (See Judges xviii. and *Dictionary of the Bible*, "High Places.")

Chapter III. Lesson 11.

1. Why did the men of Israel desire a King? What were the advantages of monarchy? Illustrate from the Old Testament, from the History of Rome, and from that of Italy in the middle ages, or from any other source.

2. What were the disadvantages of monarchy?

3. Shew, from the biographies of Hezekiah, Ahaz, Josiah, and Uzziah, the influence which the Kings of Judah and Israel exerted for good or evil.

Chapter III. Lesson 12.

1. What were the advantages given by the Temple to the nation? Illustrate from the reign of Jeroboam.

2. What were the disadvantages of the Temple? Illustrate from Isaiah i. and from Our Lord's saying about the Temple.

3. Point out the want which the Prophets arose to meet.

Chapter III. Lesson 13.

1. What were the effects of the secession of the ten tribes—(*a*) for ill, (*b*) for good?

2. Shew that there had been anticipations of secession in the spirit of Ephraim towards Judah in previous times.

3. Give a life of Ezra. What effect did the institution of synagogues produce upon the Jews?

4. Give a brief sketch of the Wars of the Maccabees, and shew what influence they exerted upon the Jewish nation.

CHAPTER III. LESSON 14.

1. Sum up the effects of the national training of nineteen centuries at the time of the birth of Christ.

2. Compare Isaiah and Hillel. (See *Dictionary of the Bible*, "Scribe," vol. iii. p. 1166.)

3. What does St. Paul say about the difference between the "letter" and the "spirit"? What does he mean by it?

CHAPTER IV. LESSON 1.

1. What do we mean when we say "a man sells his goods at a *sacrifice*"? Distinguish this use of the word from the Old Testament usage.

2. What constitutes the difference between a good or a bad *sacrifice*? Illustrate the latter from heathen sources.

3. Shew that a *sacrifice* is a kind of acted metaphor, and expand the metaphor into a simile.

CHAPTER IV. LESSON 2.

1. Why was the death of an animal peculiarly appropriate as an emblem of the spiritual act of *sacrifice*?

2. What was meant (*a*) by sprinkling the blood of the victim upon the sacrificers, (*b*) by "laying the sins" of the sacrificer on the head of the victim?

3. Whence sprang the heathen custom of offering hecatombs? Shew that this abuse is condemned by Horace, as well as by the New Testament.

Chapter IV. Lesson 3.

1. Illustrate the heathen theory of *sacrifice*, (*a*) by the worship of Moloch, as described in the Old Testament, (*b*) by the story of Polycrates of Samos.

2. Shew from Isaiah that the ordinary sacrificers of Judah in his time had lost the true meaning of *sacrifice*. Illustrate from the Psalms.

3. What does the Epistle to the Hebrews say about the inefficacy of the blood of bulls and of goats? How far was it efficacious, how far inefficacious?

Chapter IV. Lesson 4.

1. For what purpose were Priests instituted?

2. With what truth can it be said that the Priests of the Old Testament were types of Christ?

3. With what truth can it be said that the sacrifices of the Old Testament were types of Christ?

Chapter V. Lesson 1.

1. What is the meaning of "Prophet"? Shew by reference to Isaiah that prophecy does not merely mean prediction.

2. Illustrate by the parallel passage in St. Matthew, the words in St. Mark: "And some began to spit on him and to cover his face, to buffet him, and to say unto him, *Prophesy.*" Hence deduce the meaning of the word *prophesy*.

3. What is the great moral principle pervading the works of the Prophets? Illustrate by quotations.

Chapter V. Lesson 2.

1. Mention the figurative expressions by which the Prophets described the punishments of God, and trace the continued use of these expressions in the New Testament.

2. What is there unusual in such prophecies as Isaiah xlv. 1, 1 Kings xiii. 2?

3. Shew by references that many prophecies which appear not to have been ultimately fulfilled till the coming of Christ, had primary fulfilments contemporary with the Prophets.

CHAPTER V. LESSON 3.

1. It has been said that the language of the inspired authors is often "too vast for the special events" to which they allude. Explain this.

2. What is the difference between the Prophets' conception of heaven, and ours?

3. What inference has Warburton drawn from the omission of all mention of a second life in the books of Moses? (See *Dictionary of the Bible*, vol. i. p. 74.)

CHAPTER V. LESSON 4.

1. Trace the growth of a belief in the immortality of the soul among the Jewish people.

2. Shew by quotations that the Prophets interested themselves in the affairs of foreign nations.

3. According to what principle did the Prophets predict destruction for certain foreign nations? Illustrate your answer by references.

CHAPTER V. LESSON 5.

1. With what qualifications may it be said that the Prophets treated of politics?

2. In what aspects do the Prophets describe the Kingdom of God? Compare their descriptions with those given by Our Lord.

3. Describe and explain Psalm cxlix. In what way ought we as it were to appropriate and Christianize the Psalms?

Chapter V. Lesson 6.

1. Give a brief sketch of Isaiah's allusions to the suffering Deliverer. What lesson may we learn from these prophecies?

2. Mention the passages in the Prophets which illustrate the belief in the future inclusion of the Gentiles within the pale of the promises of Jehovah.

3. Briefly describe the work of a Prophet.

Chapter V. Lesson 7.

1. Illustrate the individual peculiarities of expression in (*a*) Isaiah, (*b*) Jeremiah, (*c*) Ezekiel, (*d*) Amos.

2. Illustrate the development of God's revelation through visions, from the time of Abraham to that of Our Lord.

BIBLE LESSONS.

PART II.
NEW TESTAMENT.

BIBLE LESSONS.

Part II.—*NEW TESTAMENT.*

CHAPTER I.

THE TIMES OF CHRIST.

Teacher.—By what name did Jesus allude most frequently to Himself?

Pupil.—By the name of "Son of man."

Teacher.—What did He mean by that?

Pupil.—I suppose to identify Himself with men and men's infirmities.

Teacher.—Did He habitually call Himself by the other title of the "Son of God"?

Pupil.—I cannot remember a single instance.

Teacher.—There is one in the Gospel of St. John (ix. 37), but there are special circumstances that may explain it. But did not His disciples address Him by that name—St. Peter, for example?

Pupil.—Yes. St. Peter said, "Thou art the Christ, the Son of the living God."

Teacher.—When had Jesus told Peter this?

Pupil.—Never that we read of.

Teacher.—And I suppose from the reply of Jesus to Peter we may infer that the knowledge came from God above. "Blessed art thou,

Simon Bar-jona; for flesh and blood hath not revealed it unto thee, but my Father which is in heaven."

Pupil.—Yes.

Teacher.—Elsewhere Jesus says, "No man can come to me, except the Father draw him." But how are men drawn to Jesus—by remaining in ignorance, or by obtaining knowledge about Him?

Pupil.—By learning to know Him.

Teacher.—And how do you learn to know Him?

Pupil.—Of course, by the Gospels.

Teacher.—Yes; but what is it in the life and character of Jesus, which when you know you may be said to know Him. It must be admitted, I think, that many now read the Gospels and never learn to *know* Jesus. The Pharisees had nearly, though not quite, the same opportunities as St. Peter had for knowing Him; yet they did not know Him. Can a man be said to *know* Jesus because he knows the date and place of His birth, the names of His brethren and disciples, the details of His working and teaching, and, in a word, all that may be called the statistics of His life?

Pupil.—No; because a man may know all these facts about Jesus, and yet not know Jesus Himself or love Him at all.

Teacher.—What further knowledge is wanted then?

Pupil.—A knowledge of His character, His love, sympathy, justice, and wisdom.

Teacher.—But do you know nothing of a man from his deeds and words?

Pupil.—Yes, if you know the spirit and motives of his deeds and words.

Teacher.—Then I gather from your answer that if we desire to know Jesus, we ought to try to know not merely His words and deeds, but also and above all His motives?

Pupil.—Yes.

Teacher.—Then if a knowledge of His motives and His spirit and character is sufficient to make us know Him, and if a knowledge of

Jesus implies[1] a knowledge of the Father, and this constitutes[2] eternal life, would it not seem that eternal life was a mere matter of knowledge, depending purely upon intellect, and having no connection with morality? May not such knowledge be acquired by mere study?

Pupil.—I suppose we cannot sympathise with or understand Christ's motives or character unless our hearts, like His, are simple, frank, and unselfish; and we cannot make ourselves unselfish without the help of the Father.

Teacher.—Right. We agree, then, that for the knowledge of Jesus we need, in the first place, simplicity and purity, for which we must go elsewhere than to ourselves. "No man can come to me," said Christ, "except the Father draw him." In the second place we need to know His motives. Can we know anyone's motives well, unless we know the circumstances that call forth and shape his actions? If a man kills another, are we not for a time in doubt whether to call the act bad, or justifiable, or good, until we know the circumstances of the case? And if this be so, will it not be desirable for us to know something of the times and circumstances of Jesus? We all know that the simple story of Christ's dying on the cross for men makes itself intelligible to all times and nations without study or comment. Little knowledge of circumstances is required there. But if we are to try to understand His sternness towards the Pharisees and His lenity to the "sinners," and to appreciate the meaning of much of His teaching, which on a superficial view seems inconsistent, we cannot dispense with some knowledge of the times of Christ. Let us begin with the external relations of the Jewish people. In what condition was the Roman Empire at the time of the birth of Jesus? What was the old virtue of the Greeks and Romans, and how was that virtue flourishing?

Pupil.—The old virtue of patriotism was almost extinct.

Teacher.—True.
"Et cuncta terrarum subacta
Præter atrocem animum Catonis,"

---

[1] St. John viii. 19.   [2] Ib. xvii. 3.

—if indeed even Cato can be called a patriot, and not rather the stubborn champion of a privileged and exclusive class. There was less need of patriotism, since the boundaries between nations were being broken down and all the world consolidated under one ruler. Take another virtue. Religious feeling strongly influenced the Romans when in their prime. Was that on the decline? You can answer from what you know of Juvenal, and his description of the different religions that prevailed in Rome.

Pupil.—He says that superstition was on the increase; that the gods of Asia had invaded Rome; that charms and magic were prevalent; and that morality was severed from religion.

Teacher.—Hence we gather that the old local limits which confined the Greek Apollo to Delphi and the Roman Jupiter to the Capitol, had been, or were being, swept away, and that the path was being prepared for any new faith that might claim the allegiance of all nations indiscriminately. Now pass from Rome to Palestine. Was the Chosen People contented and happy?

Pupil.—I should think not, under the yoke of Roman idolaters.

Teacher.—True. And the yoke was not an imaginary grievance. It pressed heavily sometimes. Tradition reports that our Lord's reputed parents came originally from Sephoris in Galilee. Even if it was not so, He could hardly fail to hear from them how, about the time of His birth, that town had been burned to the ground and the townsmen sold for slaves by the Roman Varus; how in the southward march of the Romans and Arabians "nothing escaped them as they marched forward, and all things were full of blood and fire;"[1] and how in the neighbourhood of Jerusalem two thousand insurgents had been crucified. Judas of Galilee had headed an insurrection against the oppressors, and though he had died fighting unsuccessfully for his country, yet his name was not forgotten. His memory was preserved by a distinct "sect" described by Josephus with the Essenes, Sadducees, and Pharisees. These "Galileans," as they were called, combined the theology of the Pharisees with a patriotism of their

[1] Josephus.

own: they refused to call any man "master," a title reserved for God alone, and they were taught by their leader to despise death in comparison with slavery. At the time when Jesus went forth on his mission, three sons of Judas of Galilee were growing up in his native Gamala, ripening for a renewal of their father's work, and destined to imitate him both in life and death. To the influence and followers of Judas Josephus attributes the final destruction of Jerusalem. We cannot doubt, therefore, that during the life of Jesus, and especially in Galilee, the patriots called "Galileans" must have been numerous, and no "Galilean" could be happy under the yoke of idolaters. I think you will easily supply for yourselves the sort of argument by which the patriots would have justified their obstinate resistance against overwhelming odds, and would have defended themselves against the charge of folly or rashness by a reference to the Scriptures.

Pupil.—They would say that in the old times of their people Jehovah had given them the victory against superior numbers of the enemy.

Teacher.—Yes. They would allege the examples of David, Gideon, and Barak, and they would say that the principle pervading the whole of the Sacred Books was that might was not right, but right was might. "What was right for David, Gideon, Barak, and in later times for Judas Maccabeus, why is that wrong for Judas of Galilee? Is not Jehovah one and the same? and if we trust in Him, will He not help us? And do we not need His help? Are we not surrounded by influences less oppressive, perhaps, but more insidiously hostile to our religion than the yoke of Jabin or of Antiochus? Are we not enslaved by Roman idolaters, corrupted by Grecian manners and Grecian literature, already almost beguiled out of the use of our native tongue? It is better to perish at once gloriously than to linger on till we have lost the last spark of national courage and piety."

That is, I suppose, how they would argue. And would they not argue well? Must not such an argument have sounded very plausible to patriotic, trustful, and unselfish peasants; though it might repel the selfish and the luxurious, the time-serving Herodian, the incredulous Sadducee, and the hard, dry Pharisee whose faith was merely in a book? What would you have had to urge against such an argument, if you had been then living?

Pupil.—I do not know; but Jesus did not assent to it.

Teacher.—Why not? Was it not right to trust that the promise of Joshua would be fulfilled, "One man of you shall chase a thousand: for the Lord your God, he it is that fighteth for you, as he hath promised me."[1] Perhaps I shall suggest an answer if I repeat the words that follow the quotation: "Take good heed therefore unto yourselves, that ye love the Lord your God. Else know for a certainty that the Lord your God will no more drive out any of these nations from before you."

Pupil.—I suppose the moral state of the nation was not such as to warrant the expectation that Jehovah would give them the victory.

Teacher.—Can you remember any instance in the past history of Israel where the nation was not encouraged by its prophets to attack or resist other nations?

Pupil.—Moses forbade them to attack Canaan, saying, "Because ye are turned away from the Lord, therefore the Lord will not be with you;"[2] and Jeremiah dissuaded his countrymen from resisting Babylon.

Teacher.—Yes. But I think we should be wrong in inferring that the only reason why Jesus refused to put Himself at the head of the Galilean patriots was because the nation was not righteous enough to obtain the victory. He felt that the mere expulsion of the Romans from Palestine was not sufficient to ensure the welfare of the nation or the advent of the kingdom of God. There was a certain class or classes of the nation upon whom He looked with peculiar tenderness and pity, as though to compensate for the contempt and hatred with which they were regarded by the rest of their countrymen.

---

[1] Joshua xxiii. 10.   [2] Numbers xiv. 43.

What names are given in the New Testament to these classes whom Jesus came especially to help?

Pupil.—Publicans and sinners. He also manifested great compassion for the diseased and for demoniacs.

Teacher.—Yes. No amount of foreign conquest could help these classes. They would perhaps have felt the consequences of the expulsion of the Roman legions in increased persecution. The publicans were regarded, and not without reason, as traitors to their country, in league with idolatrous conquerors, wringing by foreign aid unlawful gains from their enslaved countrymen; they, and the "sinners" with them, had in many cases wholly or partially cast off the allegiance of Jehovah, and adopted the customs of idolaters. They infected the whole of the nation by their guilt, they prevented the accomplishment of the promised blessings of Jehovah, and retarded the fulfilment of the prophecies of the future kingdom. They were outcasts from the respectable classes, and excommunicated from the synagogues. No attempts were made to raise or win them back to God. Sea and land were compassed to make one foreign proselyte, but hundreds of native publicans and sinners sinned on at home, hated, and not helped. If the extreme religious party could have had their will, it cannot be doubted that the sword of Phinehas would have been invoked to vindicate the sanctity of the nation, and to exterminate apostasy. Now Jesus said that He came especially to save these traitors and sinners. How was this to be done? By expelling the Romans from Palestine? Clearly not. Rather by including the outcasts once more in the Chosen People; by bringing them back to their allegiance, and making them loyal subjects to Jehovah. If in the old history of the people, Gideon, Barak, and David—if, in later times, Judas Maccabeus and his brothers—had attained all the success that could be hoped from force of arms, and yet had not been able to prevent the existence of a class of "sinners," the failure showed that the old remedy was insufficient, and a new remedy must be tried. Conquest of two kinds had been predicted of the Deliverer by the Prophets,—conquest by arms, and

G

conquest by the inherent force of goodness, by the spirit of righteousness. The first kind of conquest had been tried and found wanting; the new conquest must now be effected. It had been predicted that the Messiah must smite the Gentiles and slay sinners. That prediction must be fulfilled. Jesus felt that He must smite, but "with the rod of his mouth."[1] He must destroy sinners, or rather sin, but "with the breath of his lips."[1] Jesus would not break "the bruised reed," or quench the lingering flame of hope in the meanest sinner. Not by "striving,"[2] or "crying," or by "raising his voice in the streets," but by the peaceful quiet influence of His life and work He would "send forth judgment unto victory." I think you will now understand how it was that the Galilean patriots, sincere, trustful, and zealous as many of them were, nevertheless could not receive the complete approbation of Jesus. What are the three other sects described by Josephus?

Pupil.—I only know of the Sadducees, Pharisees, and Herodians.

Teacher.—The Herodians are not mentioned by him. They included probably all who in the upper classes were more or less disposed to support Herod in his desire to adopt the religion and spread the customs of the Greeks. But though Josephus does not mention the Herodians, he does mention the Essenes. For details of this sect you should refer to the *History of the Antiquities.*[3] I will only say that though they, like the Galileans, probably sent many disciples to Jesus, and though the purity of their lives inspired the nation with respect, yet they did not contain that aggressive spirit which was necessary to bring in the kingdom of God. The majority of them lived outside the walls of towns, and all alike were more bent upon attaining individual purity and holiness than on delivering the nation. After many years of existence, Essenism had resulted in "four thousand men" leading retired lives. Such is the account of Josephus. Essenism was a city in a valley, a candle under a bed,

---

[1] Isaiah xi. 4.
[2] Isaiah xlii. 2; St. Matthew xii. 20.
[3] History of the Antiquities, xviii. 1; Wars of the Jews, ii. 8.

clearly no principle capable of regenerating the world. Now give me briefly the characteristics of the Sadducees.

Pupil.—They did not believe in the resurrection, nor in any part of the Scriptures but the Pentateuch.

Teacher.—Many doubt the latter assertion, which you will find discussed in the *Dictionary of the Bible.* But at all events they attached more weight to the Law than to the rest of the Scriptures. They represented the Priests, as the Pharisees did the Scribes. They were aristocrats, while the Pharisees represented the middle and respectable classes. They were conservatives, and adhered to the written law; the Pharisees developed, commented, explained the stern Mosaic code into conformity with the humanized requirements of Herodian times. The Pharisees believed in predestination and in the immortality of the soul, and were led by these opinions to tend sometimes towards mercy when sitting as magistrates; the Sadducees judged men as they found them, and repudiated as new-fangled innovations, as inventions of popular Scribes, subversive of the priestly influence, all doctrines that looked beyond the present life. They were necessarily unpopular and uninfluential; they had no active spiritual vigour, and it was not from Sadduceeism that there could proceed the kingdom of God. Far more important was the sect of the Pharisees. Give me a brief description of them.

Pupil.—They are described as hypocrites, outwardly righteous, but inwardly detestable; as destroying the simplicity of the law by traditions, and imposing upon the people the burdens of new restrictions that were too hard for them to bear.

Teacher.—Yes; but now take the account of the Pharisees given by Josephus. "The Pharisees live simply and economically, not giving way to the encroachments of luxury. They yield precedence in points of honour to those who are advanced in age. The cities bore witness to the height to which they had carried the practice of virtue in all things, both as regards their way of living and their teaching." He adds that they are "noted for loving one another, and also for practising concord for the common welfare." We further know from the Acts of the Apostles, as well as from Josephus, that they held the ennobling belief in the immortality of the soul.

Pupil.—Then either Josephus must have been wrong, or our notions about the Pharisees must be incorrect.

Teacher.—That does not seem to me to follow. That the Pharisees had impressed the people with the religiousness of their lives is clearly indicated in the New Testament, as well as in Josephus. But then Jesus said that "that which is highly esteemed among men is abomination in the sight of God."[1] To understand the bitter resentment with which Jesus assailed the Pharisees is so important, that we must try to find out wherein their "abomination" consisted. We are met with a difficulty at the outset. It is not easy to obtain a fair specimen of the average teaching of Phariseeism. The Rabbinical traditional literature was not committed to writing till about four hundred years after Christ. It is most improbable that Judaic teaching and Christian teaching should run on side by side for so long a time, without mutual influence. Sometimes this influence might be of a repellent nature. For example, such a sentence as "there is no mediator between those who are called the children and their Father which is in heaven," contains in itself strong internal evidence, that it was not originated by Jewish thought, but was a protest suggested by the contrary belief of Christians. Similarly, but conversely, when we find quoted from the Talmud sayings that are very unlike the bulk of Talmudic literature, and very like the bulk of early Christian teaching, we may naturally infer that we find Christian influence again, only not now producing repulsion, but imitation. The evidence derived from the Apocrypha seems to show that in the interval between the Captivity and the coming of Christ the Jews had not learned to distinguish between sinners and sin, or to apprehend the duty of loving all men. "Give to the pious, and do not lend a hand to sinners," is the language of the Book of Tobit. The terrible punishments which are represented in the Book of the

[1] St. Luke xvi. 15.

Apocalypse, as impending upon spiritual wickedness, are described in the Apocryphal writings, as reserved for the national enemies of the Jewish race. "Woe shall come to those that rise up against my race, the Almighty Lord shall be avenged on them in the day of judgment by pouring fire and worms upon their flesh, and they shall feel it and bewail for ages," is the patriotic prediction of Judith. If, therefore, in the Apocrypha, there is little trace of the peculiar spirit which appeared in Christianity, it is a reasonable inference that in the literature which continued the Apocrypha, some of the few scattered indications of the Christian spirit may have been borrowed from Christian teaching.

One remarkable anticipation of Christian teaching is attributed on fair evidence to the great teacher Hillel. "Do nothing to thy neighbour, that thou wouldest not that he should do to thee; do this, and thou hast fulfilled the law and the prophets." But many other sayings of a Christian character seem to betray Christian influence, such as "even for a babe one may break the sabbath, for the babe will keep many a sabbath for the sabbath that was broken for him." There are many other sayings indicative of a sound and shrewd morality, which may or may not be tinged by Christian thought. One teacher protests against "laws that hang on hairs," and declares that the law was meant to be a help, not a burden, to men. A third, while he allots the sixth place in the seven classes of virtuous men to those who do right from the fear of God, allots the seventh and highest to those who do right because they love Him. Other remarkable sayings indicate the repute in which respectable industry was held by the Pharisees, and the importance attached to education and the study of the law. "A teacher is to be more revered than a father;" "a tradesman at his work need not rise before the greatest doctor;" "greater is he who derives his livelihood from work than he who fears God;" "Jerusalem was destroyed because the education of the young was neglected."[1] But, whatever may

[1] These sayings are collected from Mr. Deutsch's valuable article on the Talmud in the *Quarterly Review*.

be the origin of these precepts, there are clear indications that they do not represent the average teaching of Phariseeism. Is it not worse than absurd, is it not immoral, that the school of Hillel and Shammai should be divided on the question "whether eggs ought to be eaten when laid on festival days," or "with what sort of oil and wick are the candles of the Sabbath to be lighted"? And the immorality is unquestionable, when a Jewish debtor is prohibited, by Phariseean interpretation of the Scriptures, from paying a debt to a heathen three days before any pagan festival, and when a Jewish midwife is forbidden to assist a heathen mother in the pangs of childbirth.

The sin of the Pharisees will be illustrated by the following sentence from Josephus. "There was a certain sect of men that were Jews, who valued themselves highly upon the exact skill they had in the law of their fathers, and made men believe they were highly favoured by God; these are they that are called the sect of the Pharisees." The Pharisees were resolved to find an answer to every problem of life in the law. For this purpose they were prepared to explain everything, rightly or wrongly, into some kind of conformity with modern requirements. What they were not prepared to do was to think and feel for themselves. They believed in the letter, not in the spirit of the law. The Spirit, they thought, had once inspired the prophets, but had now long ceased to inspire the teachers of later times. They felt themselves unworthy of such inspiration, and they were loth to believe that others were more worthy. Hence when a new teacher arose, who professed to teach "with authority," given by the Spirit of God, their hostility was at once aroused. They said of the new teacher, in the words of the Apocrypha,[1] "He professeth to love the knowledge of God, and he calleth himself the child of the Lord. He was made to reprove our thoughts. He is grievous unto us even to behold; for his life is not like other men's, his ways are of another fashion. We are esteemed

---

[1] Wisdom of Solomon, ii. 13—16. This quotation is merely intended for illustration. The date is therefore of no importance.

of him as counterfeits; he abstaineth from our ways as from filthiness: he pronounceth the end of the just to be blessed, and maketh his boast that God is his Father." The precepts of the Pharisees were sometimes right, but, whether right or wrong, they were always based upon a false foundation. They worshipped a dead book, instead of a living God. They lost all sympathy with the hearts of their fellow-men. They could not answer the inquiries or satisfy the cravings of those who hungered and thirsted after righteousness. If they were asked for bread, they could only offer a stone. They clothed themselves with pedantry as with a garment, and became inextricably entangled in its folds: they loved dogmatism, and dogmatism encircled them as a girdle. They abhorred the Spirit of God, and the Spirit hovered far off from them on more congenial hearts; they honoured a teacher more than a father, a scholar more than a prophet; and, as a just retribution, they lost the spirit of sonship and the spirit of prophecy, and when at last the Father was revealed, and the Prophet of prophets came, they could discern neither Father nor Prophet.

Such was the sin of the Pharisees; a sin to which the popular teachers of every age are liable, and from which our age is probably not altogether exempt. Now I think you will better understand the resentment which Jesus felt against the Pharisees. But He called them "hypocrites." They were in error: but how does it appear that they were insincere?

Pupil.—I do not know, unless they knew the truth and taught falsehood.

Teacher.—I think any one who separates religion from sympathy, and the letter from the spirit of a law, must sometimes be insincere. Men must at times feel that they are guided by a Divine Spirit, that they are bound to think and feel and act as that Spirit dictates, and that the "Whole Duty of Man" cannot be contained in a book of reference. Men must sometimes confess the force of goodness, and must perceive that goodness must come from God wherever it is. In order to call goodness bad, as the Pharisees did, and to attribute the work of God to an evil spirit, a man must do violence to the spirit within him. He must feel one thing and say another, he must be a "hypocrite," and must sin against the Holy Spirit.[1]

It was thus that the Pharisees sinned. They stood face to face with One whom they could not but feel to be loving, wise, and powerful; or if they doubted of His wisdom, they could not doubt of His love. His infinite tenderness and compassion for the outcasts of Israel ought to have shamed them into admiration. His power of healing ought to have made them recognize a beneficent mission. But no. The law, or their explanation of the law, laid down that healing on the Sabbath was unlawful. This man healed on the Sabbath, therefore this man was a bad man, all other goodness notwithstanding. But, it might be urged, he healed with a touch, and soul as well as body; the sensualist became pure, the miser liberal in his presence. That mattered not; they could not deny the facts, but they could attribute the facts to the devil, and they did so.

Besides, the attempts to find a law for all modern life, and a solution of every modern question in the Mosaic code, must necessarily have caused hypocrisy. When teachers of a nation are ready to explain, by resorting to suppositions that have no basis, or by interpretations that contradict the laws of language; when they are even ready not to explain, but to explain away, provided that they shall be allowed to appear to explain instead of thinking for themselves; and when a system based on such wretched subterfuges, injurious alike mentally and morally, becomes recognized as the standard of national morality, and as regulating the relations between God and man, then "hypocrite" must soon become the only appropriate title for a minister of the national religion.

Now that we have passed rapidly through the different classes of Jewish society, tell me what it was that Jesus wished to introduce among them, and how far He could hope for help from them. In

---

[1] There is no evidence to show that the Pharisees, though some may have "devoured widows' houses," were as a body avaricious or immoral in their lives.

what short form do the Evangelists describe the doctrine of Jesus and the new state which He wished to introduce?

Pupil.—Jesus wished to introduce the kingdom of God.

Teacher.—Well, the Galileans were intent upon the kingdom of the Jews, the Essenes on individual purity, the Sadducees on worldly success, the Pharisees upon the popularity and the supremacy of the law. What class of those above mentioned have I omitted?

Pupil.—The publicans and sinners.

Teacher.—Who was there to help them?

Pupil.—No one.

Teacher.—True: no one. Their salvation was not of the Pharisee, the Sadducee, the Essene, or the Herodian. Therefore Jesus of Nazareth came to help the helpless: "He looked, and there was none to help; and he wondered that there was none to uphold; therefore his own arm brought salvation unto him."[1]

[1] Isaiah lix. 16.

CHAPTER II.

THE LIFE OF CHRIST.

Teacher.—Suppose you come suddenly into a class-room and hear the master in the midst of a lesson, are you likely to be able to appreciate what he is saying? And if not, why not?

Pupil.—Because I should not know how far the class had gone, what had been explained to them, and what still remained to be explained.

Teacher.—Then in order to appreciate the teaching, you ought to put yourself in the position and enter into the thoughts of whom?

Pupil.—The pupils.

Teacher.—In the same way to appreciate Christ's teaching we ought to try to put ourselves in the position and enter into the thoughts of those whom He taught. Their notions of Christ (or rather of Jesus of Nazareth, for so they regarded Him) may have been very inadequate: but if we want to understand Christ's teaching, we must understand the inadequacy of the pupils. Now, how did the Jews regard Jesus of Nazareth from the first? as the Messiah, as Divine, or as what?

Pupil.—Most of them at first regarded Him as a Prophet.

Teacher.—Can you quote me any passages which illustrate this?

Pupil.—When Jesus[1] asked His disciples what was the popular opinion about Him, they replied that some thought he was John the Baptist, others Elias, others Jeremias, or one of the Prophets.

Teacher.—There seems at this time to have been a common

[1] St. Matthew xvi. 13, 14; St. Mark vi. 15.

expectation that not merely "a" Prophet, but some one whom they called "*the* Prophet," should arise. Can you show this?

Pupil.—"*The* Prophet" is mentioned in the first chapter of St. John's Gospel (where our version has "*that* Prophet"). "Art thou Elias? And he saith, I am not. Art thou *the* Prophet? And he answered, No." And, again, "This is of a truth *the* prophet that should come into the world."[1] You told us before that Moses (Deut. xviii. 15—18) had predicted the advent of a Prophet "like unto him."

Teacher.—Well, then, since this was the point to which Christ's pupils had arrived, let us for a time lay aside, for the purposes of study, our own increased knowledge, and let us strive, like the Jewish peasants of Galilee, to regard Jesus of Nazareth as a Prophet or *the* Prophet. Then let us follow Him from His Baptism to the Temptation, from the Wilderness to Capernaum, from Capernaum to Jerusalem, listening to His teaching, observing His life and works; and let us try to receive His words as His disciples received them, and to grow in knowledge of our Master as His disciples grew. For this purpose we will pass over the description of the birth and infancy of Jesus, since these details do not appear to have been generally known or communicated to His disciples from the first; and we will pass to the Baptism, as the first public appearance of the new Prophet of Nazareth. This leads us to consider the Baptist, and the impression which Jesus produced upon him. Give a brief description of the preaching of John the Baptist, and show how he made use of the traditional imagery of prophetic expression.

Pupil.—John the Baptist, like the Prophets, predicted "the kingdom of heaven" or "salvation of God." He added that it was close at hand, and that all should prepare for it by repentance and the purification of Baptism in water.

Teacher.—Yes; but he also illustrated his mission by the traditional prophetic metaphors. Like the Prophets, he spoke of the destroying axe, the consuming but purifying fire, the winnowing fan separating

[1] St. John vi. 14.

the chaff and the wheat. More distinctly than the other Prophets, he warned his hearers not to trust in their mere descent from Abraham. "God was able," he said, "to raise up from the stones children unto Abraham." He also identified the purifying fire and the winnowing fan with the presence of a Deliverer greater than himself, who was to baptize with fire and the Holy Spirit. What distinction was drawn between purification by water and by fire in the early days of Israel? Turn to Numbers xxxi. 23.

Pupil.—Spoils taken in war were all to be purified in water and some in fire also. Purification by fire was regarded as more complete, and reserved for more precious and durable articles than those purified by water only. "The gold, and the silver, the brass, the iron, the tin, and the lead, everything that may abide the fire, ye shall make it go through the fire, and it shall be clean : nevertheless it shall be purified with the water of separation : and all that abideth not the fire ye shall make go through the water."

Teacher.—We will enter more fully into this hereafter. I will now merely ask what was the impression produced by Jesus upon John. You will remember that John said, "I have need to be baptized of thee, and comest thou to me?" How is this reconcilable with the declaration, "and I knew him not"?

Pupil.—The Baptist recognized Him, even before the Baptism, as superior to himself in purity. After the Baptism, and the appearance of the descent of the Holy Spirit on Jesus, John recognized Him as the Deliverer, and also spoke of Him as "the Lamb of God which taketh away the sin of the world," and as "the Son of God."

Teacher.—After the Baptism, Jesus is said to have been led by the Spirit into the wilderness, where He was tempted by the Devil. We shall never be able to comprehend how One whom we believe to be incapable of sin could be "tempted." Yet we are bound to believe that these temptations were real, like ours. Else there would be no argument in the words, "For in that he himself hath suffered being tempted, he is able to succour them that are tempted." But we may naturally expect the temptations of Jesus to be very different from those of selfish or vicious men, may we not?

Pupil.—Yes. And they are quite different from those of good men also. For no one, whether bad or good, would be tempted to turn stones into bread, or to worship Satan for the kingdom of the world, or to cast himself down from a pinnacle of the Temple.

Teacher.—Yet evidently we are intended to enter into the meaning of the temptations. Else they need not have been recorded, and we might merely have been informed that Christ was tempted. We ought not in considering this subject to forget the close connection in the narrative between the temptations and the Baptism which immediately preceded them. Jesus had just heard a Voice from heaven proclaiming Him to be the Son of God. Henceforward a new and more active life lay before Him. The powers, and duties, and responsibilities attending the public life of the Son of God came pressing upon Him, and hurried Him to the solitude of the desert, where He might find time for reflection and prayer. There, in the desert, with each power and duty as they passed in review before Him, came the Tempter's voice suggesting some corresponding temptation. The outward form of the temptation was different in each case, but the basis is the same throughout—"*if thou be* the Son of God." Let us now consider the first temptation. We know that the avowed purpose of Jesus was to preach the kingdom of God. Hitherto He had worked no miracles. Now, the time for working miracles had nearly arrived. He felt within Himself a Divine power to perform wonderful works in accordance with the will of God, for the furtherance of the kingdom. How might it seem that that purpose could be furthered by turning stones into bread?

Pupil.—I suppose if Jesus could have used His divine power to supply the necessities of life, He might have seemed freed from some restrictions and obstacles in the way of success. He would be independent, instead of being dependent on the charity of disciples and admirers.

Teacher.—But is not Jesus afterwards said to have created or increased bread and meat, so as to feed five thousand men with food barely sufficient for five?

Pupil.—Yes; but that was not for Himself.

Teacher.—True: the temptation may perhaps be made intelligible to us somewhat thus: " Was the Son of God to be a beggar or a poverty-stricken teacher dependent for His daily bread upon the purses of necessitous disciples, and thereby exposing Himself to the sneers and suspicions of every respectable and independent scribe? Spiritual power was good, but spiritual power aided by endowments was better. Let him make to himself friends of the Mammon of unrighteousness. For the sake of the kingdom of God, let the Son of God turn these stones into bread." Thus, then, the temptation consisted not so much in the inducement to create bread as to create bread for Himself, to supply His own wants by Divine power, and to raise Himself above the limitations of humanity. This He would not do. Do you remember what His enemies said of Him when He was on the cross, about saving Himself?

Pupil.—" He saved others; Himself He cannot save."[1]

Teacher.—The saying was true, though, like Caiaphas's utterance, the truth was beyond the reach of the utterers. It was against Christ's nature to save Himself: He not only would not, He could not do it. And in the same way it may be said with truth, " He could feed others miraculously: He could not feed Himself." A weak and selfish monarch finds the ideal of power and royalty incompatible with the wants and weaknesses of common men:

> " I live with bread like you,
> Feel want, taste grief, need friends. Subjected thus,
> How can you say to me I am a king?"

Very different was the royal ideal of Jesus, whose kingship was a supremacy in suffering, and whose crown a crown of thorns.

Now pass to the temptation to worship Satan for the dominion of

---

[1] St. Matthew xxvii. 42.

the world. How do men do homage to Satan, to the Prince of this world? By their words, or by their lives?

Pupil.—By their lives, by worldly conduct.

Teacher.—And by what kind of worldly conduct do great conquerors often obtain dominion?

Pupil.—By cruelty and unscrupulousness.

Teacher.—Yes; but most often by diplomacy, and combining tact with force, and flattery with tyranny. How had David obtained dominion for Israel?

Pupil.—By force of arms.

Teacher.—Quote a passage which shows that Jesus identified the "kingdom of this world" with warfare.

Pupil.—Jesus said to Pilate, "My kingdom is not from this world: if my kingdom were from this world, then would my servants fight."[1]

Teacher.—It would seem that to do homage to Satan for the dominion of the world would include resorting to force of arms. It might also include an unsatisfactory compromise with any dominant power or class in society (with the Pharisees, for example), for the sake of obtaining immediate success. But war was the great and pressing temptation to all good men at the time. War was the desire of the Galilean patriots, among whom Jesus had lived. But why was it wrong to fight for the diffusion of the truth of Jehovah? Was it wrong for David, Gideon, and Judas Maccabeus?

Pupil.—Surely not.

Teacher.—Was the dominion obtained by these conquerors permanent? Had it destroyed sin? Was it not confessedly imperfect? Was not Jesus looking forward to a perfect kingdom? And would it not be wrong for One who knew the perfect to accept the imperfect instead? On the other hand, do we not often do this? Are we not continually making compromises? and is it not the very essence of a compromise that it is considered as perfect by none of the agreeing parties?

---

[1] St. John xviii. 36. The A. V. has "of" in the Elizabethan sense of "from."

Pupil.—Yes. But our knowledge is imperfect. We cannot conceive of Jesus making a compromise.

Teacher.—True. And yet He Himself said that God had allowed many things "for the hardness of the hearts of men." A compromise might have secured to His side the Galilean patriots and the Pharisees, and thus concentrated the whole nation. There is nothing improbable in supposing that, if Jesus would have stooped to use force, the result of many centuries might have been anticipated, and a Syrian might have sat upon the throne of the Roman Empire. The imperial seat might have seemed a fit and influential pulpit for the proclamation of the kingdom of God. But God's ways are not our ways, and we are told that God "has chosen the weak things of the world to confound the things which are mighty,"[1] and prefers "the still small voice" to work His conquests, rather than the whirlwind and the fire.

Now pass to the third temptation, to cast Himself down from the pinnacle. This was to expose Himself to pain or death, the common lot of men; the first temptation was to deliver Himself from these evils. Can you mention any instances where Jesus avoided death and danger?

Pupil.—Yes. He retreated into a desert apart, when word was brought that the Baptist had been put to death by Herod.[2] And other cases are recorded of His escaping from His enemies when they wished to kill Him.

Teacher.—And yet, when "His hour had come," He went up to Jerusalem to meet a death predicted by Himself. Can you imagine how Jesus may have been tempted to do this before, to look danger in the face, and to refuse to escape from Herod or from His other enemies?

Pupil.—He may have disliked the appearance of fear.

Teacher.—Just so. And the temptation we are considering may have been of a similar nature. The pinnacle or battlement was proverbial for its height and dizzying prospect. The extremity of rashness that would suggest itself to those who were familiar with

---

[1] 1 Cor. i. 27. [2] St. Matthew xiv. 13.

the Temple would be to cast oneself down from so perilous a height. Though it is extremely difficult for us to comprehend it, Jesus may have been tempted to manifest His great love for the Father and His infinite faith, by exposing Himself to what would ordinarily be called certain death in reliance on the Father's power and love. The Tempter's implied suggestion that the Father might not protect His Son and that the Son had not trust enough in the Father to rely on His protection is intelligible to us just in proportion as we love and trust the Father and are jealous of His honour. To Jesus, therefore, the greatest of all temptations may have been that which is the least to us, " If thou be the Son of God, cast thyself down."

We ought not perhaps to exclude the possibility that this temptation may have also presented itself in connection with the " sign from heaven" which many of the Jews required as a test of the genuineness of the Messiah's mission. If, as there seems some reason to suppose, it was the popular belief that false gods and magicians could work signs on earth but not in heaven, then it might well seem that the most appropriate sign for one who was not a magician, the fittest "sign of the Son of Man,"[1] would be the Son of Man Himself descending from heaven in accordance with the prophecies of Daniel, and carrying irresistible conviction to every heart. Hence the error to which our Lord was tempted may have been based partly upon His willingness to show His trust in the Father, but partly also upon His desire to diffuse at once the kingdom of God, which might be effected by the sign here suggested. What name should we give to such an error in ordinary men?

Pupil.—Fanaticism.

Teacher.—Yes: the last temptation seems to have been to use spiritual power in defiance of reason. On the other hand, the first seems to have been a temptation to distrust spiritual power unless it could procure material support, a kind of religious self-distrust or quasi-prudence; and the second temptation, which suggested the propriety of an alliance and compromise between spiritual and

[1] St. Matthew xxiv. 30.

temporal power may be called worldly wisdom. And now, if we sum up the result of the temptations, we find that Jesus had determined, in preaching the Kingdom of God, 1st, not to raise Himself above the wants of human nature; 2nd, to make no compromise with worldliness in any form; 3rd, to blend wisdom with His harmlessness.

This has been a digression. For we are bent on regarding Jesus just now as a Prophet, and upon asking how at first He appeared to the inhabitants of Galilee, and we have no evidence that the narrative of these temptations was imparted at this time to His followers. Now let us return to our main subject. How far did He seem like, and how far unlike, the ancient Prophets? First, how was He like His predecessors? What did He proclaim?

Pupil.—The Kingdom of God.

Teacher.—In that respect He was like the Prophets; in what respect was He unlike them?

Pupil.—Jesus said that He came to fulfil the predictions of the Prophets.

Teacher.—Exactly. He Himself was the fulfilment; His word was the law of the new kingdom. Not content with expounding the old law like the scribes, or developing it like the prophets, He set forth a new law, higher and purer than the old, and regulating the heart instead of the actions; and this law was His own will. That the subjects of the new kingdom might be enabled to fulfil the new law, He summoned them to come to Him, to fix their hearts on Him, to suffer persecutions for Him, and to take His yoke upon them. Offences against the law were forgiven by Him. Admission to the franchise of the new kingdom was in His hands. Exclusion from the kingdom belonged to Him alone. Against dissembling and disloyal subjects He declared that He should close the gates with the words, "I never knew you; depart from me, ye that work iniquity." We have said that the will of Jesus was the new law. Yet it is equally true that Jesus expressly said He did not come to do His own will, and always subordinated His will. Can you explain this?

Pupil.—Jesus came to do the will of God, and taught His disciples to make God's will their law. But, on the other hand, His will was at one with the will of God; so it may be said that the will of Jesus was the law of His disciples.

Teacher.—Yes. He called men to come to Him because through Him they came to God the King. But He did not often call God by the name of King, though He often spoke of the Kingdom of God. By what name did He generally speak of God to His disciples?

Pupil.—As a Father.

Teacher.—And consequently all men were to be called brothers. But what name do you give to that kind of kingdom in which the king is a father, and in which all fellow-subjects are brothers?

Pupil.—A family.

Teacher.—And what is the law which unites a family and secures to each member of it his appropriate rights?

Pupil.—There is no law, and there are no rights, in a family. There is no need for such things if they love one another.

Teacher.—Then if there is to be a law at all, a family must be ruled by the law of love. This, then, was the law laid down by Jesus Christ for His disciples. His disciples were to love those that hated them, and bless them that cursed them, that they might be the children of their Father in heaven. There was to be absolutely no resistance to evil. Blows were not to be returned, robbery and compulsion not even to be avoided.

Pupil.—But is that not a mere figurative expression, "Whosoever smiteth thee on thy right cheek, turn to him the other also"?

Teacher.—It certainly cannot be called figurative, and I, for one, should shrink from calling it a hyperbole. But remember this precept does not apply to the internal relations of Christians. It regulated the conduct of the first disciples toward the Gentiles, who were to be startled and aroused into recognition of the law of love. For offences of one "brother" against another a remedy was provided, and persistent offences were punishable by excommunication.

[1] St. Matthew xviii. 17.

I believe that it was the duty of the first disciples to obey this precept of the Sermon on the Mount literally, though we all admit that it would be wrong for us to do so now. But is it not perplexing for us to find a law that was once a law, but now is not?

Pupil.—Yes, very.

Teacher.—Are there any advantages in thus being perplexed?

Pupil.—I suppose we have to think for ourselves.

Teacher.—Yes, and feel for ourselves. We are not under the law, not even under a Christian law; but under the Spirit. The Sermon on the Mount says, "Give to him that asketh thee." Is it our duty to do this, to exercise indiscriminate charity to beggars?

Pupil.—No, because it is injurious to society.

Teacher.—This, then, is another instance to show that we cannot find a code (though we can find guidance) in Christ's precepts. Now, however, to return to the new Kingdom. It was to be a family, was it not? All who did the will of God were brothers to Jesus. In this family the will of a Divine Father was to be all-powerful, so that sin was no longer to be punished, but arrested and destroyed before it took the form of action. Adultery, murder, had been condemned by the old law; the new law condemned lust and anger. Ezekiel had prophesied thus, in the name of Jehovah: "A new heart also will I give you, and a new spirit will I put within you: and I will take away the stony heart out of your flesh, and I will give you an heart of flesh. And I will put my spirit within you, and cause you to walk in my statutes."[1] This period had now arrived. Did not the Sermon on the Mount exact a great deal from the disciples? How were they able to perform it?

Pupil.—I do not know. Jesus merely says to them "Do this," or "I say unto you;" He never supposes they cannot do it.

Teacher.—How do you suppose His disciples had strength to practise so much as they did of His precepts?

Pupil.—I suppose it was because of their enthusiasm for Him. They loved and trusted Him, and that helped them.

---

[1] Ezekiel xxxvi. 26-7; compare Jeremiah iv. 4.

Teacher.—Then now you have a new point of difference between Jesus and the Prophets. Jesus not only taught men God's will, but He helped them to do it. He brought men nearer to God through Himself. Can you mention any marked change that came over the teaching of Jesus? I mean, not the substance, but the manner of His teaching.

Pupil.—He gave up the direct mode of teaching which is exemplified in the Sermon on the Mount, and began to speak in parables.

Teacher.—What reason did He give for this change, when His disciples said, "Why speakest thou to them (the people) in parables?" Point out the difficulty involved in the reply.

Pupil.—He answered, "Because it is given unto you to know the mysteries of heaven; but to them it is not given. For whosoever hath, to him shall be given: but whosoever hath not, from him shall be taken away even that he hath." These and the subsequent words seem to show that Jesus spoke in parables, because people could not understand them. That seems very difficult.

Teacher.—Which is better, that people should not understand and should know they do not understand, or that they think they understand without really understanding?

Pupil.—The former.

Teacher.—Well, it seems that when Christ preached the kingdom of God a great deal of His teaching was not understood. It was admired at the time, but made little definite impression. The very first of the parables shows this: "The seed of the word" had been sown broadcast, but very little of it had brought forth fruit; only that which "fell on good ground." "Whosoever hath," said Jesus, "to him shall be given: but whosoever hath not, from him shall be taken away even that he hath."[1] Only those few hearers who had sincerity, patience, and a strong desire for truth, had received the seed, and brought forth fruit. The rest, who had not these virtues, had not understood the truth; they had lost rather than gained by fancying they understood it. Hence Jesus now adopted the parable,

[1] St. Matthew xiii. 12.

in order that those who would not think might not understand, and might not deceive themselves into the belief that they understood; while those who would make the effort might understand all the more because of the effort. You have said that the teaching of Jesus changed its *form;* did it not in some degree change its substance? In the parables themselves, can you not point out a difference between the tone and the subject of the first and the last?

Pupil.—As a rule, the first parables treat of the nature of the kingdom of God, its influence and extension, the duty of forgiveness, and the love of the Father towards "sinners:" the latter parables describe and explain how the kingdom is rejected, and the consequences of the rejection.

Teacher.—Tell me, when first did it distinctly appear that a certain section of the people were determined to reject Jesus?

Pupil.—On the return of the Twelve from their proclamation of the Kingdom,[1] Jesus declared that the Father "had hidden these things from the wise and prudent, and had revealed them unto babes;" that is, I suppose, to the simple and uneducated.

Teacher.—Why had the Pharisees rejected Him?

Pupil.—Because Jesus, according to their notions, violated the Sabbath.

Teacher.—That was their alleged reason, and no doubt actually one of their reasons; but I imagine the real cause for their rejection of Him was that His principle was entirely different from theirs. They were for the old law: He was for a new law, or rather for a new spirit. Did the Galileans reject Him?

Pupil.—Many for a time received Him, and were desirous of making Him a king by force; but when they found He would not take their path, and was content to teach, and heal, and proclaim mystical doctrines, many of them deserted Him.

Teacher.—And John the Baptist, did he desert Jesus, or recant his recognition of Him?

[1] St. Matthew xi. 25.

Pupil.—No.

Teacher.—But you cannot forget that even the Baptist sent two of his disciples to Him, asking Him whether He was the future Deliverer, or whether men must look for another. We need not suppose that John had lost faith in Jesus. He still believed Him to be the Deliverer, but perhaps desired by this appeal and remonstrance to incite Jesus to more active measures. How did Jesus meet this message? Was He incited to aggression? You know He was not. He replied in the presence of the people that the Baptist, though not (as they might imagine from his apparent vacillation) a reed shaken by every breath of popular opinion, nor a fawning courtier of Herod's, was nevertheless inferior to the very lowest in the new kingdom of God, whose subjects did not use the sword as their weapon.

This incident shows how naturally doubts might suggest themselves even to the most zealous of the followers of Jesus. Much more natural was it that the unintelligent crowd should, after the first burst of admiration, be driven into a reactionary disappointment. We have now, therefore, come to the time when Jesus had lost his previous popularity, and had incurred the enmity of the Pharisees. Can you tell me how he had also made an enemy of Herod Antipas?

Pupil.—By his public condemnation of the marriage of Herod with the wife of his half-brother, Philip.

Teacher.—That will account for the constant mention of the subject of divorce and remarriage. It had a great political importance at the time, and furnished the enemies of Jesus with a kind of interrogatory pitfall. Had Jesus taken a lax view of Herod's conduct, He would have offended the stricter part of His disciples; by His stern condemnation He incurred the enmity of Herod. Now, tell me, soon after the execution of John the Baptist, what great change took place in the conduct and teaching of Jesus?

Pupil.—He began to speak about His approaching death.

Teacher.—Yes, and He took the ready way to meet His death by going up to Jerusalem. Now that He had been despised and rejected by those whom He had come to save, Jesus felt that His hour was come. "From this time forth," says St. Matthew,[1] "began Jesus to show unto his disciples how that he must go unto Jerusalem, and suffer many things of the elders, chief priests, and scribes, and be raised again the third day." Here, then, you have one more feature in the life of Jesus not to be found in the lives of previous prophets. This unbounded faith in Himself and in His work, a faith which set death at defiance, cannot be paralleled, even from those prophets who seem to have had a partial revelation of the resurrection. The difference is stupendous. It is true that the prophets (whose writings, as Jesus continually repeated, were to be fulfilled in Him) had prophesied rejection, suffering, even death for the Deliverer, and they may be thought to have implied His resurrection. But, unless the words of Hosea,[2] "After two days will he revive us: in the third day he will raise us up, and we shall live in his sight," seemed applicable to the Messiah, the confidence of Jesus in predicting His resurrection rested entirely on His own knowledge that He could not fail or perish, that He was one with God, the Word of God, and though "the grass withereth and the flower thereof fadeth," yet "the Word of the Lord abideth for ever."

Beside the introduction of the references to rejection, another new element may be found in the parables of this period. I mean the new allusions to the Gentiles. Do you recollect the answer of Jesus, in St. Matthew xv. 24, to the Syrophœnician woman?

Pupil.—"I am not sent but unto the lost sheep of the house of Israel."

Teacher.—Almost in the same words He had instructed His disciples to avoid "the Gentiles and Samaritans"[3] and to "go rather to the lost sheep of the house of Israel." But the faith of the Syrophœnician had induced Jesus to heal her daughter, and the faith of the centurion had not only procured the aid of Jesus, but had made Him marvel.[4] Hence He had declared that many should "come from

[1] St. Matthew xvi. 21.
[2] Hosea vi. 2.
[3] St. Matthew x. 6.
[4] Ib. viii. 10.

the east and west and should sit down with Abraham, and Isaac, and Jacob in the kingdom of heaven." Similar predictions had been made by Isaiah and other prophets, who had endeavoured in vain to expand the narrow patriotism of their countrymen. But now an additional prediction appears. "The children of the kingdom shall be cast out into outer darkness : there shall be weeping and gnashing of teeth."

This leads us to consider the dark side of the kingdom of God. The triumph of righteousness, you will remember, is inseparably connected in the Prophets with the destruction of sinners. Sinners were to be destroyed like stubble in the fire, whirled from the earth like chaff before the wind, swept away like stones in a mountain torrent. The same images are repeated in the New Testament. The destroying fire, the "fan" with which Christ was to separate the chaff from the wheat, and the flood that was to sweep away the house founded on the sand, are familiar to all. But a new description of punishment had been given in the Book of Ecclesiasticus. "The vengeance of the ungodly is fire and worms."[1] So Judith: "Woe to the nations that rise up against my kindred; the Lord Almighty will take vengeance of them in the day of judgment, in putting fire and worms in their flesh, and they shall feel them and weep for ever."[2] The last page of the prophecy of Isaiah contains a prediction that all flesh "shall come to worship" before God in "the holy mountain, Jerusalem," and concludes with the words, "they shall go forth and look upon the carcases of the men that have transgressed against me : for their worm shall not die, neither shall their fire be quenched; and they shall be an abhorring to all flesh."[3] Similar expressions are used by Jesus to denote the terrible punishment that awaited all who were not included in the kingdom. What is the origin of the word translated "hell," which is so often mentioned by Jesus?

Pupil.—It is "Gehenna," properly two words, "Ge" (the valley of) and "Henna" (Hinnom), and meant originally the valley of

---

[1] Ecclesiasticus vii. 17.   [2] Judith xvi. 17.   [3] Isaiah lxvi. 20, 23, 24.

Hinnom, where the carcases of malefactors were habitually allowed to putrefy till they were consumed by fire.

Teacher.—That latter statement of yours, though very common, is very questionable. What is certain is that the valley had been occasionally used for the cruel worship of the fire-god, Moloch. For this reason it had been turned into a cesspool by Josiah. It was thus formally polluted, and the name Gehenna was associated in the mind of every Jew with the notion of a receptacle of corruption. The refuse of the city was to be cast there. Thus therefore to say that a man was to be cast into Gehenna, or the valley of Hinnom, was a metaphorical expression. Expand it.

Pupil.—As decaying and putrefying matter is cast out of a city into its fit receptacle, so a man who is dead in the sight of God is to be cast out from the community of the living.

Teacher.—But it still remains to expand the metaphors of the fire and the worm.

Pupil.—As the bodies of the unburied dead are preyed upon by the fire and the worm, so the evil spirits of those who are spiritually dead shall be devoured by some corresponding spiritual agencies.

Teacher.—Yes : perhaps by the sense of the wrath of God, which may be represented by fire, and by remorse, which may be represented by the worm. We must not shut our eyes to this the gloomy side of the preaching of Jesus. Let me ask you whom did He speak of as liable to Gehenna ; was it the "sinners"?

Pupil.—No, it was those who rejected Him ; all who would not enter the kingdom.

Teacher.—True. All who were useless, all who were selfish, all who were faithless. In the Parable of Lazarus and Dives, Dives is cast into Gehenna simply because he "received his good things" on earth, and felt no sympathy or pain for the beggar at his gate. Jesus often warned his hearers that the road to destruction was broad, and taken by the majority; that many were called, but few chosen, and that His followers must allow no considerations of personal comfort or safety to stand between them and the kingdom. "It was better,"

He said, "to enter into life maimed, than having two hands to go into Gehenna, into the fire that never shall be quenched; where their worm dieth not, and the fire is not quenched."[1] It might seem a strong objection to the preaching of Jesus that apparently it resulted in misery. Can you mention any passage where He accepted the misery as a necessary result of His mission, and declared that He came to cause trouble and dissension?

Pupil.—" I am come to send fire on the earth. . . . . Suppose ye that I am come to give peace on earth? I tell you, Nay; but rather division."[2]

Teacher.—In what way did Christ cause dissension?

Pupil.—He set the members of Jewish households and the Jewish nation at variance.

Teacher.—And did He do good to all whom He taught? To the Pharisees for instance, who mocked Him, and called the Spirit of God Beelzebub. Did He do them good or harm?

Pupil.—Harm. They were made worse instead of better.

Teacher.—If Jesus had prevailed, He might have concentrated the whole nation round Him, and, humanly speaking, the Jewish people might have flourished in concord. As it was, what was the end of all this embitterment and discord?

Pupil.—The destruction of Jerusalem and of the Temple, and of the nation as a nation.

Teacher.—Then it must be confessed that Jesus brought fire and dissension, or, as St. Matthew expresses it, "a sword" to the whole Jewish nation.

Pupil.—But is it not horrible to think that Jesus should do harm?

Teacher.—Does the Bible, the best of books, do good to every one? to a hypocrite, for instance, who quotes it, and lives contrary to it? Does health do good to a man who uses health as an instrument for excessive vice? Does food or wine do good to gluttons and drunkards? Do you not see God's imperious law that every blessing

---

[1] St. Mark ix. 43.   [2] St. Luke xii. 51.

of His shall become a curse if we will make it a curse? Every one of God's blessings is a kind of "criterion" or judgment, distinguishing between the good and bad, and the greatest blessing to the good becomes the greatest curse to the bad. What is the Latin proverb about the "corruption of the best"?

Pupil.—" Corruptio optimi pessima."

Teacher.—Then we may well believe, since Jesus was the best, that of all the terrible retributions that ever fell on the heart of man, none equalled that which followed the Pharisaic "corruption" of His teaching, and perversion of His motives. What is the name given by Jesus (beside the "kingdom of God") to the opposite of "darkness," punishment, and "fire"?

Pupil.—Eternal life.

Teacher.—And what definition did Jesus give of eternal life?

Pupil.—" This is life eternal, that they might know thee, the only true God, and Jesus Christ, whom thou hast sent."[1]

Teacher.—Then it would seem that eternal life might begin even on earth in any human heart that attained to the knowledge of God, and in the same way the kingdom of God might and would exist on earth wherever God's will was willingly done by men. You perhaps remember a passage where Jesus was asked when the kingdom of God should appear. What was the reply?

Pupil.—" The kingdom of God cometh not with observation. Neither shall they say, Lo here! or, Lo there! for, behold, the kingdom of God is in the midst of you."[2]

Teacher.—We are now considering Jesus as a Prophet. We have found that the Prophets, speaking of a day of deliverance or judgment, often predicted some national deliverance, that took place shortly after the prediction, though the terms of the prophecy were "too large" to be completely fulfilled in any contemporaneous event. Now, can you tell with what event Jesus associates the day of judgment and the subsequent deliverance?

---

[1] St. John xvii. 3.   [2] St. Luke xvii. 20. A. V. "within."

Pupil.—The capture of Jerusalem.

Teacher.—What special importance had this event above the capture of an ordinary capital or fortified town?

Pupil.—It brought with it the destruction of the Temple, the disuse of the Temple worship, and the abrogation of the letter of some part of the law; so that it might be said to have to some extent done away with the dispensation of the old age, and prepared the way for a new age and a new dispensation.

Teacher.—In accordance with what moral law would one of the ancient prophets have prophesied the fall of Jerusalem, just as they prophesied the fall of Tyre or Babylon?

Pupil.—They would have said that the hypocrisy and cruelty which had culminated in the condemnation and execution of Jesus must bring upon the city inevitable retribution.

Teacher.—They might have added that the Temple, which was intended to be an emblem of God, had become a mere place of formal worship; an idol, instead of an emblem. Hence it must fall. Now give me the words in which St. Luke describes the fall of Jerusalem, and the subsequent deliverance.

Pupil.—"And Jerusalem shall be trodden down of the Gentiles, until the times of the Gentiles be fulfilled. And there shall be signs in the sun, and in the moon, and in the stars; and upon the earth distress of nations, with perplexity; . . . for the powers of heaven shall be shaken. And then shall they see the Son of Man coming in a cloud with power and great glory. And when these things begin to come to pass, then look up, and lift up your heads; for your redemption draweth nigh." But surely these words did not refer to any event that was then close at hand?

Teacher.—Read the following verse, the thirty-second, and then read St. Matthew x. 23.

Pupil.—The verse in St. Luke says, "Verily I say unto you, This generation shall not pass away till all be fulfilled;" and in St. Matthew Jesus tells His twelve disciples, when they are persecuted in one city to flee to another, and adds, "For verily I say unto you, Ye shall not have gone over the cities of Israel till the Son of man be come."

Teacher.—Beside you will find that in St. Matthew xvi. 28, and in the parallel passages in St. Mark and St. Luke, Jesus says to His disciples, "There be some standing here which shall not taste of death till they see the Son of man coming in his kingdom." And what event in all the three Evangelists follows that prediction?

Pupil.—The transfiguration.

Teacher.—In which Jesus appeared to His disciples as the glorified Son of God, superior to the two representatives of the Law and the Prophets. We see, therefore, that every glorification of Christ may in some sense be regarded as a "coming." The "coming" of Christ is not a mere change of place, but a "coming" into the hearts of men, by which He impresses Himself and His will and His kingdom upon our thoughts and deeds. After the fall of Jerusalem, when the altar and the sacrifice were taken away, the new sacrifice of Christ would impress itself with new force upon the world. Then Christ's claims would be universally acknowledged, and His kingdom would "come." The expression "signs in the sun and in the moon" is frequently used by the Prophets for mysterious changes in the great national powers of the world. Now, I dare say you feel that this fulfilment of Christ's prediction is not complete, and indeed is unsatisfactory, do you not?

Pupil.—Yes, I do.

Teacher.—I believe it is intended that you should. The ultimate fulfilment of this prophecy, the ultimate "day of decision," and the ultimate deliverance are probably as yet far off. False deliverers and false prophets will still arise; faith and love will grow cold; all the evil that is in mankind will be brought prominently forward, and then, amid the mourning of men, God will send His messengers and divide good from bad, punishing the one while He rewards the other. And this will happen perhaps many times in the history of the world before the "coming" of that final judgment and deliverance which shall completely fulfil Christ's prophecy. You will remember the parable of the sheep and the goats, in which Jesus speaks of this final judgment. Tell me, what difficulty is there in the last part of this?

Pupil.—I do not know. It says, "And these shall go away into everlasting punishment, but the righteous into life eternal." I do not see any difficulty.

Teacher.—What is punishment? How does it differ from torture?

Pupil.—Punishment is pain inflicted to reform an offender, or to deter others from offending. Torture is pain needlessly inflicted.

Teacher.—What need or purpose can we see in the unending pain here mentioned, inflicted apparently neither to reform nor to deter?

Pupil.—But must we not believe what is written in the Bible?

Teacher.—I am far from saying you must not. But I wish to prepare you for the difficulty which must sooner or later suggest itself or be suggested to you. Like the existence of sin or temptation, so eternal punishment is logically irreconcilable with a belief in an all-powerful and all-loving God. It is a case where faith must supply the place of logic. Either we may have mistaken the meaning of the words, or there is some purpose in it unknown to us, or there is some other explanation which we have not yet attained, and for which we are perhaps not yet prepared. All that we know is that nothing whatever, not sin nor hell itself, can destroy the truth that "God is love." Some have endeavoured to show that the word translated "eternal" means "for ages," but I am sorry to say I do not believe such a translation expresses the original. Now let us return from the consideration of the teaching or prophesying of Jesus, and ask what were the opinions about Him held by His disciples,—by Peter, for example?

Pupil.—Peter believed that He was "the Christ, the Son of the living God."

Teacher.—Had this belief never been entertained before by any of the disciples?

Pupil.—Yes. Andrew is recorded to have said to Peter, his brother, "We have found the Messias."[1]

[1] St. John i. 41.

Teacher.—I thought Jesus said to Peter, " Flesh and blood hath not revealed it unto thee, but my Father which is in heaven."

Pupil.—I do not understand how to explain this difference.

Teacher.—Well, I suppose no mere testifying or "saying" of Andrew could ever make Peter believe that Jesus was the Deliverer, until he came to know and trust in Jesus, and feel that He, and He only, could be the Deliverer. I say, Deliverer: a Deliverer from what?

Pupil.—A Deliverer from all evil that can befall body or soul.

Teacher.—Until a man feels evil, he cannot feel the need of a Deliverer from evil, can he?

Pupil.—No.

Teacher.—Then until a man felt the burden of sin, could he feel the need of a Deliverer from sin, such as Jesus was?

Pupil.—No.

Teacher.—Then Peter, like all others, needed to have his sins revealed to him, and then to feel that Jesus could forgive them, before he could say, "Thou art the Christ;"—*i.e.* the "Anointed (Deliverer);" and this necessary revelation and faith is said to come from the Father. Can you call to mind many instances where Jesus told any one that He was the Christ?

Pupil—No; I do not know of any.

Teacher.—There are perhaps two instances.[1] In neither was the utterance public, and yet the people were continually saying to Him, "If thou be the Christ, tell us plainly." Why did He not tell them?

Pupil.—I suppose, because He wished to lead them, like Peter, to feel that they needed a Deliverer, and that here was the Deliverer they needed. And if they did not come to Him in that way, they would come with false notions and expectations of deliverance, and their coming thus would be worse than not coming at all.

Teacher.—Hence you can better understand the importance attached by Jesus to this, the first confession of faith. If it had been

---

[1] St. John iv. 26; ix. 33.

the mere repetition of something which He Himself had taught, it would have been useless. But it was more; it was the first expression of heartfelt faith, the first token that Jesus had *not* lived in vain, and that the structure of the Church of Christ had now begun. Christ had before declared that whosoever built upon His will was building upon a "rock." He alluded to Himself on another occasion as "the chief corner-stone:" and in after-time the Apostle St. Peter, addressing the scattered Christians of Asia in a letter, and recalling, as it would seem, the present occasion, speaks of "the Lord" as "a living *stone*—to whom coming ye also as lively *stones* are built up, a spiritual house, an holy priesthood." Many of our Lord's disciples had deserted Him. They had built upon the sand, and their work had been swept away. The structure, of which the first stone was at this moment laid, was not built upon the sand, but on a rock, and was destined to last for ever. The rock had been in existence from the first, but it had been obscured from human view. Now, by the revelation of St. Peter, it was definitely revealed and cleared and made ready for the superstructure, and St. Peter himself (whose name denoted "stone") was to be the first stone of the "spiritual house." "Thou art Peter (stone[1])," was the reply of Jesus, "and on this foundation-stone,[2] *i.e.* the Messiah revealed to thee, will I build my church, and the gates of hell shall not prevail against it."[3] We estimate things from their consequences. Jesus saw the future in the present, and in this mustard-seed of genuine faith He discerned the future tree of the church.

It was not till this confession of faith had been elicited that Jesus spoke to His disciples of His coming rejection and death. It was

---

[1] πέτρος.

[2] πέτρα. I have attempted to keep the similarity of the words in the original.

[3] I have been led to this interpretation by a closer consideration of the passage in St. Peter's Epistle alluded to above. The context in itself fully justifies those who interpret "this rock" as referring to St. Peter, or (which was my own view till recently) to the principle of faith in Christ, which found its first exponent in St. Peter, and might, therefore, be identified with him, just as in the parable of the Sower the Word of God and the person who receives it are both called "the seed."

necessary that He should die, and their faith in Him should perish for a time, that He might rise in glory, and their faith in Him might be purified and bring forth fruit. " Except a corn of wheat fall into the ground and die, it abideth alone; but if it die, it bringeth forth much fruit." Did the faith of Peter and the other disciples at this time include all that we mean by "faith in Jesus"?

Pupil.—No; for they did not believe in His coming death or resurrection.

Teacher.—True. Let us make a brief review of the life of Jesus at the time when He took His last supper with His disciples, knowing that He was soon to be parted from them. What had been achieved as the result of all His teaching and miracles? He had from the first repelled the upper and middle classes of His countrymen. He had estranged many of the peasants whom He had at first attracted. The train of Galileans who had escorted Him into Jerusalem were still under the delusion that Jesus would be a second David. His earlier teaching had been misapprehended, His parables only partially understood, except by the inner circle of His disciples; and even the Twelve were so dull and incapable of recognizing the spiritual law of triumph through failure, and life through death, that they could not believe that Jesus would die. They were affectionate, it was true, and ready to fight for their Master; but they were not prepared to undergo apparent failure with Him. Now I ask you, what legacy had Jesus to leave to His disciples, who were in a few hours to be left helpless by His death?

Pupil.—There was His teaching.

Teacher.—But how could they understand the teaching when the Teacher was gone? And besides, did we not say that the precepts of Jesus, considered as a code, are imperfect, and indeed were not intended to be received as a code? The mere letter of His teaching was surely not sufficient, even as a legacy, still less as a substitute for the Teacher. Tell me, had not Jesus previously given His disciples a remarkable promise connected with prayer?

Pupil.—He had said that wheresoever two or three were gathered together in His name, there would He be in the midst of them.

Teacher.—In other words, He had promised His presence; He had promised Himself to His disciples. This was all He had to give. He could not, like Moses, leave them a legacy of law, or, like Joshua or David, traditions of conquest or successful administration. His law, if it could be called a law, was Himself—participation in His spirit. His conquest and success were apparent defeat and failure. Therefore Jesus, at His last meal with His disciples, celebrating, as it were, His own funeral feast, having no code, nor conquests, nor anything that the world calls substantial, to leave behind Him, bequeathed, by His last will and testament, His perpetual presence, His very self, to His disciples, bidding them partake of bread which He called His body, and of wine which He called His blood.

Now we must pass to the agony of Jesus in the garden of Gethsemane. Is it possible for us to comprehend that?

Pupil.—Surely not. Jesus is so infinitely superior to us that we ought not to hope to comprehend His feelings at such a time.

Teacher.—We certainly ought not to expect to *comprehend* it. But the fact that some details of it are recorded by the Evangelists, indicates that we are intended to study them, and to try to *apprehend* something of it. There is a danger, if we pass over the passion of Jesus even in reverence, and resolve not to think about His motives, that we may unconsciously attribute unworthy motives to Him. Read me the description given in the Epistle to the Hebrews, v. 7.

Pupil.—"Who in the days of his flesh, when he had offered up prayers and supplication with strong crying and tears unto him that was able to save him from death, and was heard in that he feared, though he were a Son, yet learned he obedience by the things which he suffered."

Teacher.—You find it there implied, that Jesus offered up prayers in order to be saved from death; and the account of the agony given by the Evangelists is to the same effect. But many good and brave men have encountered death without a murmur, for their country, for their honour, or for their friends. It cannot, therefore, have been for His own sake that Jesus prayed that the cup might pass from Him, and that He might be saved from death? However deep and mysterious the motives of Jesus, we are warranted in believing that they are infinitely unselfish, are we not? and that He who came to die for sinners, identified Himself with sinners more than it is possible for the most unselfish of us to do?

Pupil.—Yes.

Teacher.—Even when hanging in torture on the cross, He did not lose His thoughtful care for His mother. And must we not love Him the better for believing that, during His agony, His chief thought was about His unprotected and affectionate disciples, who were destined in a few minutes to be scattered in faithless flight; about the sinners whom He had come to save, and of whom so many remained unsaved; about the Pharisees and others whom He had harmed instead of helped, made worse instead of better; in a word, about sin? We have seen, and shall see more clearly, that Jesus sympathised with sinners as no one else ever did. He could forgive sin because He was pained by it. Even we feel shame and sorrow for the sins of those who are closely connected by family ties. We blush for the faults of our brothers. To Jesus the whole world was a world of brothers; and, therefore, on Him now fell the thought of the wretched and sinful world left desolate for a time without its Redeemer. The burden of all the sins of all the world descended at this moment upon Him, each sin an agony to Him. He had been tempted before by the devil to distrust God; and the baffled tempter had only retired "for a season." Now again he was present. What may have been the suggestion which on this occasion the "Prince of this world" set before Jesus, we cannot tell; but the very title, "Prince of this world," indicates the sovereignty which the evil spirit claims over men as his natural subjects, to the manner born, intended for sin and impurity, oppression and deceit—creatures for whom it was not worth while to live, much less to die. What other suggestions of Satan may have depicted darkness on earth, and darkness beyond the grave, we shall never know. It is enough for us to know that there was more here than the mere fear of humiliation and physical pain, and that the agony of Jesus must have been consistent with His life. The same remarks apply to His crucifixion and death. Now tell me, what were the last words of Jesus recorded in St. Matthew?

Pupil.—" My God, my God, why hast thou forsaken me?"

Teacher.—Had God forsaken Jesus? What is meant by God forsaking a man? And what men is God said to forsake?

Pupil.—God is said to forsake men with whom He is angry. He leaves them for a time to follow their own devices, that they may learn by bitter experience, since they will not learn from His warnings.

Teacher.—But such forsaking is in anger. Could God be angry with His Son? Had Jesus done anything but what was perfectly good?

Pupil.—Of course not. But had not God laid upon Jesus our sins?

Teacher.—Yes, and we shall study presently the meaning of this; but meantime is it possible for an infinitely good and truthful God to be angry with one who is infinitely good and truthful?

Pupil.—No, it is impossible.

Teacher.—It is utterly impossible; and though some might use the expression, God punished Jesus for us, I do not think any one would venture to say God was angry with Jesus for us. But remember that Jesus, who was sympathising with and bearing the sins of others, and completely identifying Himself with sinners, must have felt at this moment, in a degree inconceivable to us, the repugnance between God and sin. Sin and death are connected as cause and effect in the Old Testament. Death is treated as a curse pronounced by the Father upon sin; and Jesus was undergoing, as far as outward appearance went, the Father's curse. The gradual failure of vital force and spirits, the sinking of the whole human fabric of will and sense and intellect, must be painful to all, and more painful in proportion as the organization of the sufferer rises higher in the scale of humanity. Identifying Himself as He did with sinners, or, as St. Paul says, "being made sin for us," and now being in the act of receiving the final blow that sin can strike, Jesus represented the whole sinful world in its agony of doubt and despair, when He cried aloud, "My God, my God, why hast thou forsaken me?"

But another important explanation must be added. Where do these words occur, and what is the context?

Pupil.—They are the first words of the twenty-second Psalm. The Psalmist, after using these words, goes on to say that he was despised by all that saw him, who said to him, "He trusted in the Lord that he would deliver him; let him deliver him, seeing he delighted in him." He continues by appealing to God to help him. "Thou art he that took me out of the womb; thou didst keep me in hope when I was upon my mother's breast. I am poured out like water, and all my bones are out of joint: . . . and thou hast brought me into the dust of death; for dogs have compassed me: the assembly of the wicked have inclosed me; they pierced my hands and my feet. I may tell all my bones; they look and stare upon me. They part my garments among them, and cast lots upon my vesture." Shall I go on? The whole of the Psalm seems applicable to the Crucifixion.

Teacher.—I think the whole of the Psalm was in the mind of Jesus at this time; but I do not think the whole applies to the Crucifixion. Look at what follows. "But be not thou far from me, O Lord: O my strength, haste thee to help me. . . . I will declare thy name unto my brethren; in the midst of the congregation will I praise thee. Ye that fear the Lord, praise him; all ye the seed of Jacob, glorify him; and fear him, all ye the seed of Israel. . . . For He hath not despised nor abhorred the affliction of the afflicted; *neither hath He hid his face from him; but when he cried unto him, he heard.* . . . All the ends of the world shall remember and turn unto the Lord. . . . For the kingdom is the Lord's, and he is the governor among the nations." The Psalm ends with a prediction that the deliverance of the Psalmist shall be declared to future generations. "They shall come and shall declare his righteousness unto a people that shall be born, that he hath done this." You see, though the Psalm begins with lamentation, it ends in triumph.

Pupil.—Yes. Is it known under what circumstances David wrote this Psalm?

Teacher.—We have no evidence but the title, that David wrote it; and many commentators believe that the titles of the Psalms were added long after the Psalms themselves, and have not much authority. It is thought by some to have been written by a martyr suffering for the cause of Jehovah during the Captivity. But whoever was the author (and for our purpose the authorship is of little importance), the Psalm embodies more than any other the spirit of martyrdom, the cry for help, the misery and the patience, ending in the certain hope of a lasting deliverance. I do not think it is in the least unnatural to suppose that Jesus used the first verse of this Psalm (which was, of course, a household word to every Jew) in order to express the whole. He identified Himself with the suffering Psalmist in his triumph as well as in his appeal, and while He uttered the opening cry, "My God, my God, why hast thou forsaken me?" He implied at the same time the conclusion, "All the ends of the world shall remember and turn unto the Lord."

And now, putting ourselves in the position of the disciples, we have to regard the life of Jesus as ended. And what should we have felt? What did they feel?

Pupil.—Intense sorrow, apparently unmixed with hope.

Teacher.—Do you think their hopelessness diminished their love and longing for His presence?

Pupil.—No; intensified it.

Teacher.—A few minutes before His death we find the Twelve disputing about precedence, and apparently looking forward to high places in the Messiah's court. What of such desires now?

Pupil.—They would all vanish in the intense desire for His presence.

Teacher.—They had "all deserted him and fled." Would not a sense of shame prevent their desiring to see Him face to face again?

Pupil.—No; they would know He would forgive them, and they would long to show their gratitude and love.

Teacher.—They were helpless, and surrounded by powerful and implacable enemies. Would not their position engage them in self-regarding thoughts about their own safety?

Pupil.—Perhaps their helplessness would make them feel how He had helped them.

Teacher.—Yes. They had grown accustomed to be helped by Him, and they would feel that they could not live without His help now. They would not fear death now, nor poverty, nor shame. All these thoughts and fears would be lost in the sense of their loss of Him who was their life. But is it not true that the Twelve had followed their Master in part from self-regarding motives, asking, "What shall we have therefore?" and desiring to sit on twelve thrones judging the twelve tribes of Israel?

Pupil.—Yes; but they would not desire Jesus for such reasons now: they would desire Him, not as an earthly conqueror, but as a Deliverer from wretchedness, despair, and the sense of helpless desertion.

Teacher.—And that is what Jesus came to do, is it not?—to deliver men from wretchedness, not to conquer by force?

Pupil.—Yes.

Teacher.—Then you mean to say the disciples would now desire Jesus as He intended to be desired, whereas before they had desired Him in a different way?

Pupil.—Yes.

Teacher.—Then they would understand Him better now, recall His words and works with greater vividness now, and in fact realize Him now that He was dead better than they had done when He was alive?

Pupil.—Yes.

Teacher.—And the more they could realize Him, the more they would love and long for Him, and, feeling His presence a necessity, they would say to themselves that He must not, could not, abandon His disciples?

Pupil.—Yes.

Teacher.—Thus, then, they would be trained to know Jesus, and would be prepared by faith to recognize Him. And when they were prepared, He rose from the dead and appeared unto them, and convinced even doubters of His presence. He told them that all power was given to Him in heaven and earth, and that His disciples must go forth to the world and teach His doctrines. Afterwards He ascended into heaven.

Now we must sum up. We have been trying to regard Jesus as a Prophet. Step by step we have been led up into a higher atmosphere, and find ourselves above prophetic regions. The Prophets seldom or never spoke about themselves,[1] but about the will of Jehovah. The "word of the Lord" was always their description of their message, and the last of the prophets preserved the traditional self-subordination when he described himself as "a voice." Jesus, on the other hand, told His disciples to follow Him, to suffer persecution for Him, to do His will, to pray and work in His name, to trust in His presence, to hope for the Spirit that He would send, to feed upon His body and His blood. Yet all this while Jesus proclaimed the will of Jehovah as effectually—more effectually than any of the Prophets. If He taught people to look to Himself, it was because by looking to Him they would see God. "He called God His Father," said the Pharisees, "making Himself equal with God." This was not true: He did not claim equality, but He claimed something more. He claimed oneness, and declared that He and the Father were one. When one of His disciples prayed for a glimpse of the Father Himself, Jesus replied, "Have I been so long time with you, and yet hast thou not known me, Philip? He that hath seen me hath seen the Father."

---

[1] If they spoke of themselves, it was of themselves as "signs" in the hand of Jehovah exhibited to a rebellious people.

Then what have we in Jesus? A man, it is true, capable of all the sufferings and sorrows of humanity, and indeed of more real suffering and more true sorrow than we can feel; a man tempted in all points as we are, but at the same time One whose word or touch produced righteousness and health, whose professed object it was to forgive sins, to save the lost, and to give His life for the salvation of mankind; who claimed the allegiance of the world, and not only spoke of God as His Father, but declared that He was one with God. Death had not power to keep Him in the grave. He rose and appeared to His disciples, and after promising them His perpetual help He ascended into heaven, where the first Christian martyr looked up to Him and said, "Lord Jesus, receive my spirit." By this time surely we must recognize the full force of the distinction implied in the opening of the Epistle to the Hebrews, "God, who at sundry times and in divers manners spake in times past unto the fathers by the prophets, hath in these last days spoken unto us by his Son." I think we may add our belief that the Son of God, though parted from us in the flesh, still helps us and hears our prayers, as He heard Stephen's. He is still the source of forgiveness, peace, and eternal life. Whenever we think of Him, He will be one with the Father in our hearts; and whenever we see Him with the eye of faith, we shall have seen the Father also.

CHAPTER III.

CHRIST'S MIRACLES.

Teacher.—Ought we to believe in the truth of a teacher who works miracles? If so, why?

Pupil.—We ought; because miracles are supernatural, and show that a teacher is supernaturally helped.

Teacher.—What do you mean by miracles being supernatural? Suppose a teacher declares that God is an evil spirit, and, to prove this, causes a tree to be uprooted and to walk reversed upon its top; that would be supernatural, would it be a miracle?

Pupil.—I suppose it would; but I should not believe such a teacher.

Teacher.—No; you would not. You would say the miracle was either an imposture or, if supernatural, supernaturally bad, proving that the teacher was aided by an evil, not by a good being. Were there ever such cases? Is it worth while considering them?

Pupil.—I do not read of any but good miracles.

Teacher.—That is, because our translators use two different English words to express the same Greek word in the New Testament. Have you forgotten the meaning of the Greek word translated "miracle" in the Gospel of St. John?

Pupil.—Sign.

Teacher.—And do we not read[1] that false christs and prophets should arise, and "show great *signs* and wonders," insomuch that, if it were possible, they should "deceive the very elect"? It seems,

[1] St. Matthew xxiv. 4.

then, that there are, or may be, bad miracles or signs, as well as good. How are we to distinguish the good from the bad?

Pupil.—I do not know.

Teacher.—I think we shall be helped if we use the word sign instead of miracle. A miracle means simply something wonderful. A sign is an imperfect term, suggesting the need of further definition. What further question does the word sign suggest?

Pupil.—It makes us ask, "A sign of what?"

Teacher.—Apply this to the case above mentioned—the uprooted tree moving on its top. What is that a sign of?

Pupil.—Power.

Teacher.—Then you may believe that the man who works such a sign is powerful, but you need believe no more. But does this represent the signs worked by our Lord? I do not say that there are not one or two that seem mere signs of power. But the majority of our Lord's signs, what were they, and of what were they signs?

Pupil.—They were works of healing; and they showed that He had power to heal supernaturally.

Teacher.—Our Lord once worked a miraculous cure, when a number of Pharisees were present. He prefaced the act by saying to them, "But that ye may know——" What was it that this act was to make the Pharisees know? Simply, that He had power to heal supernaturally?

Pupil.—No; that He had power on earth to forgive sins. "But that ye may know that the Son of man hath power on earth to forgive sins."

Teacher.—What connection is there between sin and disease, forgiving and healing? Express it in a proportion.

Pupil.—As disease is to the body, so is sin to the soul; and as Jesus could supernaturally heal disease, so could He heal or forgive sin.

Teacher.—Exactly so. The Pharisees said Jesus had no right or power to forgive sins—only God could do that. Jesus replied that He could prove that He could do the invisible work of healing the soul, by doing the visible work of healing the body, and that by a mere word. The words, "Thy sins are forgiven thee," and "Arise, and walk," were easy. The deeds were difficult. He would prove that the first expression, which could not be tested, was more than mere words, by using the second expression, which could be tested, and by showing that it underwent the test. But did not the Pharisees say that He healed the diseased and the possessed by the help of Satan? In fact, did they not make the same objection to Christ's signs that we have made above to bad miracles? And how did Christ meet this objection?

Pupil.—He said that an evil spirit could not work deliverance from misery and evil, that all good actions must come from a good being—God.

Teacher.—This is in accordance with the books of the Old Testament. Health and prosperity are regarded as blessings bestowed by God on those who obey Him. Hence when Jesus worked a work of healing, that was a sign of what?

Pupil.—That the work and the worker came from God.

Teacher.—But when a skilful physician cures a patient, despaired of by all his friends, is that a sign that the worker comes from God?

Pupil.—No.

Teacher.—I suppose it is a sign of intelligence and skill that comes from God. But if the physician feels no interest in his work or in his patient, and does it only for reputation or money, the worker cannot be said to come from God. St. Matthew, describing the manner in which Jesus healed all that were possessed and diseased, considers the healing as the fulfilment of an ancient prophecy. Quote the prophecy.

Pupil.—"Himself took our infirmities, and bare our sicknesses."[1]

Teacher.—Can you mention any case where a sign of healing was performed without a word from Jesus?

Pupil.—The woman who touched Him in the throng was healed at once.

---

[1] St. Matthew viii. 17; Isaiah liii. 4.

Teacher.—And what did Jesus say to those who expostulated with Him for saying, while pressed on all sides by the crowd, "Who touched me?"

Pupil.—"Somebody hath touched me, for I perceive that virtue is gone out of me."

Teacher.—Then what difference is there between the works of a physician and those of Jesus considered as *signs?* Of what are they respectively signs?

Pupil.—The former are signs of acquired skill and knowledge, the latter of innate power and sympathy. The physician does not bear the sicknesses of his patients, and, though he heals, may not sympathise at all. Christ is said to bear them, and to heal them by a power coming out of Himself, out of His own nature.

Teacher.—Why did Christ perform these signs?

Pupil.—To prove His mission from God.

Teacher.—But in many cases, as in that of Peter's mother-in-law, He worked signs among friends who were convinced of His truth; while, on the other hand, He refused to perform a sign for the Pharisees, though they were not convinced, and required a sign for conviction. Surely you cannot say that He healed the daughter of the Syro-Phœnician in order to convince her or any one else of His power or truth? Again, take the first cure of a leper recorded by St. Mark (i. 41). Jesus is there said to have emphatically enjoined secrecy on the leper. But besides, a motive is there assigned for the act. What is it?

Pupil.—It is said that Jesus, "*moved with compassion*, put forth his hand, and touched" the leper, and said, "Be thou clean." But if these acts of healing were signs of His loving power, must not Jesus have performed them to show His love and power?

Teacher.—Are not honest actions the signs of an honest man? Yet surely an honest man does not perform them *to show* that he is honest, but *because* he is honest. So Jesus healed men, not *to show* them that He loved them, but *because* He loved them and sympathised with them. We call His signs supernatural, and so they are, for they are above the powers of our ordinary nature; but to Jesus they were natural, the most natural expressions of His sympathy for suffering humanity. Hence, though St. John calls the works of Christ "signs," the first three Evangelists simply use the term "mighty works." We lose a good deal if we suppose that Jesus simply cured the sick in order to convince bystanders of His own power. Indeed we know that where there was a good deal of incredulity, and where proof might have been supposed most needed, Jesus not only did not, but could not, work a sign. Read St. Mark vi. 5.

Pupil.—"And he *could there do no mighty work*, save that he laid his hands upon a few sick (infirm) folk, and healed them." But surely Jesus could have done a mighty work if He had pleased?

Teacher.—Could Jesus do wrong? Could He turn stones into bread for His own pleasure? Could He cast Himself down from the pinnacle of the Temple? Could He ask His Father to send twelve legions of angels to save Him from the cross? In one sense He *could* do all these things; in another, and the most natural sense, He *could* not. And the original in St. Mark is very definite: "He *was not able* to do any mighty work there." Why not? Answer from the context.

Pupil.—Because of the unbelief of the villagers. They took offence at His high profession because they knew Him from His childhood, and His family also, and they despised Him as the result of familiarity.

Teacher.—Mention any case where Jesus made the working of a sign contingent upon belief.

Pupil.—Before He healed the lunatic boy, He said to the boy's father, "If thou canst believe, all things are possible to him that believeth." [1]

Teacher.—It seems strange, does it not, that those who had faith already could obtain a sign from Jesus, while those who had no faith could not? In accordance with what spiritual law is this?

[1] St. Mark ix. 23. There are unimportant variations in the reading.

Pupil.—" Whosoever hath, to him shall be given, and from him that hath not shall be taken away even that he hath."

Teacher.—Most of our Lord's signs were works of healing. Can you show from the Old Testament that health was regarded as a blessing on faith and obedience towards God, and sickness as a punishment for disobedience?

Pupil.—In the Book of Deuteronomy (vii. 12—15) the people of Israel are thus addressed : " If ye hearken to these judgments . . . . thou shalt be blessed above all people, and the Lord will take away from thee all sickness."

Teacher.—Yes : Isaiah prophesied, and Jesus accepted, as a sign of the kingdom, that the blind should see, the lame walk, the lepers be cleansed, the deaf hear, the dead be raised, and the poor have the Gospel preached to them.[1] And do you remember any passage where our Lord speaks of illness as coming from Satan, who, as we saw above,[2] is said to execute the wrath of God?

Pupil.—Seeing a woman in the synagogue who "had a spirit of infirmity eighteen years, and was bowed together," Jesus released her from her infirmity by laying His hands upon her; and He described her as "a daughter of 'Abraham, whom Satan hath bound, lo, these eighteen years."

Teacher.—True : and note that in this case Jesus is not here said to have "cast out" any evil spirit; nor does this appear to have been regarded as a case of "possession." We must now touch lightly upon the cases where Jesus is said to have cast out evil spirits. I will simply give you my own opinion about it. I do not think it a matter of great importance, except that use has been made of it to throw discredit on the Gospel history.

Cases of "possession" were very common during the period of the Gospel history, not only in Palestine, but in other parts of the Roman Empire. They are not found in the early history of nations. The case of Saul is almost unique in the ancient times of Israel. Latterly, as men became less patriotic, simple and warlike, more self-

---

[1] St. Luke vii. 22; Isaiah xxxv. 5.   [2] Part I. p. 18.

introspective, melancholy and superstitious, lascivious and vicious, for want of occupation, "possession" became more common. It raged like an epidemic in Galilee and in provinces exposed to the influence of Grecian idolatry, and distant from the quieting solemnities of the Temple worship: but Judæa was comparatively free from it. Consequently St. John, writing of Jerusalem, mentions no cases of possession; and though the three first Evangelists, as long as they speak of Galilee and the North, often allude to them, yet when Jesus journeys southward, all mention of them ceases.[1] The mischief was so common as to give rise to various impostures. It became a lucrative profession to cast out devils. A Jewish exorcist is said by Josephus to have cast out an evil spirit in the presence of Vespasian and his sons. The spirit was extracted from the nostrils of the man possessed, and was forced by the exorcist to overthrow a bucket of water in his flight, as a proof of his expulsion. Such evident impostures have caused many to deny the reality of "possession." But though such expressions as "the devil went out," and others implying motion, may be figurative, yet at the present time there are cases where the shortest and most real *description* of the patient's state (no complete *explanation* perhaps is or will be possible in this world) is to say, "a man is not himself," "he is out of himself." By these words we imply that another self has "possession" of the man. One patient imagines that his stomach is full of toads; another feels himself consumed by an inward fire; a third sees blood-red flames before his eyes; he hears loud roaring noises or thundering cannonades; sulphurous flames are in his nostrils; lifeless objects assume life to threaten him, and the pitying face of a friend becomes a grinning demon.[2] The insane fit ceases sometimes, only to give way to convulsions, which in turn are succeeded by recurring insanity. Sometimes two different and discordant voices issue from the man, suggesting a struggle between two con-

---

[1] This meets the objection of Strauss that the omission of all mention of "possession" in the fourth Gospel discredits the mention of it in the first three Gospels.

[2] Maudsley's "Physiology and Pathology of the Mind."

tending wills within him. In these unhappy men the intellect sometimes retains a partial and fitful life, but the moral affections are invariably destroyed. The shames and decencies of humanity are removed. A spirit indeed unclean takes possession of the man, and he freely indulges the instincts of the animal.

I think that Jesus would have treated such modern cases as cases of "possession;" and it seems to me to be the most accurate description of such men to say that they are "possessed" by an evil spirit. They deserve, and gained from Jesus, the most sincere sympathy. Often they are paying the penalties of their own sins, but sometimes of the sins of others. The drunkenness or vicious excesses of one generation are visited on the second or third, in the form of melancholy, mania, or imbecility. To these wretched beings, who seem to have crowded the streets of every village of Galilee, Jesus extended the same compassion that He did to "sinners." Sunk in almost bestial habits (for habit, and not sin, seems the appropriate word where the will is destroyed), they were half repelled and half attracted by His voice proclaiming God the Father, and all men brothers, forgiveness for the past, light and life for the future, and, above all, God seeking the lost sheep of the house of Israel, and caring more for the one lost than the ninety-nine that were safe in the fold. Their lower self, the evil spirit in them, cried out to be left alone, their human self implored help: in this distraction they often burst out in the synagogue, interrupting Jesus. Then came the voice of the Healer: "Hold thy peace, and come out of him;" and with a loud cry, sometimes accompanied by convulsions, the man was healed. So much about "possession," and the healing of the "possessed" and the sick. Did the disciples of Jesus ever fail in an attempt to work a miraculous cure?

Pupil.—Yes; they could not cure the lunatic because of their unbelief.[1]

Teacher.—Unbelief in what?

Pupil.—In their power to heal miraculously.

[1] St. Matthew xvii. 19.

Teacher.—Then if a child, or if an uneducated ignorant man, supposed himself able to heal disease, felt quite certain of it, he could do it?

Pupil.—No.

Teacher.—Why not?

Pupil.—His faith would be false faith, founded on ignorance.

Teacher.—Then the true faith, by which the disciples cured the sick, was founded on knowledge—knowledge of what?

Pupil.—Knowledge of Jesus and of His power, and of their participation in His power, and knowledge that it was the will of God that the sick should be healed.

Teacher.—Bear this in mind for what follows. These signs of healing, as you are probably aware, did not at once become extinct among the followers of Christ. There is considerable evidence to show that in some degree they continued even after the Apostolic period. Now, however, most of us believe they are extinct. All would admit that they are rare. What is the reason for this? Is it not now, as much as then, the will of God that the sick should be healed?

Pupil.—Perhaps it is because of our unbelief.

Teacher.—Perhaps it is, in part. But are not the blind, the lame, and the dumb, now, in modern times, healed to an extent unparalleled in ancient times?

Pupil.—Yes, but that is by natural means.

Teacher.—True, but every time that God reveals to us some new scientific method of preventing or curing disease, He thereby indicates that it is His will that disease shall be thus prevented or cured; and we become less and less inclined to attempt a cure by any other means. It is quite conceivable that the knowledge ot God's will, which we are daily deriving from the growth of scientific knowledge, may have the same special fitness for our times that the "signs" or "mighty works" of healing had for the early Christian period. Science has, in the same way, influenced the objects for which we feel justified in praying. We do not pray that a child may not catch the small-pox when we have vaccination. This point, however, can be more suitably discussed when we come to the subject of prayer. Are all the signs of Jesus works of healing?

Pupil.—No. There is the destruction of the fig-tree, the coin in the fish's mouth, and the destruction of the swine.

Teacher.—I am not prepared to discuss these miracles in detail with you. All I will say is, that since the general purpose of our Lord's mighty works is clearly beneficent, we need not allow our faith to be shaken by a few exceptions liable, perhaps, to misunderstanding, or capable of various explanations. Jesus was asked repeatedly by the Pharisees for a sign. What sort of a sign?

Pupil.—A sign from heaven.

Teacher.—Yes, they seem to have thought that an impostor could work signs on earth, but not in heaven. They were prepared to believe Jesus if He would have stopped the sun, or caused some fiery apparition in the sky. Why did not Jesus give this sign?

Pupil.—Because, as you said above, they had not faith.

Teacher.—But He cured the palsied man in part, at all events, to convince the sceptical scribes[1] that He had power on earth to forgive sins. If He cured the palsy, why not stop the sun?

Pupil.—I suppose He felt the cure was a natural sign. Stopping the sun, for no reason, would have been unnatural.

Teacher.—Of what was the cure a natural, and the other (stopping the sun) an unnatural sign?

Pupil.—Of His love and power.

Teacher.—But the reign or kingdom of all-powerful love, which Christ introduced, was called by a certain title. What was it?

Pupil.—The kingdom of God.

Teacher.—Then signs of the kingdom must be appropriate to the kingdom. When the disciples wished to call down fire on their enemies, He did not say it could not be done; but "Ye know not of what spirit ye are." It would have been unnatural; so when He was asked to give a sign from heaven He refused, for the same reason

---

[1] St. Mark ii. 10.

that He would not say He was the Messiah. And what was that reason?

Pupil.—Because saying would not have been revealing: because He wished men to believe in Him for Himself; and if He had said He was the Messiah, and the Pharisees had believed in Him, they would have been believing in the Messiah, but not loving Jesus of Nazareth.

Teacher.—For the same reason, if He had stopped the sun, the Pharisees would have believed in Him. But how? As an omnipotent worker of wonders. Jesus did not want that belief; He wanted to be trusted in as the Healer, the Forgiver of Sin, the Saviour of the lost. Stopping the sun would not have been a natural sign that He could and would forgive sin. In the circumstances in which He stood, it would have been a *wonder*, not a *sign*. There are three words used in the New Testament for works of this kind—"sign," "mighty work," and "wonder." The distinction in some of the later books is not always maintained, but in the Gospel our Lord's works are called "signs" and "mighty works," but never "wonders."

Before we close the lesson, let me put before you the usual objection to Christ's miracles, which must present itself to you sooner or later. It is said that they are against the laws of Nature, and that the more we study Nature, the more invariable her laws appear. What would you say to this?

Pupil.—May not God, who made the laws of Nature, also reverse them?

Teacher.—But when a man lays down rules and afterwards breaks them, we seem to see want of forethought and wisdom. Besides, have we not admitted that Christ's miracles themselves proceeded on certain laws? In certain contingencies "He could do no mighty work."

Pupil.—Then are we to say that God's laws come into collision with one another?

Teacher.—What is the law of gravitation?

Pupil.—That every particle of matter attracts every other.

Teacher.—And therefore that the earth attracts all bodies to itself. This feather, as you know, placed in an exhausted receiver will immediately fall to the ground. It will fall by a law of nature. But now let in the air, and the feather, instead of falling, hovers. Again, it hovers by a law of Nature. Now waft it towards the fire: it is caught in the draught of the chimney, and hurries up in the current. Once more, we may say it ascends by a law of Nature. Ascent is as natural now as descent was then. Just so with the works of Christ. They are unnatural for us, they were natural for Him. Faint traces of the health-giving influence of trust and hope upon the human frame, exerted by human beings on one another, are recognized even now, particularly in the treatment of nervous diseases. Faint as they are, they are sufficient, in my opinion, to prove that the healing power of Christ was based on the same spiritual law which we find in them. If it were possible for a second Jesus of Nazareth to appear on earth, as successful in dissipating the suspicions and winning the trust and faith of sinners, he too, I doubt not, would have the same power of healing the body through the spirit.

The works of Christ, it is true, were not all works of healing. The destruction of the swine, the attraction of the fish to the nets of Peter and his companions, the blasting of the fig-tree, the discovery of the coin in the fish's mouth, and the miraculous increase of food as well as the change of water into wine, and perhaps the sudden healing of the ear of Malchus, are works that rest on a different footing. Some of them are attended with great difficulty. All should be examined with due reference to the context and to the evidence on which they severally depend. Even those who reject this or that miracle on critical or other grounds—as for example, because it is only contained in one of the Gospels, and shows signs of interpolation—are not bound to reject the great body of our Lord's miracles. Others, who accept the miracles without exception, may fairly argue thus: "We admit the difficulty in this or that miracle which you assail, we certainly cannot in this case trace a law, or any appearance of a law; but we view it in connection with Christ's other miracles, which do contain traces of a law, and hence we infer that there is a law in this case also, which, though at present concealed from us, may hereafter be revealed by science or by other means. The general tendency of order and law in the works of Christ is so strong, that we do not think that one or two isolated cases of difficulty ought in themselves to prevent us from believing that all, without exception, partake in the general tendency. We would sooner suppose that the account of any particular miracle was based on some misunderstanding, than that it was against this tendency, but at present we do not see sufficient reason for such a supposition." Miracles like these may come like certain comets, once in a hundred or even in a thousand years; they may come but once only in the history of the world, and that once, when Christ comes; but, for all that, they are according to law, just as the seemingly irregular comet obeys the same laws as govern the planets and the stars.

A law of Nature, so far as it is absolutely true, relates to the past: when it relates to the future, it is a probability. Though expressed in the present tense, and implying the future, (as, for instance, "every particle of matter attracts every other," really means "is attracting and will attract,") it is really only a compendious record of the past, with an implied inference, derived from the *likeness* of sequences of phenomena in the world, that it is *likely* (and often extremely *likely* or, as we are in the habit of saying, *certain*) that the past is now being, and will be, repeated. There is therefore no necessity or inevitability in a law of nature, except that which springs from a feeling that God reveals His will to us in an orderly manner, and does not break His order. The existence of humanity depends upon the preservation of the order, and therefore we believe the order will be preserved. If the sun rose one day and not another, if water and air and earth changed their specific gravities, if the law of gravitation were suspended, men would cease to exist. A belief in order is therefore inherent in those who believe in God as a Father of men. But how is this belief incompatible with the belief that the central figure of humanity, the Son of God, coming into the world for an express purpose, performed works specially adapted to that purpose? Though there may be some misunderstandings in the accounts of some of these works, yet surely the great bulk of them are such that we should at once say, that for a Son of God they are *natural*. Of course if a law, as it generally does, implies repetition, induction from several instances, there is a contradiction of terms in saying that Christ's works are according to law. His works cannot be repeated, unless Christ Himself is repeated. But if law means the will of God, tending to the development of material and spiritual order, free from caprice and change, working on lines that have been immoveable since the creation, then in that sense of the word the miracles of Christ are according to law, for they were "prepared by the Father before the foundation of the world."[1]

[1] The miracles of the Old Testament are not here discussed.

CHAPTER IV.

CHRIST'S SACRIFICE.

Teacher.—What did we say[1] was the meaning of sacrifice?

Pupil.—The consecration and devotion of one's will to God, of which the expression in words is "Thy will be done," and in emblems the sacrifice of an animal.

Teacher.—And how is it that Christ, and only Christ, can offer up the perfect sacrifice?

Pupil.—Because He alone could offer up His will perfectly to God.

Teacher.—When did He offer up this sacrifice?

Pupil.—At His death.

Teacher.—That was the final and culminating expression of the sacrifice. But was that the only occasion on which He offered up His will to the Father? What did He say was the purpose of His coming into the world?

Pupil.—He said, "I came down from heaven not to do mine own will, but the will of him that sent me."[2]

Teacher.—Then the purpose of His whole life was a sacrifice, and every day of His life was a part of that sacrifice, as well as the day of His death. Sacrifice with us implies effort, struggle, and pain. Can it have been an effort to Jesus to offer up His will to the Father, since He was one with God? Where was the pain, if there was any?

Pupil.—I do not know. But Jesus is described as "a man of sorrows, and acquainted with grief."

[1] Part I. chapter iv., where the nature of sacrifice is discussed.
[2] John vi. 38.

Teacher.—And can you not tell what it was that caused Him sorrow and grief? By what is Jesus said to have been "grieved"?[1]

Pupil.—By the hardness of heart, and the incredulity of the Pharisees.

Teacher.—And when is He said to have wept?

Pupil.—After the death of Lazarus, when the friends and sisters of the deceased were mourning around Him.

Teacher.—A kind-hearted surgeon or minister of religion, even after long practice, can scarcely fail to be touched with sorrow at the sight of the disease and misery and sin with which he is brought into contact. Can we then suppose that He who not merely cured, but is said to have "borne our sicknesses and carried our infirmities," who not merely forgave sins, but is said to have borne our sins, and to have been made sin for us, was altogether free from pain?

Pupil.—I suppose not.

Teacher.—Whether we can say that it was an effort to Christ to live His life I do not know. He was tempted, and temptation seems to imply a conflict, and a conflict, effort; but in any case Christ's life was a life of pain. His human will may have shrunk from contact with so much sin and wickedness; but He came "not to do his own will, but the will of God who sent him." Why do we not feel the same pain and pity for the sins and miseries of other men?

Pupil.—I suppose partly because we have not the same power of sympathy and love, and the same deep horror of sin which Christ had.

Teacher.—Then the better men are, the more they will be pained by the sins and sorrows of their fellow-men; and therefore Christ, the perfect man, must have been pained by them in proportion to His greatness. His pain must therefore have been infinite—inconceivable to us. You know how intensely He felt for the "sinners," the "lost sheep," the "little ones." In proportion to this intense anxiety and love must have been His sorrow and distress at their wretchedness. You know that He claimed the power of forgiving sins. Now no man can forgive a sin without sympathising with the

[1] St. Mark iii. 5.

sinner, and to some extent being pained by the sin. Pain was therefore a necessary condition of this power of forgiveness. Perhaps, however, you think that Christ's trust in the goodness of the Father, His insight into God's purposes, and His certainty of the ultimate triumph of righteousness, took away all pain at men's sin.

Pupil.—I should have thought His sorrow was certainly alleviated by His trust in the Father.

Teacher.—So it was, no doubt. But remember, the higher an ideal one has formed of mankind, the more one must be pained by departure from that ideal. Jesus knew, as none of us can know, what God had intended man to be: "how noble in reason, how infinite in faculties, in action how like an angel, in apprehension how like a god." Must He not have been pained then, to a degree inconceivable to us, at witnessing the noble image of God polluted and almost effaced as it is and was, by ordinary selfish human beings, and God's noblest piece of work degraded to a mere "quintessence of dust"? Do we not love Him the more for knowing that He must have been thus pained?

Pupil.—Yes.

Teacher.—Thus far we have been trying to apprehend something of the reality and purity of Christ's sacrifice. Now let us consider its influence upon us. How were the old sacrifices useful to men?

Pupil.—As emblems of the sacrifice of the heart, which they helped men to express.

Teacher.—Yes, but only as emblems. They impressed upon the sacrificer the necessity of dying to sin and living to God, and they taught him the mischief of sin, and the connection of sin with death. But we know from Isaiah that sacrifice was often misunderstood, and offered up by hypocrites and sinners who had no intention of repenting. The blood of bulls and goats could not in itself take away sin. The blood of Christ, we are told, can take away sin. Whence this difference?

Pupil.—The death of an animal was involuntary on the part of the animal, and merely the sacrificer's act, teaching nothing but what the sacrificer knew before. The life and death of Christ constituted a voluntary sacrifice, and taught men new truths about sacrifice.

Teacher.—What new truths?

Pupil.—That there is an infinite power in human nature of sacrificing oneself for others, and that this is the noblest kind of sacrifice.

Teacher.—But was it enough to know new truths about sacrifice? Was it not necessary to participate in the sacrifice, to be, as the saying goes, "sprinkled with the blood of Jesus"? How can men be thus "sprinkled"? How can they participate in that sacrifice?

Pupil.—By faith in Christ's sacrifice.

Teacher.—Do you mean by merely believing that Christ did as a fact offer up Himself for men? Suppose a man believes this and does not love Christ? Suppose, as St. James says, a man "believes and trembles"?

Pupil.—It is necessary, besides believing in the life and death of Christ as historical facts, that the man should also trust in and love Christ, and should feel that His sacrifice is infinitely good and unselfish, acceptable to God and worthy of the homage of men.

Teacher.—And is it possible that a man should thus love Christ and trust in Christ, and realize in his heart the purity and perfection of His sacrifice, and yet himself be hard and cold, unsympathetic and selfish?

Pupil.—No, it is not possible.

Teacher.—Then the sacrifice of Christ will have the effect of raising those who believe in it out of themselves into a region of purity and unselfishness by the side of Christ. The sacrifice of a lamb simply gave an impressive form to the imperfect meaning of the sacrificer himself; the sacrifice of Christ reveals the perfection of sacrifice, the beauty of it, the divinity of it. More than reveals, it attracts and assimilates men, conforming them to Christ's pattern. Christ is more than a mere example. We are taught to believe that He "draws men unto him." It is not merely we that think of and copy Him; He also moulds and shapes us to His image. By all our thoughts of Him, as forgiving, as healing, but by none more than our thought of Him as dying on the cross for us, He day by day draws us nearer towards Himself, towards God. I say towards God; and now I ask when are we drawn near to God? when are we at one with Him?

Pupil.—When we love Him and trust Him.

Teacher.—And is it possible for us to be at one with Christ, to feel that we are under Christ's protection, recognized as brothers by Christ, and not at the same time to feel that we are recognized as children, and loved as children by the Father?'

Pupil.—No.

Teacher.—Then by Christ's sacrifice we are made *at one* with the Father; hence it is called the "atonement."

Pupil.—Is it not called the atonement or propitiation *for our sins?* How are our sins removed by Christ's sacrifice? Did He not bear the punishment of our sins?

Teacher.—He bore the terrible consequences of our sins—pain, sorrow, and death; which to us are a punishment, though they cannot strictly be called a punishment to Christ. But He bore more than the consequences of our sins, He bore our sins, and by bearing them He forgave them. When we consider the nature of forgiveness, we shall investigate the connection between forgiving and self-sacrifice. Meantime, do you know of any historical instance of self-sacrifice? I wish to point out the dissimilarity between Christ's sacrifice and nay other. Take the story of Calais.

Pupil.—Eustace de St. Pierre devoted himself to a shameful death to save his fellow-citizens from destruction.

Teacher.—He was spared: but that does not diminish the nobleness of the act. We may call it a sacrifice, for, as far as motive went, he sacrificed himself for his countrymen. Now can you not feel that all the citizens of Calais must have been morally raised by such a sacrifice? Not merely gratitude and admiration, but a sense of self-respect and of the noble acts a man may do must have sprung up in many hearts; a keen desire to go and do likewise, a feeling that the citizens of Calais were intended by God to do noble acts, and of all noble acts self-sacrifice as the noblest. Now Eustace offered his life for Calais. Christ died for the world. What the citizens of Calais felt about themselves and their duty, as an inference from the sacrifice of Eustace, that all human beings must feel in an infinitely greater degree about human nature and human duty, as an inference from the sacrifice of Christ. So far there may be thought to be some kind of similarity. Now for the great, the all-important difference. What is it?

Pupil.—Eustace devoted himself to save his countrymen from death;—Christ to save the world from spiritual death.

Teacher.—I do not think that the great difference. At least the difference is not fully explained. Many men, some of the martyrs and missionaries for instance, have died for the moral and spiritual benefit of their fellow-men. But wherein has this sacrifice often consisted, and how is it limited? It often consists, does it not, in the simple devotion of their lives in the cause of duty, and it is often limited to the moment of their death? No doubt a man who gives up, as it were, his death to the cause of duty must, for the most part, have previously given up some portion of his life. Eustace, I dare say, was not made noble and unselfish for the first time at the moment of his noble sacrifice. He had doubtless been prepared by a life of previous unselfishness to forget himself in the engrossing pity for a despairing city. But often men have died for their fellow-men, who, during their lives, have been unforgiving and unsympathetic. We cannot too distinctly remember that voluntarily dying, like every other action, is only so far good and noble as it expresses good and noble motives. The perfection of Christ's sacrifice consisted in this, that it was not an isolated act, but the consistent and final expression of a perfect love and sympathy for mankind, and it is not difficult to feel how the worst may be affected by such a sacrifice.

Imagine one of the most degraded "sinners" who had seen and known Christ, some sinner of sinners, impure in thought and act, worldly and selfish, debased by want of respect for himself both from himself and others, a kind of reptile among men, who has never heard a loving word since he was a little child, standing before the cross of Christ and arguing, or rather feeling, thus: "Here is one whom I could never understand, any more than earth can comprehend heaven. He is the Son of God and one with God. He loved goodness and hated sin, more than the best of those who look down on me. He knew all my faults and meannesses, my hard ingratitude, my impurity, my covetousness, my cruelty, knew them better, and hated them more keenly than my most malignant enemy. He saw me through and through; I could hide nothing from Him, and yet He saw something to love in me. He loved me and pitied me all the more, because no one else felt either love or pity for me. How He must have loathed my sins, and yet He tolerated me! How He must have abhorred the very atmosphere of my thoughts, and yet He sat at my table and took part in my pleasures! If before I could scarcely believe that it was possible that He could love me, I can disbelieve it no longer now, for there He hangs upon the cross, dying for me. But, if He loves me, God may perhaps love me instead of hating me; nay, God must love me, for the Crucified must have been true, and He told us that God was our Father. And if God loves me, is there not something in me, even in me, which men have not seen and I have not seen—some image of God in my heart deserving love? Yes, even if there is nothing left, even if the image is obliterated, I feel that I am meant to be loved by God, and that God will do what He means with me, and love me, and conform me once again to His image, that is to His Son, to Him in whom alone I live henceforth. Henceforth I am one with Christ, and nothing shall separate me from Him. Never again need I offer a sacrifice. There is my sacrifice. That is what I mean or ought to mean, but can never express. Take, O God, whom I may now call Father, that sacrifice for mine. It is mine; for henceforward the life that I live, it is not I that live it, but Christ that liveth in me."

I do not say the man would utter this. The less he uttered perhaps the better. But I think he might feel something like this.

CHAPTER V.

LOVE.

Teacher.—Why ought we to love one another?

Pupil.—Because we are commanded to do so by Christ.

Teacher.—True, but why did Christ command us to love one another? Suppose you were poor and ill, in great distress and need of help, and a man came to your bedside bringing you food and medicine, clothing and money, you would be inclined to feel gratitude to him, indeed a kind of love, would you not?

Pupil.—Yes.

Teacher.—But suppose your benefactor said to you, "All this I do, not because I love or like you for your own sake, for I can see nothing to like in you. You seem to me a degraded and brutalized creature, whose nature it is to be sensual and sinful. What I do to you I do, not for your sake, but for the sake of a friend, and because that friend bade me do it." Would not you feel strongly inclined to repel his gifts? Would you feel any love for him?

Pupil.—No, I could not.

Teacher.—Would such a man be fulfilling Christ's precept?

Pupil.—No, for Christ did not say, "Do good to one another," but " Love one another."

Teacher.—But how can we love a dull, stupid, commonplace, artful, mean, flattering creature?

Pupil.—We must love him because Christ died for him.

Teacher.—But suppose a man comes to you with professions of love, and you ask him what he sees to love in you, and he replies,

"Nothing. But Christ loves you and died for you, and therefore I love you." Would you not feel that though the man *said* he loved you, he was really only trying to love you, and had not yet succeeded? If one of your own brothers were to love you in that way, not because he loved you for yourself, but because your father loved you, would that be brotherly love? Would it not really be love for your father, not really for you? Would it make you love your brother back again?

Pupil.—No.

Teacher.—Then why must we love a sinful and bad man?

Pupil.—We must love, not his badness or sinfulness, but himself. We must distinguish the sinner from the sin. We may hate the deed, while we love the doer.

Teacher.—But by what right do you separate a man's bad acts from him, and love him in spite of his badness. Is not that as unreasonable as to separate a man's good acts from him, and hate him in spite of his goodness?

Pupil.—I don't know. Yet I feel there is a difference.

Teacher.—Could you love an evil spirit; a being that could say "evil is to me what good is to men"?

Pupil.—I feel it hard to comprehend the existence of such a being; but love would be out of the question in such a case.

Teacher.—You can sometimes forgive and love a man who has committed a murder; can you forgive or love a wild beast who has done precisely the same thing? You feel that forgiveness is here altogether out of place: tell me, then, why can you forgive a bad man, but not an evil spirit or a wild beast?

Pupil.—You cannot forgive a wild beast, just as you cannot feel any resentment against it. You may have to destroy it, but you would be childish to be angry with it. It is acting according to its nature.

Teacher.—You cannot be angry, then, with anything for acting according to its nature?

Pupil.—No.

Teacher.—But are not men naturally inclined to sin? And does not St. Paul say "we were by nature the children of wrath"? and if so, can you fairly be angry with men for sinning, if sin is in accordance with their nature? And yet what do we mean by an "unnatural" father, or by "unnatural" cruelty?

Pupil.—We mean a father who does not love his children as he ought; and cruelty we call "unnatural" when it passes the bounds of ordinary humanity, and is excessively bad.

Teacher.—Then, you see, in our ordinary language we seem to admit that badness is unnatural for men, and wrong, and that we may be fairly angry at it; and yet St. Paul talks about men being "by nature the children of wrath," and we ourselves say that it is natural to err, and on that account we claim forgiveness and deprecate anger. Can you explain this?

Pupil.—No.

Teacher.—Is it the nature of a clock to indicate the time?

Pupil.—Yes.

Teacher.—The right time, I suppose you mean?

Pupil.—Of course.

Teacher.—And yet out of a thousand clocks scarcely one will indicate the correct time to a second, so that it may be said, strictly speaking, that no clock, or hardly any clock, indicates the correct time, and that it is the nature of a clock to deviate from the right time, and to indicate the wrong time.

Pupil.—Yes; but the purpose and object of a clock is to indicate the right time, and a good clock will deserve its name in proportion as it fulfils the purpose of the maker, and indicates the right time.

Teacher.—Then when you say it is the nature of a clock to indicate the right time, you mean the object or intention of the maker, to which all clocks approximate, but never, or hardly ever, exactly attain. When you say it is the nature of a clock to indicate the wrong time, what do you mean by *nature* then?

Pupil.—I mean what the clock does, its actual working—its custom, so to speak.

Teacher.—Now I think you can apply this to the case of men.

Pupil.—It is the nature of a man to do right, for that is the purpose of the Maker in making him; and a man deserves to be called a man in proportion as he fulfils this purpose, to which all men approximate, but none attain. On the other hand, since all men are imperfect, and continually do wrong, it is the nature of men (in the sense of habit or custom) to do wrong.

Teacher.—Which is the higher and nobler sense of the word "nature"?

Pupil.—The former.

Teacher.—Is a man likely to do right when you tell him it is his nature to do wrong, unless you carefully explain what you mean by "nature"?

Pupil.—No. But surely we cannot ourselves do right by nature. Does not St. Paul say that "in ourselves," that is, in our flesh, "dwelleth no good thing"?

Teacher.—Quite so. We ourselves, unaided by God, cannot do what is right, and yet it is the nature of men to do right. What is the inference?

Pupil.—That every man is by nature aided by God.[1]

Teacher.—Yes. You may say, like a man of the world, that every man has "something good at bottom;" or, as Moses says, that men are "made in the image of God," and even in their present state contain some traces of that image; or, like St. Paul, that Christ, or that the Spirit of God, dwells in the hearts of men. All these expressions—even the first, though very imperfectly—indicate that all men have something divine in them whereby they resemble God, and claim the love of men. And what did we agree[2] that this was, this faculty in virtue of which men resemble God?

Pupil.—The power of loving. But how can it be said that the heathen before the time of Christ had the Spirit of God?

---

[1] Compare St. Paul's Epistle (Rom. ii. 14): "When the Gentiles, which have not the law, do by *nature* the things of the law."

[2] See Part I. chapter i.

Teacher—Did they ever do—the ancient Greeks and Romans—anything that was right and painful? Were any of them unselfish, generous, kind, and truthful?

Pupil.—Yes.

Teacher.—Then they must have had the Spirit of God. As St. Paul says, men cannot do what is right unaided by God. Clement of Alexandria said that God trained the heathen by philosophy, as He trained the Jews by the law, for the reception of the truth of Christ. But I think the ties of family and country exercised more influence than philosophy. Wherever two or three have been gathered together in family or country, loving one another, there the Spirit of God has been at work: for no man can love another without the aid of the Spirit of God. But this mention of the heathen is a digression. Let us return to our subject. We agree that every man contains in himself, do we not, some trace of the image of God which claims our love?

Pupil.—Yes.

Teacher.—Now who will best be able to love other men? Will it not be the man who has the best eye for discerning this image of God beneath all manner of obscuring defilements?

Pupil.—Yes.

Teacher.—And no one, surely, will be so skilled in discerning this image as the man who has seen the image as it is, and loves it and longs for it, and is always on the search for anything that can remind him of it?

Pupil.—No one.

Teacher.—And what is this image, "the express image of God"?

Pupil.—Christ.

Teacher.—Then it follows that the man who loves Christ best will find it easiest to discern something worth loving in men, and hence Christianity and philanthropy are immediately connected together, according to our Lord's saying, "By this shall men know that ye are my disciples, if ye have love one toward another." Therefore, if we see a man degraded, apparently below the possibility of restoration, literally brutalized, brought down to the level of the brutes by sin, what ought we to feel about him?

Pupil.—I suppose we ought to try and recognize something in him that is worthy of love.

Teacher.—Yes. And if we cannot see it, we ought to blame our own blindness and inability to discern the image of God. And the lower the man is sunk, and the more he differs from that image, and the greater the contrast between the glorious possibility for which he was created and the pitiful fact, the more we ought to feel—what?

Pupil.—Pity.

Teacher.—Who, above all men, by affinity would naturally have the power of recognizing and loving the faintest trace of God's image in the hearts of men?

Pupil.—Christ: for He was that image.

Teacher.—"He knew what was in men." Did He love men less because He knew men more? You know it was not so. And what was the effect of His love upon publicans and sinners? Did it encourage them to continue in their extortions and sins?

Pupil.—No; they repented.

Teacher.—The "sinners" had been told by the Pharisees that they were sinners, and had been treated as though it were their nature to sin, and they had sinned accordingly. Christ came, telling them that He loved them, and came to save them just because they were sinners, and they became conscious of a new power of righteousness. Zaccheus the extortioner became Zaccheus the just. But, even without referring to the Gospels, I think ordinary life might show not only that a man is morally raised by receiving respect and affection from his neighbours, but also that every man has something in him worth loving; for, if a man had nothing good in him, and were utterly bad, then those who knew him best would hate him most, whereas who are those who generally like a man best?

Pupil.—His parents and brothers.

Teacher.—Well, then, the purpose of Christ was to make the world a family, a brotherhood, recognizing and loving in one another

Himself, the likeness of the heavenly Father. Such love is twice blessed, for it not only blesses the man who bestows it, but raises the man on whom it is bestowed, giving him self-respect and the consciousness of a divine power of doing right. This effect of love will be explained more suitably under the head of forgiveness in the following chapter.

CHAPTER VI.

FORGIVENESS.

Teacher.—What is meant by forgiveness?
Pupil.—Letting a man off.
Teacher.—Letting him off what?
Pupil.—The penalty of his fault.
Teacher.—Is it? Take the following case. A servant, we will suppose, has defrauded his master. The fault has not been, and perhaps may never be, detected. But the man is weighed down by the consciousness of his sin, and longs to confess, and to be forgiven. He comes to his master and tells all. The master replies, "Go to your work as usual. To prosecute you would injure my business. The money which you have stolen is of little importance to me, but I will take effectual precautions that you shall never have a chance of stealing again." The penalty is here remitted; but is that forgiveness?

Pupil.—No. The master remits nothing in reality. The penalty is a mere nothing to him.

Teacher.—Imagine a different reply from a somewhat different master, more good-tempered and easy than the last, and more sensitive to the distress of others, but worldly, and without much sense of sin except as an inconvenience. He says, "I know men will take advantage of their employers. You have been many years with me; I don't like to part with you; I'll say nothing about the money, though I don't like to lose it. I know you cannot easily work it up. For the future I must look after you, though." Is that forgiveness?

Pupil.—Not exactly. Not like Christ's forgiveness.

Teacher.—Why not? The penalty is remitted.

Pupil.—Yes; of course. That is a necessary part of forgiveness; but something more is wanting, which I cannot easily express.

Teacher.—Take a third reply, and see whether that will help you. This third master says, "I can scarcely believe you can have thus deceived me. I trusted you implicitly, and I am pained more than I can express. Still I do believe in you even now. There must have been some unusual temptation or unusual weakness in you at the time. I feel sure you will not do it again. I'll tell you what I shall do. I can't afford to lose the money, nor do I think you ought to wish to avoid making compensation. You must work it up, and I will give you time. I know you will find it hard, but if I were in your place I should want to make compensation, and I think you ought to do the same. But you shall never hear a single word from me again about it. I shall take no additional precautions to prevent your deceiving me again. I feel sure I may trust you. I forgive you from my heart, and henceforth I forget it." Not every offender can deserve to have this said to him; still less can every forgiver say this with sincerity. But if a man can say it and believe it, is it not forgiveness?

Pupil.—I suppose it is. Yes, it must be. But why, then, is the remission of the punishment so often considered a necessary part of forgiveness?

Teacher.—Because it is the outward sign of the inward and spiritual act of forgiveness. Writing "forgive" for "repent," we may say—

> " The world will not believe a man *forgives*,
> And this wise world of ours is mainly right."

It is a very easy thing to say "I forgive," but very difficult to forgive from the heart. Most men would suspect their own honesty and sincerity if they said "I forgive," and added "but I must have my penalty." Few spectators would believe in the reality of such a forgiveness, still fewer that were thus forgiven. But though the remission of the penalty is generally necessary as a test of the sincerity of the forgiver, and as a means of impressing the person forgiven, yet it is but the outward sign. There may be exceptional cases, as above, where the penalty is not remitted because it is best that it should not be remitted. Similarly, a drunkard may feel that God has forgiven his past sin, and yet the penalty of chastening disease may not be remitted in this life. But if the remission of the penalty is merely the outward and visible sign of an inward spiritual act, what is that inward act?

Pupil.—Pity or sympathy.

Teacher.—Pity for what? Take the above case. Was it pity because the man was poor and could not easily make restitution? or pity for any other reason?

Pupil.—Pity for his degradation, sympathy with his shame and penitence.

Teacher.—What is the burden that is weighing down the sinner?

Pupil.—Sin.

Teacher.—And what is the meaning of "sympathy"?

Pupil.—"Suffering with."

Teacher.—Then the forgiver suffers, or bears with the sinner the burden of his sin?

Pupil.—Yes; but if a man has not sinned, how can he bear another's sin?

Teacher.—If your or my brother were detected in some shameful sin, could we help feeling shame, even though we were quite innocent ourselves? Should we not feel, though we could not explain it, that the sin was brought close to us, and, as it were, weighed upon us?

Pupil.—I think we should.

Teacher.—Then the more all men are regarded by us as our brothers, the more we shall feel their sins; and unless a man feels our sins he cannot forgive us. Suppose you desire forgiveness for committing some sinful act against a neighbour, and your neighbour has no idea of sin, except as something inconvenient and annoying to others. He pities you, we will suppose, sincerely, because you have lost money and reputation; he expresses himself kindly about your fault, and says he will forget it. He will forget it, and easily; for sin leaves no impression on his mind; but will he have forgiven it? You are weighed down by the sense of guilt and degradation, moral purity defiled, estrangement from God, and the loss of self-respect; he does not feel the weight. You want sympathy, and he gives you geniality. Will you feel, as you go out of the presence of such a man, forgotten, that you have been forgiven?

Pupil.—No. I should be grateful for his kindness, but I should not feel forgiven.

Teacher.—But now take the third case mentioned above, where the master did not remit the penalty, but yet forgave; would not you feel, though you might not be able to explain how, that by such a forgiveness your sin was really lightened, your self-respect increased, your power of doing right greatly strengthened?

Pupil.—Yes, I should.

Teacher.—In what consists the difference between this, the real forgiveness, and the two former false imitations of it?

Pupil.—The true forgiver was pained by the sin, and sympathised with the degradation of the sinner, feeling the sin to some extent as if it were his own. Again, he had so much trust in the sinner that he could say, "I feel sure it is not your nature to sin like this."

Teacher.—Then there are two requisites for performing the operation of forgiveness. The man who forgives must to some extent be pained by the burden of the sin which he forgives, and must place some trust and faith in the man whom he forgives?

Pupil.—Yes.

Teacher.—But is that last requisite always possible? Can one always trust that a thief will never rob again, or a Pharisee never dissemble again, if once forgiven?

Pupil.—No.

Teacher.—Then can you forgive the thief who asks for forgiveness, while all the time you fear that possibly, if not probably, he will take to stealing again when a week is out?

Pupil.—I do not know what to say: for it seems impossible to forgive without trusting, and we cannot always trust. And yet, on the other hand, our Lord teaches us to forgive after repeated offences.

Teacher.—Can you, even when you feel most trust and most pity, ever hope to forgive a man in the way in which Christ forgave? Does not a perfect forgiveness require perfect faith in human nature and a perfect power of sympathy, or of bearing the sins of others? And can you ever hope to attain to this perfect power?

Pupil.—No.

Teacher.—No indeed. But does it follow, because you cannot perfectly forgive, that you should not be able partially to forgive, and to grow continually in the power of forgiving, as you grow in faith, and trust, and sympathy? When your faith and trust are small, your power of forgiving will be weak, and comparatively ineffectual. But in the case of every man who turns to you and says, "I repent," you can at least believe some good of him. He may have given no signs of true repentance, he may seem likely to commit the same fault "seven times in a day," as our Lord says. But even in that case you can believe that he has the germs of a better life in him, that Christ died for him and loves him, so that he must have something that deserves love in him; and you may trust that hereafter God will develop this dormant seed of righteousness into a tree of spiritual life. It is well that we should understand our very limited power of forgiving. We may use exaggerated language sometimes, which will do more harm than good. If we say that we will "completely forget the past," while nevertheless we show by our conduct that we have not quite forgotten it, but are only trying to forget it, we do harm to the man whom we are trying to forgive. At the very moment when we use the exaggerated language, the exaggeration is often felt, and produces a sense of an imposture, and a feeling of suspicion and uneasiness. Forgiveness is the most difficult task that God has imposed on men, and it will never be perfectly performed by us in this life. I said just now that exaggeration produces a sense of imposture. What expression of St. Paul suggests, upon a superficial view, the notion that there is something unreal about forgiveness, something imputed that has no existence?

Pupil.—The imputation of righteousness.

Teacher.—Give me an instance of "imputed righteousness."

Pupil.—Abraham's faith was "imputed unto him for righteousness."

Teacher.—But is not faith the source of all righteousness? May not faith (if it be real or, as St. Paul says, living faith) be compared to a tree that will inevitably bring forth the fruit of righteous action? And if the All-seeing sees the oak in the acorn, can He not see the righteous act in the germ? Is there any fiction in calling a faithful man righteous? It may seem new and startling to a nation of formalists and Pharisees, but do we not continually impute righteousness in the same way, and say that it is the motive and not the action that makes a man good or bad? and is not that true morality?

Pupil.—Yes. But I thought only God imputed righteousness to men. Do men impute righteousness to one another?

Teacher.—Do they not, whenever, as the saying goes, they "take the will for the deed?" Every man imputes righteousness when he forgives another. And this imputation is also a source of positive strength and righteousness in the man to whom righteousness is imputed. Let me try to explain this. Suppose a father and his young son are trying to swim for their lives from a shipwreck to the shore. The father knows that the distance is almost too great unless the boy is in good health and spirits; but just now he is terrified and nervous, and cannot do himself justice. In his present state of mind he could barely swim three-quarters of the distance. The father, making up his mind that his son's life will be saved, persuades both himself and his son that the distance can be accomplished. The boy has never swum so far before; but the father assures him that he can do it, promises him that he shall do it. The boy believes his father's assurances, strikes out cheerfully, swims boldly and steadily, gains courage, and finally reaches the shore. Now the child could not have done this, if the father had not told him he could do it. The father imputed, as it were, strength to the child, knowing that the imputation would realize itself, and the child, through faith in his father, acquired strength. There is no fiction here. It is a law of human nature. And in the same way the imputation of righteousness rests on a law of our spiritual nature. We have power by faith and trust to impute righteousness, as St. Paul says, to one another. This imputation is based upon the truth that men were made like, and are being made more like, God. In proportion as we believe in this truth, and trust that God will fulfil His purpose, we shall have power to impute righteousness, and thereby to strengthen, and to forgive. Forgiveness is a paradox, like the saying in the Gospel, "I believe, help thou mine unbelief." Just so it is our duty to trust in men, partly because they are worthy of trust, and partly in order that they may become worthy of trust.

But ought we to forgive an unrepentant man, an unjust and proud oppressor, a malignant and successful slanderer? Is it not our duty, if possible, to put down oppression and to punish injustice?

Pupil.—Yes: and forgiveness seems incompatible with vengeance; and yet our Lord teaches us to forgive our enemies.

Teacher.—Did Christ forgive the Pharisees? What did He call them?

Pupil.—He called them "serpents," a "generation of vipers," and He did not speak as though He forgave them.

Teacher.—No. He implied that, if they persisted in calling good evil, to suit their theology and their interpretation of the Bible, good would become evil to them, and they would become like Satan, beings whose nature fed on evil, incapable of forgiveness and regeneration. Besides, He laid down a rule for one's conduct towards a fellow-Christian who persisted in injustice. And what was that rule?

Pupil.—The offender was to be requested to make compensation, and if he refused he was to be treated as an outcast from the Christian society.

Teacher.—And yet Christ also bade us forgive "our brother" even though he injured us "seven times in a day," if he came to us and said "I repent." What, then, ought to be our attitude towards offenders who have not made, and are never likely to make, compensation for their faults? Perhaps they have forgotten they ever committed the faults. We cannot perform an effectual and complete forgiveness, we cannot lighten the burden of the sin, for the offender does not feel it to be a burden; but we can banish all personal vindictiveness, we can still, I suppose, think charitably of the offender, and believe that he is better than he appears to be, and that his sins do not represent him; we can be ready to forgive him, can we not, should he ever turn to us and say " I repent "?

Pupil.—Yes.

Teacher.—But suppose a man offends you in such a manner that you feel it natural to punish him. Suppose he strikes you in the street, may you strike him back again if he persists?

Pupil.—I suppose not.

Teacher.—May you hand him over to the policeman?

Pupil.—Yes.

Teacher.—Then he will be punished by the law, and if he does not desist he will be struck by the policeman. What is the difference between your punishing him directly, through the policeman, and indirectly, so far as the law allows you, with your own hand? Again, if you see the same man striking a woman or a child, may you not strike him to make him desist?

Pupil.—Yes.

Teacher.—Then why may you strike the man in the one case, but not in the other?

Pupil.—It is wrong to allow any one to be illegally oppressed; and the law enjoins on us to stop it, when the officers of the law are absent.

Teacher.—Then if the law does not allow any one, neither does it allow you to be illegally oppressed. It therefore enjoins on you to resist illegal oppression directed against yourself, when the officers of the law are absent.

Pupil.—But is that in accordance with the precepts of Christ?

Teacher.—I told you before that the precepts of Christ were intended, at the time when they were given, to be literally obeyed by the first disciples, and there may come a time when we ought to obey them literally again; but at present literal obedience might be injurious to society, and, therefore, not in accordance with Christianity, *i.e.* the Spirit of Christ. But we may learn much from the spirit of Christ's precept. Why does the law not allow us, when the officers of the law are present, to execute the law ourselves, unless in aid of the officers?

Pupil.—I suppose because there is danger that we should be too passionate and vindictive.

Teacher.—Then it is right to punish, but there is a feeling which tends to make punishment excessive and unjust. What is that feeling?

Pupil.—Anger.

Teacher.—I should not call it anger. You are angry when you see the weak oppressed, and that is right; but when we are injured in our own persons, we are sometimes disposed to be excessively angry, not because the injury is wrong, but because the injury affects *us*. That is wrong. What name do we give to this latter feeling of self-regarding desire for vengeance? Give me the Latin-derived word.

Pupil.—Vindictiveness.

Teacher.—I should say then that anger is indifferent, sometimes right and sometimes wrong, but vindictiveness gives a selfish character to anger, and is always wrong. There is an anger that is always right, such as one feels at the sight of cruelty, injustice, and oppression, a moral recoil of sentiment from evil. "Recoil of sentiment"—express that in a French-derived word.

Pupil.—Resentment.

Teacher.—Remember, then, that resentment is a virtue, and that a man who feels no resentment at the sight of injustice is destitute of a true sense of sin. There is almost as great a deficiency of resentment in the world as there is an excess of vindictiveness. Vindictiveness is clearly inconsistent with forgiveness: is resentment also?

Pupil.—I scarcely know.

Teacher.—Have we not agreed that resentment, *i.e.* the unselfish recoil and feeling of anger at injustice, is a virtue? Therefore, as long as the injustice exists our resentment ought to exist also. But when the injustice has passed away, either by being owned and compensated for, or by being put down and punished, the resentment is modified. In the former case, when the man confesses his sin, we dissociate the sin from him and resentment vanishes, having nothing to subsist on. In the latter case, where the oppressor is punished, but does not own or feel his sin, we cannot fully forgive, we can only forgive as far as we are concerned, being always ready to offer forgiveness. Resentment cannot in this case disappear, but we do not feel that unmixed anger with which we recoil from successful and exultant injustice, or thriving hypocrisy. The sin is punished; the sinner is taught, at all events, that sin is painful, and the feeling of pity, which ought always to co-exist with anger, now predominates. Resentment is, therefore, inconsistent with a complete forgiveness, but not with the attitude of forgiveness. Now let us return to the important question which we touched on above. Is it possible to forgive and to punish at the same time? Can we sincerely say to a man who has robbed us and begs us to pardon him, "I forgive you, but I must hand you over to the law"?

Pupil.—The man, at all events, would not be likely to believe in our sincerity.

Teacher.—I don't think he would; and many of us would be inclined to suspect our own sincerity. The words "I forgive" are so easy and so cheap that one feels ashamed at uttering them, unless one proves by action that they mean something. Yet we said above that it is possible, though very difficult, to forgive and to punish. And take another case. Imagine the first Brutus judging his traitorous sons and condemning them to death. It is quite possible that he may have condemned them in stern resentment; but it is also conceivable, is it not, that he may have spoken to them previously in private, have mourned over them and with them, like a father with children, have comforted them and encouraged them to meet death bravely, and then, after heartily forgiving them as a father, he may have ascended the public seat of justice, and scourged and beheaded them as a consul? It is conceivable, is it not, that, even while the rods of the lictors were striking them, or while the axe was in the act of falling, the two sons may still have seen in the consul's face reason for believing in the forgiveness of their father? And why?

Pupil.—Because they would know he was pained.

Teacher.—Then we come to the same conclusion as before, that it is not necessary that the forgiver should remit punishment, if only he himself feels pain.

Pupil.—I think so.

Teacher.—You don't mean pain unconnected with the forgiveness. Pain of what kind, then?

Pupil.—Pain arising from pity for the offender—sympathy.

Teacher.—Forgiveness, then, requires sympathy with the offender as well as the complete banishment of personal spite or vindictiveness. Surely this implies a considerable effort. By what metaphorical name (the name of a bodily desire) is the craving for vengeance often expressed?

Pupil.—We call it a "thirst" for vengeance.

Teacher.—Yes; and we find the Homeric heroes, as well as the Northmen and most other warlike tribes, feeling this desire as really as we feel thirst; ready to give up everything—life itself—if they could set foot on their enemy's throat, and in his sight tear the armour from off his limbs and insult him before he died, and then give him the final stab. Now to give up the satisfaction of this feeling is to give up a great deal; and for whom does one give it up?

Pupil.—One gives it up because it is right, because it is the will of the righteous God.

Teacher.—And when a man gives up anything for Him, whether the offering be visible or invisible, by what name do we call it?

Pupil.—Sacrifice.

Teacher.—Then we see that the spiritual law of forgiveness, and the spiritual law of sacrifice, are connected together. A man can forgive best when he can best give up all personal vindictive feeling; that is, sacrifice his will to God: and no man can perfectly forgive another unless his will is one with God's, unless he can offer the perfect sacrifice of the will. And who alone could offer that?

Pupil.—Christ.

Teacher.—Therefore Christ alone could perfectly forgive: and we, when we forgive, only so far forgive as we enter into the sacrifice of Christ, and are thereby ourselves enabled to offer up our wills to God through Christ. In other words, we cannot forgive (and from the beginning of the world no one has ever forgiven) except through the Spirit of Christ.

We have now to put ourselves in the position of the person forgiven, and to ask what is requisite in order to accept forgiveness. Jesus did not say to the Pharisees, "Your sins are forgiven you," though they needed forgiveness as much as any one. He could not forgive them, for they did not wish for forgiveness. If they had said, "We are blind," He could have given them light, but they said, "We see," therefore they remained in darkness. Not all a giant's strength can lighten the yoke on the shoulders of the complacent fool who appropriates his burden as his clothing or ornament, as part of himself. We may, therefore, take for granted that no man can have his sin forgiven or *borne* by another, unless he feels his sin as a burden, and desires to be forgiven. Let us consider the other requisites for accepting forgiveness. When He forgave the palsied man, what is Jesus said to have noted previously?

Pupil.—The faith of those who took the trouble to let the sick man down from the roof.

Teacher.—Yes. We may fairly suppose that the sick man had asked his bearers to take this trouble, and that it was his faith as well as theirs that Jesus noted. Now let us consider this further. If a man when forgiven by another suspects the forgiver of being actuated by interested motives, or of not thoroughly forgiving him, can he feel forgiven?

Pupil.—No; he must have faith in the forgiver's truthfulness.

Teacher.—This, then, is the first requisite. Again, we agreed, did we not, that he must also feel that the forgiver has an adequate notion of the *sin*, as distinct from inconvenience or penalty?

Pupil.—Yes; he must believe that the forgiver is good and hates sin, and is pained by his sin.

Teacher.—But supposing he believes both in the forgiver's truthfulness and goodness, and yet says to himself, "He is too good to understand me: he does not know how bad I am: I have been bred up to mischief since I was a child, and it is in my blood. He says he trusts and feels sure I shall go right, but I know I shall not. I cannot help going wrong: I am born to be a sinner." What then?

Pupil.—If he feels sure he will go on sinning, he is likely to go on sinning.

Teacher.—Then the forgiveness, though freely offered, will have had no effect, will not have lightened the man's sin or made him stronger. What third requisite ought to have been present to make the forgiveness efficacious?

Pupil.—He ought to have believed that he was not born to sin, but that God created him for righteousness, to be a child of God.

Teacher.—True. He ought to have had faith in God. But we are supposing a man who has very little, if any, faith in God. Would not a kind of substitute be found in faith in an all-knowing and forgiving man? Suppose the man believes that the forgiver is not merely truthful, but also perfectly within the compass of his knowledge when he says, "You were not born to sin. Your sins are forgiven you. You are intended to be a child of God"? Will not the consequence be, he will believe first in the man who tells him that God loves him, and then in a loving God?

Pupil.—Yes.

Teacher.—Hence it was that Jesus carried the hearts of men, through Himself, up to the throne of the Father. "He knew what was in men," St. John says. Men knew that He knew them, and that, in spite of His knowledge, He loved them and assured them the Father loved them. They therefore believed in Him, and through

Him in the Father. All good men have some slight power of thus raising up weaker men to God; but it is as slight compared with Christ's power, as our goodness is slight compared with His goodness. We agree, then, that faith is the great requisite for receiving a true forgiveness when truly offered. I say requisite. Is, then, God's forgiveness conditionally offered?

Pupil.—Yes. God will forgive us only if we have faith.

Teacher.—Do you mean also that God will forgive us because of our faith?

Pupil.—Yes.

Teacher.—I should not say that. Does God give us light *because* we have eyes, or air *because* we have mouths?

Pupil.—No. He gives us light and air, and we receive them *by means* of our eyes and mouths.

Teacher.—Exactly so; and do we not continually say that God's forgiveness in the same way is freely offered, as free as air or light, and we have only to accept it? Faith is the instrument by which we accept it, the eye or mouth of the soul. We cannot buy God's forgiveness by faith or prayers or tears, any more than by alms, or a life of righteous deeds. Else faith itself would be degraded to the level of what St. Paul calls a "work," *i.e.* a deed not voluntarily done out of love. It is apparently as much a law, and a necessity, of the spiritual world that God does not forgive us without the use of faith, as, in the material world, that He does not give us light without the use of our eyes. But both the eye and faith are instruments, not causes. Is there any other restriction mentioned in the New Testament on the acceptance of forgiveness?

Pupil.—It is said that if we do not forgive the sins of others, God will not forgive ours.

Teacher.—But I thought we agreed that God's forgiveness is freely offered, and we have but to believe in it to accept it.

Pupil.—But perhaps this is an exception.

Teacher.—I do not think it is. Can you really believe in the just God and in His forgiveness of you, and not at the same time feel that you are very sinful, and that He loves you for something that is not very prominent in your nature or apparent to your neighbours, and that if He can forgive you, with all your petty faults, your weakness or stubbornness, your insignificance or hardness, there is not much more reason why He should not pardon others, even the worst? Can you really believe in God as your Father, without feeling that He is your Father in virtue of a principle that is common to all men, so that He is best addressed by each individual man as " *Our* Father," and not "*My* Father"? In a word, is not your faith in God closely connected with your faith in human nature, the handiwork of God?

Pupil.—Yes.

Teacher.—Then if you disbelieve in human nature you disbelieve in God. If your faith is not sufficient to enable you to forgive, neither is it enough to enable you to receive forgiveness. If you think it right to be hard and unforgiving to others, you convert your thought of God, the Supreme Right, into a Supreme Wrong, and you worship a false god, not the true God. Thus there is nothing arbitrary in the statement that God will not forgive the unforgiving. An unforgiving temper implies want of faith, and without faith a man cannot be forgiven any more than he can see without eyes.

CHAPTER VII.

FAITH.

Teacher.—Is faith a virtue?

Pupil.—Yes; it is classed by St. Paul along with hope and love, as one of the three great virtues.

Teacher.—What do you mean by faith? Faith in what? It is evident that faith in wealth, or in power, or in one's self, is not a virtue. What do you understand as the object of faith when you call it a virtue?

Pupil.—I mean, by faith, faith in Christ.

Teacher.—That answer will want explanation presently. But meanwhile is not faith mentioned as a virtue in the Old Testament before Christ came upon earth? Give me instances of heroes in the Old Testament, who are said to have achieved great deeds by faith.

Pupil.—Gideon, Barak, Jephthah, Samson, and many others who are noted for their patriotism, are said to have done what they did by faith.

Teacher.—By faith in what?

Pupil.—In God.

Teacher.—But do you mean that a mere belief in the existence of a God could stimulate Gideon, Barak, and Jephthah to patriotic deeds? Did not the Ammonites and Moabites also believe in the existence of a God? What was the difference of belief between a patriot of Israel and a Moabite or Ammonite patriot?

Pupil.—I suppose the Ammonite or Moabite who believed in many gods, gods of many wills, and variable imperfect natures, would not feel the same confidence in an eternal, unchanging righteousness, and in the triumph of right over might, which would be felt by one who believed in the One God, the unchanging and perfectly righteous Jehovah.

Teacher.—We said above, that patriotism need not always be a virtue. Sometimes it degenerates into pride and injustice. Yet even in a Cato, with his "delenda est Carthago," patriotism may give rise to many unselfish actions. But if one can feel while fighting for one's country, that one is fighting for truth against falsehood, for oppressed righteousness against oppressing tyranny, will not one's patriotism ally itself with all that is highest and noblest, and most unselfish? And if common and degenerate patriotism stimulates us to noble deeds, shall we not be much more stimulated when the cause of our country identifies itself with the cause of righteousness and with the will of God? And now tell me what was this faith of Gideon, Barak, and the rest, that enabled them to contend successfully against overwhelming numbers, and to deliver their country from oppression?

Pupil.—Faith in one unchanging, all-powerful, and all-righteous God.

Teacher.—Yes; and consequently faith in a perfect future, faith in an ultimate deliverance, and in the fulfilment of all those promises of God which are implied by the natural aspirations of men. Many heathen men and women have had some portion of this faith, and have been raised by it above the level of average selfishness to deeds that must command the respect of Christians. They have believed in the beauty and the power of justice, temperance, bravery, and they have been consequently made just, temperate, and brave. But the men of Israel, who believed in a personal Being, including in Himself all goodness and power, were more influenced than the nations to whom the several virtues were so many abstract ideas, or else so many different gods. And, rising in the climax, we ought to be more powerfully influenced than the men of Israel by our faith in Christ. And why?

Pupil.—Because the belief in a perfectly good God was faint and weak till Jesus Christ revealed God to men.

Teacher.—But does not St. Paul say that there is no other name given under heaven by which men can be saved except the name of Jesus? What, then, are we to say about the faith of those who lived before the Christian era?

Pupil.—God will not expect faith in Jesus from those who never heard of the name of Jesus—from the Patriarchs, for instance.

Teacher.—Yet our Lord says that Abraham "looked forward to *His day*, and was glad." And what did we say was the use of sacrifices? To what did they point, and to what did they wave forward, as it were, the attention of the sacrificer, at all events when they were rightly offered?

Pupil.—They pointed forward to the ideal sacrifice, the sacrifice of Christ.

Teacher.—Yes; and similarly the promises of a Deliverer, and the faith in a Deliverer, pointed forward to the ideal Deliverer, that is, to Christ. Remember that Christ is said to be the Word of God. Ever since the creation of the world, the Father has been asking men by His word to trust in Him. The word of God has been teaching us to recognize and love in Him justice, righteousness, and mercy, speaking to us, partly by the beauty and order of the material world, partly by the relations of the family and the country, and partly by thoughts and ideas which have impressed us as being direct messages from God. Every revelation made by the Word of God has required from us a corresponding faith; faith in the Maker of the world, faith in the God of the Spirits of all flesh; faith in Him who ordained the ties of family love; faith in Him who made of one blood all nations of men for to dwell on all the face of the earth, and hath determined the times before appointed and the bounds of their habitation: but all these revelations and all these kinds of faith are but as it were "broken lights" of that Supreme Revelation which is granted to us in Christ, and of the faith in Him. Hence it may be said, with truth, that all the real good that has ever been in the world comes from Christ. The wars and arts, the science, literature, and policy of the past, so far as they have been founded upon falsehood or selfishness, or the mere love of pleasure, have produced, or are destined to produce, none but transitory effects. But so far as they have been inspired by unselfishness or by the genuine love of truth and beauty, they partake of that "Word of God" which can never pass away.

Now let us consider the nature of that particular kind of faith which is most commonly alluded to in the books of the New Testament; first in the Gospels, and afterwards in the Epistles of St. Paul and St. James. Jesus often praises the faith of those for whom He wrought miracles. How did their faith, the faith of the centurion, of the Syrophœnician woman, the penitent thief, and others, differ from our faith in Christ?

Pupil.—It was simpler.

Teacher.—Yes, very much simpler. The faith of these persons could not have included faith in many of the dogmas which we now profess; for example, not even a distinct faith in the resurrection of Christ. On one occasion Jesus described the faith which He expected from some blind men whom He proposed to heal. Do you remember His words, and what followed?

Pupil.—He said, "Believe ye that I am able to do this?" and upon their saying "Yes," He healed them.

Teacher.—Here, then, a mere faith in the power of Jesus to heal supernaturally was sufficient to procure the supernatural cure. But is faith in power necessarily good?

Pupil.—No. But this was faith in the power of Christ to do good.

Teacher.—Exactly. It was the kind of faith that a child has in his father. We know it better by the more familiar name of trustfulness. In such a faith love and trust are necessary components. These blind men, and others who were similarly healed, believed that Christ was able and willing to help all men. They felt also with more or less distinctness that there were no limits to His power. We believe more definitely that Christ helps us spiritually as well as bodily; that He bears our sins; that He is present everywhere; that He is eternal, and has triumphed over death; and that He is all-powerful, as being one with the Father. But our faith, though more definite, is not different in kind from the faith of these blind men, whose simple confession of faith amounted to no more than this, "Thou art able to heal us." The peasants of Galilee, who believed from their hearts that Jesus of Nazareth was sent by God, and had from God a divine power of healing, must have believed a great deal that we regard as high and ennobling, and find it difficult to believe. They must have felt sure that God was good and loving, and they must have believed that He was represented fitly by one who, at all events for a time, did not appear as a King or a Conqueror, but as a poor wanderer, not having where to lay his head, despised and rejected by the upper classes of his countrymen. The Pharisees and Sadducees could not believe this. The impure could not see God in Christ: the unmerciful could not believe in the teacher of mercy; the covetous and self-complacent could not believe in the representative of a righteousness for which they could feel no hunger nor thirst. It was not easy then, as it is not easy now, heartily to believe or trust in Christ. But those who could believe in Him were wonderfully influenced by their belief. And the influence was manifested in actions, not in words. Men gave up their property and left all they had to follow Him. Men and women, whose whole lives had been spent in sin, suddenly appear to the world patterns of righteousness and purity. It was enough for Christ to say "thy sins be forgiven thee," to change the whole course of their existence. How could faith in Christ produce these results?

Pupil.—We cannot understand how.

Teacher.—We cannot completely comprehend it, because we cannot fathom the abysmal goodness or power of Christ. But we can apprehend it. We can see in Christ's influence upon men the complete fulfilment of the same spiritual law which is discerned in the influence of men upon one another. Bacon, in his Essay on Atheism, traces the influence of faith or trust in developing the powers even of the brute creation. "Take," he says, "example of a dog, and mark what a generosity and courage he will put on when he finds himself maintained by a man, who to him is instead of a God. So man, when he resteth and assureth himself upon divine protection and favour, gathereth a force and faith which human nature in itself could not obtain." And we all know how powerfully children are influenced by their parents, and in after life by others whom they love and trust. In this way (perhaps also in other ways) Christ influences us to an infinite degree. There are few cases of men being instantly changed by a word, or by a sudden impulse of trust in another man. But both history and fiction tell us that men who have lost the power of believing in anything that is pure and noble have sometimes been raised up again by the influence of a single person whose purity and nobleness were beyond doubt. Conversely, men have been sunk, like Timon of Athens, from the level of humanity to that of beasts or devils, by meeting with ingratitude and selfishness, which have forced the inference—

> "There's nothing level in our cursed natures
> But direct villany. Therefore be abhorred
> All feasts, societies, and throngs of men.
> His semblable, yea, himself, Timon disdains."

It is not uncommon to say that Christian faith is a mere speculative theory, which cannot practically influence men's actions. The answer to such an assertion is, that faith in Christ influences us as naturally as faith in a friend or in a father. Let us endeavour to ascertain how faith in Christ influences our relations towards God, our neighbour, ourselves, sin and death, and the final consummation of things. If we thoroughly believe in Christ and Christ's teaching, what must we consequently believe about God?

Pupil.—That He is our Father.

Teacher.—Yes; and that He is an all-powerful Father, able to hear prayer and forgive sin; and if we are tempted sometimes to think that God is no more than a First Cause, or a Law, or a Being who made the world, and then left it to work like a machine by itself, what does Christ teach us to the contrary?

Pupil.—That God clothes the grass of the field, and adorns each flower, and that not a sparrow falls to the ground without His knowledge, nor a hair of the head of His children can be harmed.

Teacher.—And as regards our neighbour, how is it possible for us to believe in Christ, and at the same time to entertain mean or ignoble views about other men? How does the Lord's Prayer at its very outset protest against the notion that men are to be despised or hated?

Pupil.—We are taught to call God our Father, and hence to call men our brethren.

Teacher.—Yes; it is not enough to believe that Christ is a man, if we do not also believe that He represents humanity, and that men are intended to be, like Christ, the children of God. I mentioned the example of Timon of Athens just now. Can you remember how in his misanthropic degradation he was influenced by meeting an honest man? Turn to Act iv. sc. iii. line 503, and read the passage.

Pupil.—

> "I do proclaim
> One honest man—mistake me not—but one;
> No more, I pray.
> How fain would I have hated all mankind!
> And thou redeem'st thyself: but all, save thee,
> I fell with curses."

Teacher.—If we treat Christ in the same way, we shall stop, like Timon, proclaiming one pure ideal, but "no more," and our conduct will not be affected by our belief. We are to go further towards our fellow-men, to believe that Christ represents human nature as it was created, and as it will be perfected by God. This belief will extend to ourselves as well as our neighbours; and how shall we be influenced by believing that we are individually recognized by Christ as brothers, and as the children of God?

Pupil.—We shall be stimulated to justify the recognition by behaving like God's children.

Teacher.—Next as regards sin. Believing that Christ came to save us from our sins, that He was pained through life by our sins, that they formed His burden, and the chief part of His bitterest agony in the hour of His death and passion, can we possibly regard sin as a mere bagatelle? Shall we not rather take the Hebrew view, which looks on sin as a disease?

Pupil.—Yes, a disease of the soul.

Teacher.—As an incurable disease?

Pupil.—No; as a disease that can be cured by Christ.

Teacher.—And if we believe in God as a Father, and Christ as a forgiver, how must we think we can attain forgiveness—by any price or gift of ours to God?

Pupil.—No, the Father cannot bargain. He freely offers forgiveness through Christ, and we must have faith that He means what He says, and must freely accept it.

Teacher.—But can we sin as we like every day, and ask and receive forgiveness every evening, and thus go on from year to year, perpetually being forgiven, and as perpetually sinning?

Pupil.—No; for we cannot receive forgiveness of sin without feeling sin as a burden, and if we thus feel it we shall hate it, and hating it, we shall not persist in it.

Teacher.—I am not sure of that. Many men feel sinful habits—drunkenness for instance—to be a burden indeed; but a burden that they cannot at once shake off. But this we may say, that a belief in Christ will give the strongest possible motive for resisting sin, or, perhaps we ought to say, for doing what is right; and a perfect belief and union with Christ would make us perfectly sinless and righteous. Next, as regards death, what effect on our way of regarding death will be produced by faith in Christ? You know how the ancients regarded it, either as the annihilation of body and soul, or else as bringing after it a second state, which even at its brightest was a pallid and shadowy reproduction of earthly life. The pious King Hezekiah shrinks from it. "The grave," he cries to God, "cannot praise thee; death cannot celebrate thee: they that go down into the pit cannot hope for thy truth."[1] But if men regard themselves as one with Christ, and Christ as the conqueror of death, triumphant over the terrors of the grave, surely they may naturally call death a sleep, as the early Christians did, and may declare with St. Paul that death has lost its sting, and the grave its victory. Sorrow for the loss of friends may be, and is, natural and justifiable, as the expression of our own sense of desolateness and bereavement; but to speak of heaven as our home, and yet to mourn over those who have gone to heaven, to make death terrible by gloomy obsequies and trappings, to pore over the coffin and the grave, and never to mention the names of the departed without some epithet of commiseration, all this may be common, but is none the less an evidence of want of faith in Christ, is it not?

Pupil.—Yes, it must be.

Teacher.—Lastly, as regards the consummation of all things, the day of the Lord, the day of "decision" or "judgment," to which all the Prophets looked forward. What will be the belief of those who regard Christ as not dead but living, seated at the right hand of God?

Pupil.—They will be assured that Christ is ruling, and will rule, all things according to His will.

Teacher.—Yes, and what does that imply? Does it not mean that Christ is even now, in spite of all appearances to the contrary, directing to His own ends the actions of kings and nations; that His Spirit is even now brooding on the troubled sea of humanity, preparing it for the final spiritual creation; and that He will eventually subdue all things that seem antagonistic to Him—death and hell, and sin and sorrow?

Pupil.—Yes.

Teacher.—Nothing, then, can be more constant and truly happy amid all the fluctuations and sorrows of this transitory life than the man whose faith is firmly fixed on Christ. If we are wavering and unhappy, that only shows our want of faith in Him. Even a faith

[1] Isaiah xxxviii. 18.

in justice and righteousness can support a man through many trials. What does Horace say of the "man who is just, and holds his purpose fast"?

Pupil.—"He is not moved from his fixed purpose by the wild clamour of a misguided people, nor by the angry eye of an imperious tyrant, nor by the boisterous storm wind that marshals the waves of restless Hadria, nor by the great hand of thundering Jove. Were the round world to shatter in fragments on his head, the ruin might strike him, but could not make him tremble."

Teacher.—Nothing in ancient literature can exceed the beauty of this description of the power of the faith in righteousness to banish fear; but there are enemies more terrible than either the storms of Hadria, or even a universe destroyed—there is sin. A man who may not blench before "the face of an imperious tyrant," may be appalled at the thought of the degradation and wretchedness of his fellow-creatures, and the apparent impossibility of rescuing the human race from spiritual death. How, then, does St. Paul describe the conquest of a Christian over the assaults of tribulation, and his inseparableness from Christ?

Pupil.—" Who shall separate us from the love of Christ? Shall tribulation, or distress, or persecution, or famine, or nakedness, or peril, or sword? Nay, in all these things we are more than conquerors through him that loved us. For I am persuaded that neither death, nor life, nor angels, nor principalities, nor powers, nor things present, nor things to come, nor height, nor depth, nor any other creature, shall be able to separate us from the love of God, which is in Jesus Christ our Lord."

Teacher.—So much, then, for the nature and power of faith. Now, what apparently contradictory statements are made about faith by St. Paul and St. James?

Pupil.—St. Paul says that we are "justified by faith without works," and St. James that "faith without works is dead."

Teacher.—How do you reconcile the two statements?

Pupil.—I suppose we receive Christ's forgiveness by means of faith, and not because of any works or merits of ours; and on the other hand, faith in Christ, if it be true faith, cannot but express itself in actions.

Teacher.—Exactly; the works are the necessary consequences of faith wherever there is time and opportunity for them. Sometimes, as in the case of the penitent thief, there may be no opportunity or time for actions; but in the ordinary course of things, actions follow faith as fruit springs from a fruit-tree. God can recognize faith without actions, and can distinguish the fruitful tree before it has brought forth fruit: but men are taught to test faith by its fruits. Now let us consider another "hard saying" on this subject. What does Christ say to His disciples about the all-powerful nature of faith?

Pupil.—" If ye have faith as a grain of mustard seed, ye shall say to this mountain, Be thou removed, and cast into the midst of the sea, and it shall be done."

Teacher.—Can you understand that?

Pupil.—I can understand it; but it is difficult to realize.

Teacher.—Exactly. Neither Christ nor any of His disciples ever cast a mountain into the sea. Why did they not? Christ had infinite faith, and His disciples, after His resurrection, had faith enough to perform miracles. If they did not work this miracle, it was not for want of faith.

Pupil.—I suppose there was no need of such a miracle.

Teacher.—Why not? Would it not have convinced many unbelievers?

Pupil.—Yes. But in the lesson on miracles it was agreed that a disorderly or portentous miracle, wrought merely for the sake of forcing conviction, is not such a " sign " as Christ exhibits.

Teacher.—Exactly. By what metaphor do we illustrate the operation of faith?

Pupil.—We call it the eye of the soul.

Teacher.—By faith, then, we discern the will of God. If our faith be living, and capable of life and expansion like a seed, though it be at first as small as a grain of mustard seed, we can so discern God's will, and so assimilate our will to His, that whatever we desire will be accomplished. Some have treated this expression about the mountain as a merely figurative expression; but there is no metaphor here. It is quite possible that there might arise circumstances when it might be seen to be God's will that even a mountain should be uprooted and cast into the sea. Then a man who had a living faith would say, "Be thou uprooted," and it would be done. It is possible also that by some law which is beyond our comprehension, we are enabled to co-operate with God by means of faith, just as we are in the habit every day of co-operating with Him by means of actions. This we shall consider more fully under the head of prayer. Now let us conclude the present subject by asking, How can we obtain faith? How can we believe in Christ? How must we begin?

Pupil.—I suppose we must begin by believing in His existence, and by ascertaining the truth of the Gospels and Epistles.

Teacher.—And how must we do that?

Pupil.—By reading them carefully and comparing them together, and by examining the internal and external evidence in their favour.

Teacher.—In a word, by studying some such a book as Paley's "Evidences of Christianity"?

Pupil.—Yes.

Teacher.—But that is not the way in which you and I attained to a belief in Christ. How did we attain to it?

Pupil.—We were taught when children to love and trust in Christ by our parents and teachers.

Teacher.—Then we believed in Christ at first because we believed in our parents and teachers?

Pupil.—Yes.

Teacher.—And afterwards?

Pupil.—Afterwards we believed because of the historical evidence.

Teacher.—But do you mean that your belief in the existence of Christ was based on exactly the same grounds as your belief in the existence of Julius Cæsar?

Pupil.—Not quite. Our belief in the existence of Christ was based from the first in a great measure upon our love of Him, and our feeling that the Gospel is too good to be false, and that the world would be desolate without Him.

Teacher.—So, then, your belief in Christ is founded partly upon authority, partly upon evidence and inference, and partly upon the character of Christ Himself, and a feeling that the Gospel must be true because we wish it to be true. In this threefold composite belief, which element influences your actions most?

Pupil.—The belief in Christ's character. The belief that Christ must have lived because we cannot do without Him.

Teacher.—If, therefore, we want to believe heartily in Christ, we must try to love Him and need Him. This we shall do if we love purity and righteousness, and hate sin and selfishness; if we are dissatisfied with the present state of infirmity and sinfulness in which we are placed, and earnestly look forward, like the ancient Prophets, to another and a better state, where goodness and righteousness shall be triumphant for ever, and there shall be no more evil. A spiritual and hopeful life is the best possible preparation and preservative for a belief in the righteousness of Christ. This hopeful spirit is something totally distinct from belief in authority or belief founded on historical evidence. It may be instilled in part by the training of parents, in part by the teaching of nature, in part by contact with the thoughts of other men, in part it may arise from some to us unknown source, so that we at once ascribe it to the suggestion of an invisible spirit; but whether we can or cannot indicate the immediate source, the ultimate inspirer of this hope is God. What did Christ say about those who came unto Him?

Pupil.—"No man can come unto me, except the Father draw him."

Teacher.—Then we see that faith in Christ is something totally distinct from an intellectual assent to the truth of the narrative of the Gospel, based upon historical evidence. But we must not despise that evidence either. Faith is allied to reason, and without reason degenerates into—what?

Pupil.—Superstition.

Teacher.—Yes. Reason, and Hope, and Action go all to the making up of Faith. As we are to love God, so are we to believe in God, not only with all our heart, but also with all our mind, and all our strength.

CHAPTER VIII.

PRAYER.

Teacher.—What is the purpose of prayer?

Pupil.—To obtain our desires from God.

Teacher.—What if our desires are hurtful?

Pupil.—To obtain from God those things which are expedient for us.

Teacher.—But what if you are met by the objection of Juvenal, that if anything is expedient for us God will give it to us, and therefore we need not pray for it; and if it is inexpedient for us, then it is foolish as well as needless to pray for it, and therefore prayer is sometimes foolish, and always needless?

Pupil.—I should say that Christ taught us to pray.

Teacher.—That would be a very sufficient answer for one who believed in Christ. And I think you might also retort the difficulty upon your objector thus: "If it is expedient for me that I should have my daily bread, God will give it me, and therefore I need not work for it; and if it is not expedient for me, then God will not give it to me, and it is foolish to work for it, and therefore to work for one's bread is sometimes foolish and always needless." How is this dilemma about working for one's bread practically answered?

Pupil.—As a matter of fact, those who do not work in some way, do not (except in peculiar states of society) get their bread, and those who work, do get their bread.

Teacher.—Then we see that human action is a means ordained by God for the procuring of certain results. This is so common as not to cause any surprise or reflection; but it is very mysterious and inexplicable. Look at it thus. We cannot conceive God to be other than all-knowing, and therefore to be fore-knowing. To suppose that anything, however trifling, the curl of an eddy in a brook, the fall of a single thistle-seed to the ground, can come to pass, and God not know it beforehand, is impossible. We may therefore suppose the future to be written as it were, if we may use a human metaphor, on the mind of the Supreme Being, and being there written it can only come to pass as it is written. Hence it might seem that no human beings, who believe that God is all-knowing, would take the trouble to act, for whether they act or not, all things must happen in one pre-arranged, predestined manner. Yet, as a fact, we all do act, and we know that if we act certain results will follow, which will not occur if we do not act. God has so constituted the world and human beings, that men can co-operate with Him. Men change forests into cities, deserts into gardens, dry up marshes, pierce an isthmus, thrust back the ocean, and materially change the face of the earth, and alter the climates of its different regions. If, then, by means of our actions we are thus enabled to co-operate with God, and materially alter the world which He created, it is clearly conceivable that we may co-operate with Him in other ways, by prayer for instance. I do not as yet say it is demonstrable, but conceivable. All the objections which are directed against prayer from the foreknowledge of God are equally capable of being directed against action. Yet we act. Why, then, should we not pray? Now I think that you will feel that all this is not quite convincing; that there is a great difference between our grounds for acting and praying, and more reason for the former than for the latter. Try and express the difference.

Pupil.—We are taught every day the use of action, and we know by experience that we cannot do without it. But we are not taught so plainly by experience the use of prayer.

Teacher.—Exactly. In all that has been said above there has been no proof, or attempt to prove, that prayer *does*, like action, produce certain results. We have only shown that it is conceivable that prayer, like action, *may* produce results. For proof, more is wanted. Ordinary experience is not enough. A particular kind of experience is required. The lightning struck iron many times, but this repeated experience did not prove that iron attracted lightning till Franklin sent up his kite to draw the lightning down. What name do you give to such experience as Franklin's?

Pupil.—Experiment.

Teacher.—Exactly. No scientific truth can be considered established till it has been tested by experiment. But do you not see a difficulty in applying this test to prayer?

Pupil.—Yes. It must be difficult to pray earnestly, and at the same time to feel that one is experimenting with God.

Teacher.—More than difficult; I should say impossible. "He that prayeth to God," says St. James, "must pray, nothing wavering." It is one thing to say, "I do not know whether it is God's will that I should obtain my wish; if it is not God's will, His will, not mine, be done," and quite another to say, "I do not know whether prayer is of any use, but I will try the experiment in order to see whether it is of use." Since, therefore, experiment is out of the question the utility of prayer cannot be scientifically demonstrated. Of course there may be several instances, beside those recorded in the Bible, where prayer has procured rain, or stilled a storm, or healed the sick. But experience without experiment is seldom sufficient for scientific demonstration. All that we can prove by reasoning is that there is no more inherent *a priori* improbability in producing results by action than by prayer. As yet, then, we have given no positive reason for prayer. Why, then, do men pray?

Pupil.—We pray because Christ taught us to pray.

Teacher.—Yes, but more than that. Almost all nations, in almost all times, have been in the habit of offering up prayers to their gods. Why?

Pupil.—Men have felt that God would be moved by their prayers.

Teacher.—Yes, they have thought that by continual prayer they could weary the gods into granting their desires. "If Vesta is deaf to the familiar chants of her votaries, with what new prayer," asks Horace, "shall the virgin priestesses *weary* her too neglectful ear?" But is that a right feeling? God is our Father. What kind of father is it that will not grant a child's request for little, but will grant it for much, asking? Does not our Lord warn us of the error of those who "think they shall be heard for their much speaking"? This universal feeling, that God is moved by prayer, is it not an error, then, based upon an unworthy notion of God?

Pupil.—It would seem to be.

Teacher.—And yet, on the other hand, if we are praying for a sick friend, a brother, or a father who is dangerously ill, must we only pray once? May we not pray twice? and if twice, why not more often? Where are we to draw the line? And again, if we may pray for one who has very little hope of recovery, may we pray for one who has so little hope that it may almost be described as none at all, for one whose recovery would be little short of a miracle; and if so, may we go further, and pray that the miracle of Lazarus may be repeated, and that a friend who has died may be raised up? Lastly, if we may pray for fair weather when the harvest all through the kingdom is threatened with destruction, may we pray when the crops of a single county or district are endangered, or when merely our own crops are likely to be damaged?

Pupil.—I do not know what to say. There seems no rule about prayer.

Teacher.—Let us discuss the question further. You said, when we began our lesson, that the use of prayer is to obtain our desires. I think there is another way of putting this. Christ often enjoined on His disciples to "watch and pray." Why?

Pupil.—That they might not "enter into temptation."[1]

Teacher.—What tempts men?

Pupil.—The world. Pleasures that seem substantial, or near at hand, in comparison with spiritual things.

---

[1] St. Matthew xxvi. 41; St. Mark xiv. 38.

Teacher.—And what is the antidote to the powerful presence of "this present world"?

Pupil.—The perpetual sense of the more powerful presence of God.

Teacher.—And how does prayer tend to this?

Pupil.—By bringing us into communion with God.

Teacher.—Yes; by making us feel that God is real and near. God is our Father; of what sort is that intercourse between human children and fathers which tends to increase confidence and love between them? Is it constrained or reserved?

Pupil.—No; natural, free, and unrestrained.

Teacher.—Would such intercourse be natural and productive of confidence, if a child told all his desires to his companions, and perhaps to the servants of the house, but was afraid to mention them to his father? A child who talked about religion or about lessons to its father, because it was afraid to speak about its sports, would not be a very interesting or natural child, would it? And such a forced conversation would not, I think, be agreeable to a sagacious and kind father, or tend to the increase of mutual confidence.

Pupil.—No, it would not.

Teacher.—A wise father would, therefore, encourage his child to communicate to him his little hopes and fears, his pleasures and his pain; and not to conceal his desires, although they might be very childish, and sometimes very foolish?

Pupil.—Yes, he would.

Teacher.—In that way, not only would confidence be generated, but the folly and thoughtlessness of some desires might be kindly pointed out and gently checked; and so the child would grow in thoughtfulness and in harmony with his father's spirit. Often there need be no explanation or check of any kind. A foolish wish would be discovered by the child to be foolish because it was not granted.

Pupil.—Yes; but what if the child expressed some wish that was selfish or even vicious?

Teacher.—A good question. But I think that a child, who was in the habit of confiding his secrets and desires to his father, would soon imperceptibly fall into a kind of likeness and harmony with his father's disposition. The fully developed selfish or vicious desire would have had its germ in some half-selfish, half-thoughtless desire, which would have been rebuked or checked before. The child would therefore know that he dare not express such a desire, except in the way of confession. More than this, his constant intercourse with his father would do more than merely make him conscious that his desire would be unsuccessful; he would also feel that it was wrong; and, if he loved his father, he would struggle against it. But in the way of confession, and in the hope of being freed from it, even a wrong desire might be expressed. Now, let us apply this illustration to answer our question, What may we pray for? The answer is, we are to pray for everything that we feel it to be natural to wish for and to pray for in the presence of the heavenly Father. We shall not pray for results that can easily be secured by action, because to pray for these is trifling; nor for results that may benefit us at the expense of our neighbours, because we shall feel such prayers to be unworthy; nor for anything that we know to be wrong, for we shall be prevented by fear and shame. Also, we shall feel a reluctance, increasing as we grow older and wiser, to pray for any material advantages that can apparently not be obtained except by a seeming modification or violation of the ordinary laws of nature. We may often form unwise desires, and express them in unwise prayers; but the constant repetition of such ungranted prayers in the immediate presence of the Father will gradually teach us that they are not in harmony with His will, and that they are not, and cannot be, literally granted. By definitely expressing our wishes, and setting them side by side with the standard of God's will, we shall learn to make our will His, far more than if we continued to entertain wishes which we dared not express in His presence. There is one point, however, in which the prayers of children to their parents are not analogous to human prayers addressed to God; where is the difference? Children are often really giving their parents information of their wishes by expressing them : is it so in prayer?

Pupil.—No; God knows the wishes of all His children before they are expressed in words.

Teacher.—We spoke about confidence being established between parents and children on the basis of the free expression of the children's desires. Parents learn to know and understand the nature of their children, and to sympathise with their desires. It would seem, then, that this part of the analogy cannot apply to God, who knows and understands our nature, whether we pray or not. Yet, in one sense, the application holds. St. Paul, describing the state of Christian men rescued from heathendom, says, " But now, after that ye have known God, or rather——" What is the second, more correct equivalent which he substitutes for the first " knowing God "? [1]

Pupil.—" Or rather are known of God."

Teacher.—Yes. God cannot, in one sense, *know* selfishness or sin. God *knows* men only in Christ, in whose image He made them. There is no kindred, no point of contact, between the perfection of the Godhead and sin. Hence, in one sense, prayer may be called a means by which God knows us, as well as a means for enabling us to know Him. Now, however, for the point of difference. A child asks his father to give him something. The father gives it, and could have given it before had he known the child desired it. This seems inapplicable to God. Now, therefore, we come once more to the question, Can we regard our prayers as in any sense obtaining material benefits? Spiritual benefits are intelligible, because prayer will bring us closer to God, and make our will one with His; but can change of weather, for instance, be produced by prayer? Several very pious and very learned men have answered in the negative. For my own part, however, I cannot but think that the law of prayer is laid down in the words of Jesus, " Whensoever two or three of you shall agree touching anything that ye shall pray for, it shall be done." We have no scientific proof of this: but the authority of Christ, not to speak of the teaching of St. Paul and St. James, seems to indicate that

---

[1] Gal. iv. 9.

there are no limits whatever to the power of prayer. Do you see a difficulty here?

Pupil.—Yes, of course. Suppose people pray in opposition to the will of God; or suppose two or three Christians in France pray for one result, and in Germany, at the same time, for the opposite result.

Teacher.—Exactly; but the theory contained in the words of Christ is, that the two or three who thus agree in prayer are under the controlling influence of the Holy Spirit, who is one and the same in every country, and is also one with God. Hence, the reason why the power of faithful prayer is boundless, is because such prayer is always in accordance with the will of God, and therefore must be fulfilled. We shall see shortly that no faithful prayer is wasted.

The result of our further consideration is, that we are brought back to our old conclusion. We may pray for anything that we feel we may strongly wish for in the presence of a heavenly Father, especially when the fulfilment of the desire seems not to depend upon our own actions. This answers such an objection as the following, which I have heard urged: "If you may pray that a dying friend may be healed, may you not pray for a fortune, or for a coach and pair, or for eighteenpence?" The answer is, that such prayers as these last are unworthy of a man in the maturity of intellect and spiritual development, except under special circumstances. If eighteenpence can save a man from starvation, there is no reason why he should not pray for eighteenpence. Different prayers may be justifiable in different persons. A grazing farmer, in the midst of a district of arable land, who prayed for rain, to gain for himself a slight profit, to the great detriment of all his surrounding neighbours, would offer an unworthy prayer; and an educated man, aware of the complicated laws upon which the weather depends, and the many interests affected by rain or sunshine, ought also to hesitate before uttering a prayer that the weather may be such as to suit his interests. But then, in both cases the *wish* is as selfish and unjustifiable as the prayer. If the *wish* were right, the *prayer* would be right. On the other hand, a little child, taught that the Father in heaven loves little children, and wishes them to be happy, and ignorant of the infinite results and complex causes of the weather, may naturally pray that God may drive away the rain, so as not to interfere with his promised amusement. The child will very soon learn more of the truth, and will discontinue such wishes and prayers; but, while he feels it right to wish, he may rightly pray. And the best way to teach him that such prayers are unwise for the wise, is to let him pray till he understands why such prayers are unwise and cannot be fulfilled. Do you see any difficulty here?

Pupil.—Does not this seem a great waste of prayer? Is it right thus to let a child offer up a prayer that cannot be answered?

Teacher.—Always remember that prayer is but the expression of a wish. It is not the prayer, but the wish that is mistaken. As soon as the child is old enough to know that the wish is wrong, he should be told so; then, when the wish disappears, the prayer will disappear also. But what makes you think the prayer is wasted?

Pupil.—The weather is unchanged.

Teacher.—Do you think that Jesus ever wasted prayer?

Pupil.—Of course that is impossible.

Teacher.—But can you not recall an instance where Jesus offered up a prayer, and more than once, that was not literally fulfilled?

Pupil.—Yes, He prayed that if it were possible the cup might pass from Him.

Teacher.—And yet we know the cup did not pass from Him. And Jesus Himself, in His second prayer, expresses more distinctly that the cup could not pass from Him. "He went away again the second time, and prayed, saying, O my Father, if this cup may not pass away from me, except I drink it, thy will be done." The prayer cannot be said to have been wasted, since it gave strength and comfort. Perhaps you can tell me of a vision, mentioned by one only of the Evangelists, which gave a visible expression to the strength derived from prayer.

Pupil.—St. Luke says that "there appeared an angel unto him from heaven strengthening him."

Teacher.—Thus then the prayer of Christ, though not literally fulfilled, obtained a fulfilment. And similarly, we are taught that every sincere prayer which, like the prayer of Jesus, contains, or implies the words "nevertheless not my will, but thine be done," necessarily, by the laws of prayer, obtains its fulfilment. The fulfilment may sometimes come in a material form, sometimes not; but at all times honest prayer brings spiritual strength. The cup did not pass away, but Jesus received strength to drink it. So St. Paul besought the Lord that his "thorn in the flesh" might depart from him, but he received the similar answer, "my strength is sufficient for thee." In the strictest sense of the word, all faithful prayer may be said to be completely granted. Either the wish of the person praying is fulfilled, or else, by means of prayer, his wish is brought into harmony with the will of God, so that in either case the wish is performed. We have seen that the prayers of the young and old may naturally differ. Can you tell me of any other circumstances that may modify prayer?

Pupil.—I suppose education may. You said just now that the knowledge of the laws of nature, and the many interests affected by the weather, may render a man of science more reluctant than a farm-labourer to make weather the subject of prayer.

Teacher.—Yes; and the same difference may extend to nations and periods. The increased knowledge of causes and means to produce material results may naturally diminish the desire to pray for them, since we can obtain them by action. No one prays that a disease may be healed which can be certainly cured by a simple remedy; no one prays that a friend a thousand miles away may be moved to come at once to help us, when the telegraph can send a message in an hour; no one prays that a calm may give place to a wind when he is in a steam-vessel, where engines only await orders to get to work. By increasing our knowledge of disease, and our means of communication and motion, God, as it were, declares it to be His will that hereafter certain results shall be obtained by ordinary human actions, based upon the increased knowledge of divine laws. Hence to pray for such things seems now to be praying against the will of God. But, on the other hand, praying for fair weather is not quite like this. Why not?

Pupil.—I suppose because we have not discovered any means for modifying the weather.

Teacher.—Yes, and because God has revealed Himself as a God of order and goodness, who has prepared the earth for the support of man, and has appointed the seasons of seed-time and harvest. Hence, if we were to see the crops rotting on the ground, the labourers out of work, agriculturists plunged in immediate distress, all kinds of labour and art feeling indirectly an injurious influence in the anticipation of scarcity, the rich curtailing their expenses, and the poor dreading a winter of want, many of us might naturally feel that it is not God's will that these disorderly evils should exist, or that His gifts should thus be wasted, and we might feel it right and natural to pray that His general law of seed-time and harvest might not be broken; and as by our actions we co-operate with God, so, on the authority of Christ, we believe that we may also co-operate with Him by our prayers. So much for the nature and results of prayer, the reasons why we consider prayer not irrational, and the authority on which we base it. There is, however, one argument for the use of prayer which has been omitted; let us examine it. How do you infer, on the supposition of our being created by God, that we are intended to eat?

Pupil.—Because eating is necessary to sustain life.

Teacher.—Your argument is, I take it, that if God created us, He intended to satisfy these desires which tend to the preservation of life. This holds good of spiritual as well as animal life. If God is the author of our spirits, then He intended to satisfy these spiritual desires which tend to the preservation of spiritual life. And what is our Lord's definition of life—eternal life?

Pupil.—" And this is life eternal, that they might know thee the only true God, and Jesus Christ whom thou hast sent." [1]

[1] St. John xvii. 3.

Teacher.—Every desire, therefore, that tends to make us know God, to remind us of His presence and watchful love, to direct all our thoughts and wishes towards Him, to make us confident in Him, and one with Him, tends to preserve our spiritual life, and must be regarded as right and natural. Now prayer does all this. Prayer subjects the actions of each day as it passes, and the projects of each day as it comes, to a test, making us ask, "Are my past actions, or are my present projects, in accordance with God's will?" Prayer prevents us from supposing we can keep anything secret from the Father; prayer makes us feel that nothing is too mean or humble for His love; prayer gives vigour to our religion, and purity to our work, by connecting the two together. The labours and pleasures of every day have a tendency, by bringing us into contact with visible and tangible objects, to persuade us that these, and not the invisible attributes of God, justice, mercy, and truth, are the realities of life. Prayer neutralizes this excessive influence of the world. If we were to cease to pray, we should be in danger of gradually ceasing to feel the divine attraction that retains us in the right orbit. Were we perfect, or more nearly perfect than we are, we might strive to remind ourselves of God by meditation instead of prayer. Instead of praying, we might praise. Our sole prayer might be "Thy will be done." But our own experience of weakness, and our frequent failures in attempts to do our duty, will convince many of us that we cannot exchange prayer for praise till we reach the assembly of the saints, of whom we are taught to think as always hymning triumphant hallelujahs around the throne of God. To many others it will be sufficient to remember that Jesus, who "knew what was in man," taught us to say more than "Thy will be done," and did not think it beneath His notice to add, "Give us this day our daily bread."

CHAPTER IX.

THE SACRAMENTS.[1]

[*Teacher.*—The word sacrament does not occur in the Bible; but it is so commonly used with reference to actions described in the Bible, that I think it well to ask you what you mean by it.

Pupil.—A sacrament is an action enjoined upon His disciples by Christ Himself.

Teacher.—But you do not mean any action? "If they persecute you in one city, flee unto another." "Whatsoever is set before you, eat." Surely these actions, though enjoined by Christ, are not sacraments?

Pupil.—No. A sacramental action is the outward and visible sign of an inward and spiritual reality.

Teacher.—Then prayer is a sacrament, is it not? For *saying* " thy will be done" is the outward and visible sign of the inward and spiritual reality, *feeling* " Thy will be done."

Pupil.—Prayer was not specially enjoined by Christ. It was practised before.

Teacher.—So was Baptism by John the Baptist, and by others before John the Baptist, yet you call Baptism a sacrament.

Pupil.—Then perhaps prayer ought to be called a sacrament.

Teacher.—Take another case. Suppose a man gives, to use the words of Jesus, " a cup of cold water to one of His disciples in the name of Jesus." That is an outward action enjoined implicitly by]

---

[1] See Preface. Only so much of this chapter as bears directly upon the text of the New Testament has formed a part of my actual teaching.

[Christ Himself, and it denotes an inward and spiritual reality, viz. devotion to Christ. Is that a sacrament?

Pupil.—I really do not know. By the definition it seems to be.

Teacher.—No doubt in one sense of the word all actions done to the glory of God, and expressive of spiritual processes, such as almsgiving, praying, working, may be called sacraments. But there is a difference between these and the two sacraments called Baptism and the Lord's Supper. What difference?

Pupil.—In almsgiving the action would be done for its own sake, because it is morally good, and so would prayer; but eating bread and drinking wine have no moral significance apart from Christ's commandment, nor has washing.

Teacher.—Exactly. They are actions that are common to the whole human race, and that are necessary for the preservation of life and health. If almsgiving had been selected as a sacrament, there would have been danger of thinking that the act of almsgiving constituted the whole of the sacrament. There is no such danger in washing or eating, which are actions neither good nor bad in themselves; they may be called indifferent. Now with the exception of Baptism and the Lord's Supper, there are no other *indifferent* actions enjoined by our Lord on His disciples. Hence, though we do not deny that many other actions may be in a sense called sacraments, yet in ordinary language we restrict the term to these two. Now comes the question, of what use are the sacraments? We have said that they are signs of an inward process? What is this process?

Pupil.—We receive God's grace by the sacraments.

Teacher.—What do you mean by "grace?"

Pupil.—God's gift.

Teacher.—There are different gifts of God: health, strength, beauty, intellect, food, wine, wealth, and others. Which, if any, of these gifts do you mean?

Pupil.—None of these. I mean God's spiritual gift by which He gives Himself, His Spirit, to us.

Teacher.—Yes. God is said to take up His abode in those who] [are His children, and Christ is said to " dwell in their hearts by faith." But we are not to believe a man receives this gift of God every time he washes, or every time he eats bread and drinks wine, are we?

Pupil.—No; not unless the washing and eating are in accordance with Christ's ordinance, and in His name.

Teacher.—Can you mention an instance where partaking of the Lord's Supper is recorded to have done the partaker harm, and not good?

Pupil.—It is said that immediately upon taking the food which Jesus offered to him, Judas Iscariot was possessed by an evil spirit: "Satan entered into him."

Teacher.—But the bread and wine had been broken and blessed by Christ Himself.

Pupil.—Yes; but Judas had no faith.

Teacher.—Then a man will not receive grace as the gift of God through the Lord's Supper unless he has faith?

Pupil.—No.

Teacher.—Then, though faith cannot be called a part of the sacrament, yet it is a necessary means for receiving the grace of the sacrament, so that it may be called a necessary part of the reception of the sacrament?

Pupil.—Yes.

Teacher.—Now, suppose a man sincerely desirous of receiving the Lord's Supper, but unable in the agonies of death either to eat or drink; or suppose him sincerely willing but unable to be baptized, owing to the absence of water. What then?

Pupil.—I should think God makes allowance for such cases.

Teacher.—As far as the will and motive is concerned, the man has received the sacrament, has he not? And God is said to look on the heart, not on the deed?

Pupil—Yes; and therefore in the sight of God the man has received the sacraments.

Teacher.— Hence the famous saying of Augustine, " Believe, and] [thou hast eaten." Faith, therefore, is not only a necessary part of the reception of a sacrament, but in exceptional cases may be a substitute, accepted by God Himself, for the sacrament.

Pupil.—Yes.

Teacher.—But then suppose a man says, "I do not think it necessary ever to partake of the bread. 'I believe, and therefore I have eaten.'"

Pupil.—If he really believes, I suppose he may say this.

Teacher.—But is it possible for any one to say, I believe in Christ, and in the efficacy of the sacraments which He ordained, and my belief in their efficacy is so strong that I do not think them efficacious for myself? An angel, a being thoroughly washed in purity, living and, as it were, feeding on the perpetual presence of Christ, may not require sacraments; but can men say this?

Pupil.—No. But is there any especial efficacy in the use of bread and wine?

Teacher.—I have told you that it seems as though Christ took for His two sacraments two of the simplest and commonest actions of life: washing, which follows immediately on the entrance into life, and eating and drinking, which are afterwards necessary to support life, and made these two simple actions not merely memorials of Himself, but also means by which those who faithfully receive them may receive in addition His presence, favour, and strength—in other words, may preserve and strengthen their spiritual life. If in any country bread were unknown as a regular article of diet, it would obviously be absurd to import bread specially for the celebration of the Lord's Supper. It would be a keeping of the letter, but a violation of the spirit. It would not convey to the receiver the truth which Christ intended to be conveyed, that He intends us to find in Him not exceptional sustenance, but our ordinary spiritual food. And the same applies to wine. Now, however, let us ask what is the difference of the grace conveyed by the two several sacraments. And how shall we elicit the answer to that question?

Pupil.—By finding out what is said in the Bible about them.]

[*Teacher.*—True; but not much is said about them. And the little that is said by St. Paul, St. Peter, and others, is derived in the course of argument. What data are there for arguing about the spiritual difference between the Baptism and the Lord's Supper, and between the spiritual reality implied by eating and drinking, and that implied by washing?

Pupil.—I suppose, the material difference. The spiritual difference will be analogous to, and may be deduced from, the material difference.

Teacher.—Let us, then, begin by considering the spiritual process implied in Baptism. The outward sign is purification of the body. What would naturally be the corresponding spiritual reality?

Pupil.—Purification of the soul.

Teacher.—How could a man receive this spiritual purification? It would not be sufficient that his body should be washed.

Pupil.—No. We agreed that he must have faith; he must believe that Christ has the will and power to purify his spirit.

Teacher.—But how often may he receive this purification?

Pupil.—Once only.

Teacher.—Why only once? The Sacrament of the Lord's Supper is frequently received.

Pupil.—Christ only intended us to receive it once for all.

Teacher.—But why? If washing is as ordinary and almost as necessary as eating, why should not the Sacrament which involves the former action be as often repeated as that which involves the latter? I see you cannot answer. Tell me by what name this sacramental washing is called, "the washing of —— ?"

Pupil.—Regeneration.

Teacher.—Yes; just as a child when just born is washed and purified on entering into the life of this world, so every one on his entrance into the life of the Spirit must be spiritually purified. The washing of the body represents this spiritual washing which is connected with the new spiritual birth. Hence it is called the washing of the new birth or regeneration. And now you can see why Bap-]

[tism only takes place once, because it represents the spiritual birth, which can only take place once. The subsequent spiritual growth may be retarded or stopped, but a second spiritual birth is not regarded as possible. Now of what nature is this spiritual birth? When does it take place, and what are the signs of it?

Pupil.—It takes ,place when we are converted, and the sign of it is a righteous life.

Teacher.—But when are we converted? We are none of us perfectly righteous; we all call ourselves sinners, and confess sins daily. What amount of righteousness justifies us in saying we are born again?

Pupil.—Did not St. Paul feel a sudden change when he was converted, and might not a change assure us similarly of our conversion?

Teacher.—It might; but we are not placed in the circumstances in which St. Paul was placed. We do not become Christians in a moment from being persecutors of Christians. It is possible, is it not, that in a Christian country, loved and tended by wise and Christian parents, a little child may grow up gentle, simple, and loving, imbued from his earliest years with the Christian spirit? The effect produced upon little children by the actions, words, and even the expressions of their parents and friends, is so subtle, and at the same time so pervasive in its working, that it seems difficult to draw a line and to say, "on this day the child began to feel the moral influence of the Holy Spirit;" "on this day the child's spiritual birth was completed." Even with others who are conscious that a change has passed over their lives, and that they have exchanged habitual thoughtlessness or selfishness for habitual struggle against selfishness, it may be impossible to say, "on such a day this change took place or began."

Pupil.—Yes; perhaps we cannot always say when the change takes place, or it may take place so early as not to be felt as a change.

Teacher.—Well, it is perhaps not necessary that we should be able to mark the precise date of such changes. It is enough for us to] [know that as there is a physical life in which we naturally desire things that are pleasant and avoid things painful, so there is a spiritual life in which we naturally desire that which is pleasing to God, and avoid that which displeases Him. To this spiritual life we must all attain, and baptism is not only the sign of birth into this life, but also, through God's grace, a means by which we receive the new birth; but the precise time when the new birth takes place, whether it is gradual or instantaneous, whether and how far it is quicker with some and slower with others, these and other questions of detail we have no means of fully answering. But the following question is urgent, and presses for an answer. You know that our Lord said, "Except a man be born of water and of the Spirit, he cannot enter into the kingdom of heaven." What about the many millions who have never been baptized?

Pupil.—I should think God would make allowance for them.

Teacher.—But how can He save those who have not been baptized in the name of Christ, and have not been purified by the Holy Spirit? Does not St. Paul say that salvation is given by no other name under heaven except the name of Christ?

Pupil.—Though they may not have been baptized they may have been animated by the spirit of Christ. We agreed that the patriarchs and the men of Israel, and even the heathens, were inspired by the Word of God, that is, by Christ.

Teacher.—Then whatever may be the meaning of the passage in St. John, we need feel no fear about the fate of those who have died unbaptized in heathen times. Again, suppose young helpless children die without baptism—or suppose men, through the force of training and education, have conceived that baptism ought to be deferred till they feel some definite change called conversion, and so die before baptism; can we believe that such men, not to speak of the helpless children, will be rejected by Christ if they honestly believe that they are doing His will?

Pupil.—I should think not. But if we are equally safe whether we are baptized or not, what is the use of baptism?]

[*Teacher*.—I should say that those who, like the Phariseean friends of Nicodemus, rejected Christ's baptism with water, were in very great danger indeed; for in their case rejection betokened spiritual pride and self-confidence. Perhaps Nicodemus himself wished to be a disciple of Christ, but to avoid the public profession of discipleship implied by baptism in water. The rejection of baptism from motives such as these made discipleship impossible. But in speaking of the results of baptism, I should prefer to use the word *health* rather than *safety*. When Jesus healed the sick He is said to have *saved* them, and the Greek word which we translate by *safety* or salvation, often means sound health. Now I do not think you are so likely to have spiritual health if you remain unbaptized, prying into the corners of your heart, registering your deeds, and words, and thoughts, analysing your motives, testing each morning and each night your spiritual condition in order to see whether you are at last fit for baptism, instead of turning your thoughts from yourself to God alone, and lifting up your heart to Him. You may be honest in your belief, but you are none the less, as it appears to me, in danger of thinking too much about yourself and too little about God. Such a course of continuous anxiety and introspection does not seem the best preparation for that state of childish simplicity, trust, and confidence, which is declared to be the best state for those who wish to enter into the kingdom of God. To be obliged to say, " I am not good enough to-day, I do not feel the working of the Spirit strongly enough with me to-day to call myself the child of God, but I trust to feel good enough and influenced by the Spirit enough to-morrow," seems to me to turn the attention in quite the wrong direction. We never shall feel good enough, or possessed enough by the Spirit of Christ, to say that, in virtue of such feelings, we claim to be the children of God. It seems better that, from his earliest years, a child should be taught that he has a right, derived through the revelation of Christ, to call himself the child of God, in whose image he was made; and that he is recognized by God as His child, though it may be an erring and very unworthy child. The] [recognition does not depend upon the child's thoughts, or actions, or religious reveries. God claims all children as His children, and the baptism of each child is the outward sign that God considers the little one as His. Such are my own opinions about this matter. I know, by experience, that many who are unbaptized are far better men than many who are baptized. We ought thankfully to accept facts such as these. All good men are made good by the Spirit of God. If we call a good man bad, we sin against God's Holy Spirit. "The Spirit," we are told, "breatheth where it listeth." We are not to set up a Christian pale of our own construction, and say, "The Spirit does not breathe outside this wall of ours." On the other hand, we may still believe that those who are good and unbaptized are good in spite of great disadvantages. There are many arguments on the side of those who dislike infant baptism which deserve careful consideration. I dare say one suggests itself to you derived from the nature and definition of a sacrament. What is necessary for the reception of a sacrament?

Pupil.—Faith; and infants cannot have faith.

Teacher.—Exactly. Let us put the argument as forcibly as we can. In the Roman Church, infants are caused to partake of the bread and wine of the Lord's Supper; why is that not as reasonable as baptizing them? If baptism avails a child without faith, why not the Lord's Supper also? Further, if baptism avails a child without faith, why not baptize secretly the children of heathen and of unbelievers?

This is logical, and it is not easy to give a brief and logical answer. But it is evident that the difference between the two sacraments justifies a difference in their use. It is unnatural and harmful for a child to partake of bread and wine; that is only fit for a developed condition of life. It is natural and healthy for a child to be washed. That is necessary on the first entrance into life. And, looking at the impossibility of drawing a marked line between the time when spiritual birth may commence; believing that even the first unconscious clinging to the mother's bosom may contain in it the germs of a trust and love that by imperceptible shades will change to faith,] [how and when, we know not; believing also that, as St. Paul says, the children of Christian parents are already in a certain sense holy, and that in the ordinary course of things the Christian growth will be developed in them; and, lastly, having regard to the deplorable condition of a little child subjecting itself to self-examination and waiting till it can say 'Our Father,' we think it, on the whole, expedient to bring the very youngest infant to the arms of Christ. The faith of a father or a friend is said to have had power to procure the healing of a child or a servant. It is far more intelligible that the faith and prayers of parents and of friends believing in Christ's sacrament should exercise a spiritual effect upon a baptized infant, and should be made the means of imparting sacramental grace. For these reasons infant baptism is practised by the majority of Christians.

Now let us consider the nature of the Lord's Supper. On what point in this sacrament have the great disputes arisen which have divided Christendom?

Pupil.—On the presence of Christ in the sacrament.

Teacher.—Yes. Some maintain that the bread and wine are merely emblems of Christ, our spiritual life; others maintain that the bread and wine are partially changed by Christ's presence; others, again, that the bread and wine, though remaining visibly the same, have their substance really replaced by Christ's veritable body and blood. So many disputes have arisen in connection with these different opinions, that the original institution of the sacrament is obscured and in danger of being forgotten. Let us recur to it. How does Christ define the word blood, when He says of the wine "this is my blood"?

Pupil.—He says, "This is my blood of the new testament."

Teacher.—And what do you mean by "testament"?

Pupil.—A will.

Teacher.—Yes. The word may also mean covenant; but the Epistle to the Hebrews, after saying "He (Christ) is the mediator of the new *testament,*" adds, "for where a testament is, there must also of necessity be the death of the testator," where the word evidently implies a "will". By a will the testator bequeaths something. Moses] [bequeathed the Law to his people; what did Christ bequeath to His disciples?

Pupil.—His teaching.

Teacher.—Was that all? That was a poor substitute for Himself. What was the "promise" which He said should be fulfilled after His death?

Pupil.—The promise of the Holy Spirit, the Spirit of God.

Teacher.—You say "Spirit of God." Is not the Spirit also mentioned with relation to Christ?

Pupil.—Yes, by the name of "Spirit of Christ."

Teacher.—Had Christ previously made any promise to His disciples connected with prayer?

Pupil.—Yes. He had promised that "wheresoever two or three were gathered together in His name, there He would be in the midst of them."

Teacher.—Now what did Christ bequeath to His disciples?

Pupil.—His body and His blood.

Teacher.—Yes. But were they, then, to regard Him on whom they fed as one who had lived, but was now dead?

Pupil.—No, as living, and as seated at the right hand of God.

Teacher.—And were the bodies or the spirits of the disciples to be strengthened by this food?

Pupil.—The spirits.

Teacher.—Then we all agree that in the sacrament of the Lord's Supper, Christ bequeathed to us Himself not as dead flesh, the nutriment of the body, but as living and spiritual food; and as often as we rightly partake of that sacrament, we partake of Christ, our spiritual food? Whatever may be our points of difference we are agreed so far?

Pupil.—Yes.

Teacher.—Well, surely that is a fact of great importance; and the how, and why, and when Christ becomes our spiritual food in the sacrament are facts of secondary importance. My own opinion is that though the nutrition of our spirits by Christ in the sacrament] [is as real as the nutrition of our bodies by material food, yet there is no change whatever in the bread and wine, which are merely emblematic. It seems to me that the belief in what is called transubstantiation tends to superstition, and spiritual, as well as intellectual, weakness. But if a man believes anything, however intellectually absurd, yet comes to the Lord's table, humble, honest and sincere in feeling weakness and seeking strength, be his notions about the media through which the grace of God is conveyed as vague or false as they may, it is in accordance with what we know of God and Christ to think that such a one, doing what Christ enjoined in remembrance of Christ, does not fail to obtain some blessing. But suppose a man comes to the Lord's Supper because it is considered respectable to do so, or out of curiosity, or any other unworthy motive?

Pupil.—Such a man derives no benefit from the Lord's Supper.

Teacher.—Does not St. Paul go further than that, when speaking of those who are unworthy partakers of the sacrament?

Pupil.—He says, " He that eateth and drinketh unworthily, eateth and drinketh damnation to himself; for this cause many are weak and sickly among you, and many sleep."[1]

Teacher.—True; it would be, and still is, natural that those who come to the Lord's table unworthily should find remorse, uneasiness, and disquiet instead of peace and pardon. Body as well as spirit might naturally suffer. But the text you quote is often misunderstood, and deters persons without reason from the Lord's Supper. Tell me from the context what constituted the "unworthiness" of these communicants?

Pupil.—They came to the Lord's Supper as though it were an ordinary meal; some ate gluttonously, and some became intoxicated.

Teacher.—Yes. Strictly speaking, can we call any one "worthy" of such a legacy as Christ has left us—His body and blood?

Pupil.—No.

Teacher.—No, indeed. And therefore if people wait till they are " worthy " in that sense, they will wait for ever; and it is perhaps]

---

[1] 1 Cor. xi. 29, 30.

[better that they should wait for ever than come because they think they are at last thus "worthy." But, in a loose sense of the word, who is a *worthy* communicant? For whom is the Lord's Supper intended?

Pupil.—For those who are converted.

Teacher.—What do you mean by converted?

Pupil.—Turned towards God, disposed to do His will.

Teacher.—Do any of us feel completely disposed to do God's will? Our Lord said that His will was one with the Father's, and the object and lesson of our lives is to learn to conform our wills to the Father's will; but can any of us say we are completely turned towards God and that we never turn away from Him?

Pupil.—I suppose not. Still, must there not be a difference between the converted and the unconverted.

Teacher.—No doubt. And if a man is living in habitual and wilful sin, conscious that he is doing wrong, and yet making no effort to do right, perhaps excusing himself by saying that he is disposed to do right, but has not the power, such a man cannot be called, in any sense of the word, converted; nor can he with any benefit to himself come to the Lord's Supper; but if he is weak, yet always praying and striving for strength—deficient in faith, yet always hungering after more faith—often falling into sin, yet always struggling against sin—do you think such a one would have been rejected by our Lord when on earth, or is rejected by Him now?

Pupil.—No.

Teacher.—Then if a man says, I am a Christian, but an unworthy one; I wish to do good, but I often do wrong; I try to improve, but I do not succeed so well as I should wish; I am very weak and imperfect, and therefore I do not like to attend the sacrament: these are all so many reasons why he should attend, not why he should not attend—are they not?

Pupil.—Yes.

Teacher.—But if a man says, I am a Christian, but only because it is fashionable to be so; I have no great wish to do right, except] [where doing right is convenient; I am tolerably satisfied with my moral condition; I do not wish to make myself singular by attending the sacrament: such a man is not only unworthy but unfit for deriving any benefit from the sacrament?

Pupil.—Yes.

Teacher.—There is one other question I should like to ask. By what other name is the sacrament of the Lord's Supper commonly known?

Pupil.—Communion.

Teacher.—Give me the passage of St. Paul that explains this.

Pupil.—St. Paul calls the cup "the communion of the blood of Christ," and the bread "the communion of the body of Christ." He adds, "for we being many are one bread and one body: for we are all partakers of that one bread."

Teacher.—Then the Lord's Supper implies not merely eating, but eating in common; not merely admission into the body of Christ, but also admission in company with others. What is the spiritual action implied, not by the eating, but by the eating in *common*, by the *communion* ?

Pupil.—The spiritual concord and communion of the communicants.

Teacher.—Yes: they are to be one in Christ. You say "spiritual communion." What word implying communion, and indeed sometimes translated communion in the New Testament, is often associated with the Holy Spirit, just as "love" is with God?

Pupil.—Fellowship: "the fellowship of the Holy Ghost."

Teacher.—Well, Communion and Fellowship are the same words in the Greek of the New Testament. We might, but for the force of association, call the Lord's Supper the Holy Fellowship instead of the Holy Communion. We might similarly speak of the Fellowship of the Saints instead of the Communion of Saints. You see, then, that the sacrament of the Lord's Supper is, so to speak, of a more *social* nature than baptism. It brings into greater prominence the fact that men do not enter into the body of Christ as isolated indi-]

[viduals. Being a Christian, implies being a member or "fellow" of a society. A Christian life implies concord or *communion* with fellow-Christians. Now, what is the only sign of Christian discipleship given by Christ Himself?

Pupil.—Love. " By this shall all men know that ye are my disciples, if ye have love one to another."

Teacher.—Hence the sacrament which we call the Holy Communion implies not merely unity with Christ, and assimilation to His body, but, additionally and consequently, unity and communion with men in Christ. Regarded from this aspect, the Lord's Supper is a way of expressing, and of enabling us to realize and put in practice, the revelation of Christ that we are all members of one Body, bound to love one another as we love ourselves.]

CHAPTER X.

THE HOLY SPIRIT.

Teacher.—What is the literal meaning of the word spirit?
Pupil.—Breath.
Teacher.—Why is this name breath or spirit given to a certain part of a man and to certain other beings?
Pupil.—I cannot definitely answer.
Teacher.—Is the name literally correct? If not, how is it used?
Pupil.—It is used metaphorically, not literally.
Teacher.—Expand the metaphor implied in the word "spirit."
Pupil.—As the breath that issues from the body, though invisible and intangible, is the sign of bodily life, so something invisible and intangible in man's soul is the sign of spiritual life.
Teacher.—Well, I am not sure whether originally there was a metaphor at all. Men may have supposed the spirit not to be *like* breath, but to *be* breath. Perhaps the distinction between bodily and spiritual life is too refined for such a very primitive expression. Men may have reasoned thus: "Life in a man is marked by moving, thinking, loving. The question is, where does this life reside? What does a dead man want that a living man has? Breath. Breath, then, is probably life. Again, life is subtle and mysterious, hidden in the depths of our nature; so also is breath, a vaporous and scarcely visible thing, issuing from within the man—another reason why life is breath. Again, speech is a sign of life, and breath and speech are almost synonymous. Lastly, the energy of breath seems to vary with the intensity of life. In motion and in emotion we breathe

harder than when we are at rest. This is a corroborating proof that the breath is life in action." Hence we may see how *spiritus* (breath) or *spirit* would be used of the mind when in excitement or motion. Now comes the question, what is meant by the Spirit of God?

Pupil.—I do not know. God is a Spirit.

Teacher.—Exactly, and it seems difficult to explain the meaning of the spirit of a spirit. Perhaps, as it is impossible for us to comprehend logically the nature of God, it is impossible to attain logical accuracy in our attempts to express His nature. But perhaps we ought not to press for a full correspondence between the parts of a metaphor when applied to men and when transferred to God. It is observed that the spirit of a man passes in a sense out of him into another man, *i.e.* that one man's will and feelings become another man's. This image is transferred to God. Hence the Old Testament, when speaking of the action of God on the hearts of men, more especially when men are inspired (the very word *inspire* explains and justifies the use of *spirit*) to prophesy, mentions the agency of the Spirit of God. Such mention is very common in the Old Testament. Now can you mention any passage in the New Testament which implies that the Holy Ghost, or Holy Spirit (for the two expressions are the same), was not given to men till after the conclusion of the Old Testament history?

Pupil.—In the Gospel of St. John it is said that the Holy Ghost was not yet given, for Jesus was not yet glorified; and Jesus says to His disciples, that if He did not go from them to His Father, the Comforter (that is, the Holy Spirit) would not come to them.

Teacher.—Then is the Holy Spirit mentioned in the New Testament different from the Spirit of God mentioned in the Old Testament?

Pupil.—No; there are not two Spirits of God. I cannot explain this.

Teacher.—I think it may be explained by saying that the Spirit of God, though active in the Old as well as the New Testament, did not produce the same results. Though the Spirit was the same (St.

Peter speaks of the Spirit of Christ, even as working in the history of the Old Testament), yet the operation was different. Jesus Himself distinguished between the results of the manifestation of the Spirit in Elijah, who called down fire from heaven, and the Spirit that was to pervade His disciples. I wish now to understand, if possible, why the Spirit, in its new operation, "would not come" till Jesus had ascended. The Spirit is not merely called the Holy Spirit and the Spirit of God; it is also associated with Christ. Can you mention any passage that illustrates this connection?

Pupil.—St. Paul says, "If any man have not *the Spirit of Christ*, he is none of his;" and directly afterwards he alludes to the Spirit as "the Spirit of him that raised up Jesus from the dead."[1]

Teacher.—There are other passages[2] of a similar kind. Then we have to ask why, in order that the disciples might receive the Spirit of Christ, it was necessary that Christ should leave them.

Pupil.—I suppose they were not prepared to receive the Spirit till He left them.

Teacher.—Can you show that, while He was with them on earth, they were not prepared for His Spirit?

Pupil.—They did not understand Him or His purposes. They looked for an earthly rather than a spiritual deliverance, procured by earthly, and not spiritual means. The Gospel often tells us that their inability to understand Him was so great that the most positive declarations about His coming death and resurrection were misunderstood or neglected by them.

Teacher.—And how could the departure of Christ enable them to understand Him? If they could not understand Him when present, must it not have been more difficult to understand Him when absent?

Pupil.—They might regret Him the more and love Him the more for His absence.

Teacher.—Yes, and to love a person is the best way to understand him. Very often, when a statesman has died, regret for his loss makes

---

[1] Rom. viii. 9.   [2] Gal. iv. 6; Philip. i. 9.

his policy the more regarded and better understood. A friend who is parted from us by death or prolonged absence often influences us all the more. The personal presence and individual peculiarities of a friend are like a scaffolding that helps to raise up the structure of the friendship; but when the building is constructed, the scaffolding is useless, and now hides what it once helped to build. Hence the life of a friend often shines out in a more real and living manner when he is taken from us by death.

> "For it so falls out,
> That what we have we prize not to the worth
> Whiles we enjoy it; but being lack'd and lost,
> Why, then we rack the value, then we pride
> The virtue that possession could not show us
> Whiles it was ours. So will it fare with Claudio;
> When he shall hear she died upon his words,
> The idea of her life shall sweetly creep
> Into his study of imagination,
> And every lovely organ of her life
> Shall come apparell'd in more precious habit,
> More moving-delicate and full of life,
> Into the eye and prospect of the soul,
> Than when she lived indeed."

It may be partly, as Shakespeare tells us, that the loss of a valued friend makes us value him more. Partly, perhaps, the influence of spirit upon spirit is not restricted to mere personal intercourse, or limited by death. The true and purified "idea" of a father often comes to a son for the first time when death intervenes between the two. Then the patience, care, and forethought become more evident and lovable; the occasional sternness that was once misunderstood, the strictness that seemed to approach moroseness, the anger that almost approximated to ill-temper, the checks and chiding that once wore the marks of austerity and censoriousness, now come "apparell'd in the habit" of anxiety for a child's welfare, and are for the first time recognized and appreciated. Now for the first time the father's lessons are understood. Words and precepts long forgotten, or thought to be forgotten, are brought to the son's remembrance. The father is dead, but being dead, still speaks; his bodily presence has gone, but his spiritual influence is substituted for it. Such considerations as these may enable us to understand how it was that the disciples of Christ did not understand Him or receive His Spirit till He was taken from them. Then, and not till then, did they fully feel their need of Him; not in the capacity of a king or conqueror, but as a spiritual friend and helper. Now let us ask, how the descent of the Holy Spirit of Christ was first manifested?

Pupil.—By the gift of tongues on the day of Pentecost.

Teacher.—What was the spiritual meaning of this event? If you or I were suddenly enabled to talk Arabic, or some other language of which ordinarily we knew nothing, would that have any spiritual meaning?

Pupil.—Might it not mean that the Spirit could teach everything?

Teacher.—But if teaching were meant, the Spirit might be expected to teach other things indiscriminately—astronomy, mathematics, and other studies, not languages merely.

Pupil.—I do not know what was the spiritual meaning of the gift of tongues.

Teacher.—Let us discuss it, then. St. Paul implies that the gift of tongues was not a sign to unbelievers in Corinth. Why not?

Pupil.—He says that if all the congregation spoke "with tongues," any unbeliever who came in would say they were mad.

Teacher.—But now, suppose in London—Corinth, like London, was a great commercial city, where many languages must have been spoken and understood—a congregation of mixed persons could, under certain influences, speak, without knowing, French, German, Spanish, Italian, Dutch, and other languages; would that be considered a token of madness, and not rather a very remarkable phenomenon requiring investigation?

Pupil.—It would be thought remarkable, certainly.

Teacher.—So I think it would have been thought in Corinth. Therefore, though there are different opinions on the subject, that opinion seems most reasonable which asserts that the disciples did not speak different languages, but were understood by those who spoke different languages. I will explain this somewhat in detail. When men are deeply moved they generally make use of their own native tongue; or, if they are bred up in countries where two languages are in use, they resort to the language or dialect of their infancy. It is not improbable that our Lord occasionally used the Aramaic dialect instead of Greek in moments of deep emotion, or when He wished to appeal to the hearts of rustic people. Now when the Spirit descended on the Apostles, as "they were all with one accord" in a room of the Temple, every one began to feel the inspiration of thoughts beyond expression, crying to God as Father. Even when calmly writing of the work of the Holy Spirit in the Epistle to the Galatians,[1] St. Paul resorts to the Aramaic, as though the Greek were insufficient, and says that God sent forth the Spirit of His Son, crying, "*Abba*, Father." It is supposed that in the ecstatic moment of inspiration, the Apostles burst out into praises and prayers in a language not their own, but not necessarily a known and defined language, much more probably an inarticulate language, blended with sounds of joy and ecstasy, such as could only be intelligible to those who were strongly in sympathy with the utterers. Men from different and distant nations, from Cappadocia, from Egypt, from Parthia, coming into the room, found themselves brought beneath the influence of the same Spirit that inspired the Apostles. Such was the force of the sympathy, that the same inarticulate utterances conveyed the same meanings to different hearers; but to each hearer the meaning came clothed in the expression natural to his deepest and most emotional thought. To the Parthian it was of Parthia; to the men of Cappadocia, Cappadocian; but in reality it was of no country. It was the cosmopolitan language of the New Jerusalem, independent of intellectual forms of expression, and intelligible to all those who longed to love God as their Father, and one another as brothers. To use the words of an early com-

[1] Gal. iv. 6.

mentator, "There was but one utterance, but it conveyed many meanings." And now I ask, what was the spiritual meaning of this manifestation? How did it differ from the operations of the Spirit upon the men of the Old Testament—Elijah, for instance? Take one point of difference. Elijah, you will remember, received a revelation of God as being "a still small voice." But Elijah was alone in the desert.

Pupil.—The Apostles were together, and the Spirit was revealed, not in solitude, but through the medium of fellowship, as a spirit of communion and sympathy.

Teacher.—There was a marked distinction, recognized even by the most enlightened philosophers, between different nations. Even Plato prided himself upon the purity of Greek blood, uncontaminated by mixture with "barbarians," by which he meant foreigners. It was also a characteristic of the ancient Pagan religions that they regarded different nations as springing from different gods, to whom they were consequently bound to render homage. How was such a pseudo-patriotism affected by the revelation of the Holy Spirit?

Pupil.—It was condemned. From henceforth all men were to be brothers and children of the heavenly Father, speaking one language of love and sympathy taught by the Holy Spirit.

Teacher.—And how does this agree with the sign of Christianity given by Christ?

Pupil.—The sign of Christian disciples was to be that they loved one another, and the spiritual meaning of this manifestation of the Holy Spirit was that henceforth a new power of mutual human love was to rule upon earth.

Teacher.—How was the Holy Spirit communicated?

Pupil.—By the laying on of hands.

Teacher.—In all cases?

Pupil.—No. Sometimes the mere proclamation of the truth of Christ was sufficient to cause the manifestation of the Spirit.

Teacher.—Tell me what was the spiritual meaning of the laying on of hands.

Pupil.—I do not know. Was it not the instrument of conferring the Spirit?

Teacher.—Clearly not always, as you have yourself shown. But I mean, why select that particular bodily action? Do you think that laying the hand on the shoulder would not have had the same effect? Or, let me put it thus: Clement of Alexandria declared that women who wore false hair could not receive the Spirit by the imposition of hands. Do you think he was right?

Pupil.—No.

Teacher.—Then it was not the mere placing of the hand upon a part of the body that caused the manifestation of the Spirit. The bodily act was a sign of some spiritual act. Of what?

Pupil.—I suppose it was a sign that the person who placed his hand on the other's head imparted the Spirit of Christ from himself to the other person.

Teacher.—A similar expression occurs in the Old Testament. Elisha prayed that a double portion of Elijah's spirit might rest upon himself. This outward action seems to imply a spiritual law that God imparts the gift of His Spirit, oftenest, though not always, through human intercourse. It may not be direct intercourse, the influence may be conveyed by books or narratives; but, as a rule, the Holy Spirit does not come, like the visions that came to Moses in the wilderness, from the contemplation of the works of nature, but amid collections of human beings. The Spirit is a social spirit, and breathes upon the communion of men. Why had not this Spirit, or rather this operation of the Spirit, been manifested before?

Pupil.—I suppose because men were not prepared for it.

Teacher.—Yes; this was the Spirit of Christ. Until the revelation of Christ, the Spirit of Christ could not be manifested; and, as we said before,[1] men had to pass through the simple rules of morality before they were prepared to receive the highest moral revelation incarnate in Christ. Now, what are the results of the working of

[1] Part I. chapter xiv.

the Spirit of Christ? I do not now allude to the phenomena of "tongues." I mean, how does the Spirit influence the life of a Christian?

Pupil.—It tends to make him resemble Christ.

Teacher.—True. But how will men resemble Christ? By repeating His very words and actions? By dining with "sinners," by washing the feet of their inferiors?

Pupil.—No; by acting in His Spirit, by self-sacrifice.

Teacher.—But there are cases in life where even good men doubt which course to take. How can we tell in such doubtful cases what one ought to do?

Pupil.—The Spirit of Christ will guide us.

Teacher.—But suppose two good men, placed in the same circumstances, say that the Spirit of Christ bids them adopt opposite courses of conduct?

Pupil.—One of them must be wrong.

Teacher.—Then the Spirit of Christ does not always guide good men?

Pupil.—That cannot be.

Teacher.—I suppose the Spirit would guide us if we would listen, but we alter or misunderstand the voice owing to our own folly or evil prejudices and bad habits. But a man who is thoroughly unselfish cannot act wickedly, though he may foolishly. He that loveth his neighbour, says St. Paul, has no occasion for stumbling. You see, however, that we have no infallible, irresistible guide to direct our actions. Even when our motives are right, our actions may be, and often are, erroneous. Would it not have been well if the New Testament had given us full and minute directions to guide our every action in our several courses of life, whether we are tradesmen or merchants, artists or physicians or lawyers? Men are sometimes at a loss to know what is the Christian view of bargains and business, of politics, of science, of art, of pleasure and amusement. Would it not be well to have an infallible dictionary, so to speak, of Christian casuistry containing the whole duty of a Christian man, so that in any difficulty, we might turn to our book and say, "This, and this only, is the right way to act for a Christian?"

Pupil.—Such a book would at all events save much anxiety and prevent some error.

Teacher.—True. Would it be attended with any disadvantages?

Pupil.—It could not possibly provide solutions for all the various problems of life.

Teacher.—I grant that: but suppose it could provide for them all, would there be any disadvantage then?

Pupil.—I cannot see any.

Teacher.—Such a book would then be the infallible guide of our life, would it not? I am supposing it to be so clearly written as to give no opportunity for misunderstanding.

Pupil.—It would be an infallible guide.

Teacher.—But, at present, what or who is the guide of our life?

Pupil.—Christ.

Teacher.—Then, armed with our book, provided we thoroughly believed that this book was right, we should have no need of Christ, no need for thought or for self-questioning, no need to believe or pray that God will give us light. Would that be a condition likely to develop a high state of morality?

Pupil.—I suppose not.

Teacher.—Such a code or book of casuistry could be fairly called the Christian law. And what does St. Paul say about law as opposed to Christ?

Pupil.—He says that we are not under the law, but under Christ.

Teacher.—Yes; and though St. Paul generally means by law the Jewish law, yet his argument applies to any fixed law. Laws or rules of any kind, and the works which they enforce, are, St. Paul says, dead. A law concerns itself not with motives, but with overt acts—cannot adapt itself to continually changing circumstances, cannot fully employ the reasoning and spiritual faculties, and cannot fully develop any feelings beyond those of discipline and obedience. A Spirit can do all this. Hence the advantages of a Spirit over a Law.

You may sometimes hear complaints made that Christianity, as a scheme of morality, is very imperfect; that art, science, politics, patriotism and amusement, are excluded from the narrow field of the questions to which it furnishes answers. The reply is, that we are not under a scheme at all, but guided by a Spirit: it is not so correct to say we believe in Christianity, as in Christ. He will help us and guide us, and give us all the solutions required by all the questions that modern life may have presented, or may present hereafter. Some say that Christianity has done its work, and is now worn out, and an obstacle to the progress of society. But the Christian man is ready to accept every beneficial reformation, whether in social or political life, or in the outward expression of religious thought. He is bound to do so; and not merely to accept, but himself to suggest and reform, because he is not under a dead law, but under a living Lord, who is reforming the world in conformity to the Divine pattern. By the very nature of his creed, a Christian is a pledged Reformer.

There are one or two expressions about the Holy Spirit that require our attention. For instance, we are said to be baptized by the Holy Spirit. What does that mean?

Pupil.—Purified by the Holy Spirit.

Teacher.—Purified by the spirit of fellowship, the spirit of communion. Purified from what? the opposite of fellowship, I suppose?

Pupil.—Purified from our selfishness, made unselfish and loving.

Teacher.—On one occasion Christ says to His disciples that He has a baptism to be baptized with, and that they shall share in that baptism. Now, what kind of a baptism was that?

Pupil.—The baptism of trial and suffering.

Teacher.—Do you mean that calamity is a baptism by the Holy Spirit?

Pupil.—Yes.

Teacher.—But many men who fret and repine against calamity are made worse by it, not better.

Pupil.—Yes. Calamity is not a baptism in itself, but it is sometimes the means of trying and purifying men.

Teacher.—So, I suppose, is prosperity, though perhaps not so often. Prosperity may make men thankful to God and kind towards men?

Pupil.—Yes.

Teacher.—Then both prosperity and adversity, and, we may add, beauty and deformity, health and sickness, wealth and poverty, and indeed the world and all that in it is, are so many instruments by which the Holy Spirit is continually striving to purify us and make us unselfish. But suffering is His especial instrument, and why?

Pupil.—Because sympathy is more required by the suffering than the prosperous, and those who have suffered can, as a rule, sympathise with other sufferers. Hence suffering often makes men unselfish.

Teacher.—Another question. The Holy Spirit is said to "reprove"[1] —we ought rather to say convict, or convince—men of sin. How?

Pupil.—I do not know.

Teacher.—When is a sinner convicted—I mean made conscious—of sin?

Pupil.—Perhaps when he is punished.

Teacher—I think not. Often a criminal, when punished, thinks of nothing else but to escape or shorten his punishment. He does not realize the sinfulness, though he does the inconvenience, of his crime, a jot the more for being punished. The sternest rebukes and the severest punishments are often unsuccessful in making men conscious of sin. Yet some hardened criminals are sometimes touched with penitence; and what mostly produces this feeling?

Pupil.—Sorrow for the mischief they have done.

Teacher.—Yes; and the solitude of the prison, the sympathy of friends, and the teachings of the ministers of religion, often encourage the sorrow. But take the case of the woman who, though

[1] John xvi. 8.

a "sinner," anointed our Lord and wetted His feet with her tears. What caused her penitence?

Pupil.—Sorrow for her past life.

Teacher.—But why did she suddenly feel this in the presence of Christ, and not before in the presence of some Pharisee? She had probably been expelled from the synagogue some time before. Why should she not have felt the sorrow then? Take, again, Zaccheus, and the many others who seem to have been touched with sorrow for their sins in the presence of Jesus, and tell me, what caused their sorrow?

Pupil.—There was a feeling of the difference between the purity of Christ and their impurity—of the beauty of righteousness and the infinite value of that which they had thrown away during their past lives. Perhaps they also felt sorrow for themselves, because they saw that Christ was sorrowful for them.

Teacher.—Then the presence of Christ, and the influence of His Spirit upon men, produced at first a painful effect. It made the unclean and the impure cry, "What have we to do with thee? torment us not." Like the men in Plato's cave, who had long sat in native darkness, and therefore shrank at first from the light which showed them all things as they really were, so sinners, coming into the presence of Christ, felt at first nothing but pain at the contrast between themselves and Him. The pain was necessary. Until the hunger and thirst were felt, the righteousness that was to satisfy the hunger could not be granted. Until the burden of the sin pressed as a burden, it could not be lightened. Until pardon was earnestly desired, it could not be granted. And this is not merely true of the action of the Holy Spirit upon individuals. What does Christ say about the nature of His influence in answer to those who "supposed he came to send peace"?

Pupil.—He said that He came to send war and discord.

Teacher.—And war and discord came, not only in the hearts of individuals, the good principle striving against the bad, but also in every household, and in every nation, the new faith expelling the old.

The same spirit that prompted the Jews to reject Christ, intensified by the rejection, prompted them to rush into war against the Roman power, and brought on the destruction of their capital and Temple and the dispersion of the nation. And ever since the time of Christ, the Holy Spirit has been working in the same double way, making use of good and evil, peace and war; judging the world and separating good from evil. Religious wars, persecutions, superstitions, have sprung, or have seemed to spring, from the working of the Christian spirit. But on the whole, even in this world, where the problem of life is not, and cannot be, fully solved, we are enabled, in spite of many seeming retrogressions, to see the slow process by which the Holy Spirit is working on men, bringing good out of evil, and peace out of war, gradually destroying idolatry, polygamy, and slavery, and raising men to a higher level of morality, not directly assailing the institutions of men, but purifying their hearts first, and indirectly their customs and institutions, always working outwards from the inner.

The difference between the ancient and the Christian spirit is apparent in more than mere morality. Consider the difference between the allusions to natural scenery in ancient and in modern poetry. The ancients regarded the world as a habitation for man; rough forests and inaccessible mountains seemed to them uninviting objects to which a man might perhaps by long familiarity render himself not greatly averse. To us the foliage of the trees and the forms of the hills speak of the Creator, and the whole world has become the garment in which the Almighty clothes and partially reveals His divine attributes. The Hebrew spirit which found expression in the Psalm of Moses recognizes the Divine symmetry and order of the universe; but the suggestive and dependent loveliness of nature never found due recognition till Christ's Spirit came. Pan, and the Dryads, and the Oreads had usurped the honours due to the forests and the mountains. The usurpers were now banished, and Nature resumed her proper privilege, and in her own right, as the visible Minister of the Supreme, claimed to inspire art and point the poet upwards with a "Sursum corda," which finds its response in the lines of Wordsworth :—

> "My heart *leaps up* when I behold
> A rainbow in the sky."

The influence of the Holy Spirit extends to the intellect as well as to the spiritual faculty. As superstition dwarfs the reason, and immoral mythology deforms it, and doubt unsettles it, so the Spirit of Love and Truth strengthens and develops it. Errors in faith cause errors in science; and conversely, faith in God, when based on truth, prepares the way for the full and fair investigation of all God's truths, scientific as well as spiritual. And thus we believe that it has been, and yet will be, the work of the Holy Spirit to teach us new duties corresponding to new circumstances, to clear our reason and understanding by delivering us from false beliefs and fears, and finally, in the words of Christ, to guide us into all the truth.

CHAPTER XI.

THE TECHNICAL TERMS OF ST. PAUL.

SOME of the terms used by St. Paul have what may be called technical meanings, that is, peculiar meanings derivable from the context of his writings, and from an understanding that pervades them. Thus the word "flesh" is used by St. Paul technically. It does not denote the mere substance of which our bodies are composed, but an evil principle, antagonistic to the higher principle, the spirit in man. We will consider some of these terms in the order which they will naturally assume from the point of view whence St. Paul regarded men, as originally in the "flesh," doing by "nature" the works of the "flesh," and wholly engrossed in "this world," then introduced to "law," which brings in the idea of "sin." The "law," making man for the first time conscious of sin, seems to create sin. It does actually increase the wretchedness of the sinner, by intensifying the struggle against sin and the despair of the failure. But meanwhile the way is being prepared for something higher than "law." A desire for redemption is engendered: hence a longing for a Redeemer, and thus "law" becomes, in God's hands, the guide to conduct undeveloped humanity, like a child, to the school of the Teacher, Christ. The substitution of the perfect Teacher for an imperfect guide has not been an accident. It has been "predestined" from the first by the supreme Father, who knows His wandering children, and "foreknows" the time to recall them to the fold. Men do not choose God, God rather chooses men, or "elects" them, and "calls" them out of the world into a new existence. The message by which

He calls them is the Gospel, or good news of Christ, telling them that God is a Father, and making men at one with God. Men cannot receive this gospel without "faith," or trust in Christ. They must believe that He actually represents God, and is the Son of God; and also that He came in the flesh; further, they must believe that His is the ideal sacrifice offered up for them, and really capable of cleansing them from sin. The new sphere into which they are raised by faith is "Christ," the "body of Christ," "the Church." They are raised from "this world" high up into "spiritual places." Their old connections are broken. They are now dead to sin and alive to Christ. They are not merely living servants of Christ, they are in Christ, members of His body, partakers of His past pains and glorious future. If the body of Christ was crucified, so also has their "flesh," their "old," or "carnal man," been crucified. If Christ has died, so also have they been buried as it were by baptism with Christ, so that the "old man" has died. If Christ has risen again, so also have they risen in "the new man," the spiritual nature which already exists in earth, and will be infinitely perfected hereafter.

Into this new and blessed state men are raised by "faith," not by "works." As soon as "works" are thought of, as soon as men think they can attain righteousness for themselves, in the way of traffic, by performing a certain amount of "works," for which God will reward them, so soon God becomes a taskmaster, not a Father; and Christ, who came to reveal a Father and not a master, becomes of "no effect." God does not desire "works." He sees into the hearts and motives of men. He saw into the heart of faithful Abraham, and took the will for the deed. Abraham did no "work," yet Abraham had righteousness imputed to him. He was considered righteous and made righteous, or "justified," because he had simply believed in God, and thereby accepted the righteousness or justification which God will freely give to all who trust in Him. It does not follow that those who are in Christ should continue in sin. God forbid. Faith will naturally produce the results of faith, and these are love, joy, peace, and all corresponding actions. But these actions will not be "works," for they will not be done for wages in the spirit of servants, but out of love in the spirit of children. Now that the believer is in Christ, old things have passed away and all things have become new: he is now "sanctified." He now knows God, or rather God (who cannot "know" imperfect and sinful creatures, and therefore cannot "know" men out of Christ) knows him. He is a member of Christ's Body, and, as such, animated by Christ's vital Spirit: "Except a man," says St. Paul, "have the spirit of Christ, he is none of Christ's." All worldly distinctions have passed away; in Christ there is neither Jew nor Gentile, bond nor free.

But spiritual distinctions remain. All members have not the same purpose, but are directed by the vital Spirit to different works, according to their several capacities. There is one and the same spirit in the human body, but it gives to the hand and the foot distinct works. So the Spirit which animates the Body of Christ gives to one member the power of teaching, to another the power of ruling, and to others other powers; but to each one some appropriate power. No member of Christ is to be despised, and no work of any member is to be counted trifling or indifferent. Even eating and drinking can be done "to the glory of God," or "in Christ." These powers or faculties which are bestowed by the Spirit are called "gifts." The Spirit itself and the goodness of the Gospel come from God by His free favour, and not as wages for a "work;" they therefore might be called a "gift;" but they are called more generally "grace" or favour (*charis*), while the several manifestations of the "grace" are called "gifts" (*charismata*). The members of this great Body are all dependent upon the Head, which is Christ.[1]

Such is a brief sketch of St. Paul's account of the process by which men enter into the Kingdom of God, or, as he would rather say, into Christ. There are now to be considered a few difficulties connected with the use of some of these technical terms, arising often

---

[1] It can hardly be said there is confusion of metaphor in calling Christ both the Head and the Body. Viewed from different aspects, He is at one time the Head, at another the Body.

from the double sense in which they are used. Take for example the word "nature." Where does St. Paul imply that men are "by nature" evil?

Pupil.—In the Epistle to the Ephesians (ii. 3), St. Paul speaks of himself and his friends thus: "We were by nature the children of wrath, even as others."

Teacher.—Well, if it is men's nature to be the children of wrath, *i.e.* alien from God and sinful, then it may be maintained that in sinning men are only acting according to their nature. If that is so, then a "natural" father will be one who is unkind, and an "unnatural" father one who is kind; and instead of calling cruelty, as we do, "unnatural," we ought to call it "natural." What was the explanation that we gave of this difficulty? We took, if you remember, an illustration from a clock, and asked whether it was *natural* for a clock to indicate the right or the wrong time.

Pupil.—There are two uses of the word nature—the intention of the creator and the custom of the thing created.

Teacher.—Yes, it is men's object and nature to be conformed to the image of God, but it is also their custom and nature to differ from His image. In the truest sense of the word, it is the nature of men to do the will of God and serve Him, and St. Paul speaks about the Gentiles "who have not the law, doing by *nature* the things contained in the law." Now consider the use of the word "flesh" and the "world." Is not the flesh made by God as well as the spirit? Did not God make the world and call it very good? Why, then, does St. Paul continually speak of the "flesh" and the "world" as evil?

Pupil.—Because they tempt men.

Teacher.—Everything tempts men — health, strength, friends, wealth, genius, skill: there is no gift of God but tempts a man to misuse it. Yet we do not speak of health and strength as evil. When the flesh is in its fit place, strictly subordinate to the reason, can any one say that it is an evil?

Pupil.—I suppose St. Paul only calls it evil when it rebels against the spirit.

Teacher.—Exactly. Sometimes St. Paul uses the word literally without any notion of condemnation, and talks of his "abiding *in the flesh*" as being necessary for the Philippians; at other times, using the word metaphorically, he says "they that are *in the flesh* cannot please God."[1] And the same explanation applies to the use of "the world," or more often "this world." The world in itself is very good, and is intended to reveal the Creator. But, through the weakness of man, the world is suffered to step out of its place into the place occupied by God. We are too readily and too much impressed by what we see, and far too little by things invisible, intangible, and spiritual. What is out of sight is proverbially out of mind, and not seeing implies not believing. Hence "*this* world" (as being the more real and substantial) opposes itself to the invisible world, and imposes itself upon us as sufficient for all our needs. The present triumphs over the future, sight conquers faith. For these reasons, and from this aspect, *this present world* is treated by St. Paul as opposed to God, and almost as synonymous with the Evil Spirit. Whatever exerts this faith-destroying influence by setting the present against the future, and the visible against the invisible—whether it be pleasure or philosophy, or ambition or war or public opinion—comes under the head of "this world." In the same way the flesh, being present and powerful, and often able to secure obedience to its desires against the commandments of God, is also generally condemned as being ranged on the same side as "this world" against the Spirit of God.

Now, before we proceed to the consideration of the process of "sanctifying," let us briefly touch upon the terms Predestination and Election. What natural objection might be made by a Jew against the genuineness of a kingdom that claims to be of Divine origin, and to base itself upon the prophecies of the Old Testament, and yet excludes the majority of the chosen people. How might he use the promises in the Old Testament to show that the kingdom had no claim to be called the kingdom of God, since it excluded God's chosen people?

[1] Rom. viii. 8.

Pupil.—He might say that the promises of God were broken if the Christian Church was the promised kingdom, for it had been promised that Israel should be delivered, and Israel had not been delivered.

Teacher.—Now, how does St. Paul meet this?

Pupil.—He says that Israel after the Spirit, not after the flesh, is the true Israel.

Teacher.—But it might have been urged that such an explanation as this was a mere figment, an afterthought, and that God must have changed His mind. Moreover, it might be represented by the enemies of the early Church that the life of Jesus was a failure, and His death the seal of failure, and that it could never have been intended by God that His Son should die the death of a slave on earth. What does St. Paul say to meet such objections?

Pupil.—He says that the sacrifice of Christ was pre-ordained before the foundation of the world: that God calls His children and bestows His gifts without changing His mind: that there is no break in the series of God's plans: and that the history of the world must be taken as a whole, good issuing out of evil, the whole foreknown from the beginning.

Teacher.—Well, but if everything was foreknown, the rejection of Christ was foreknown. Hence those who rejected Him might excuse themselves by saying that it was predestined. In fact, we are landed in the difficulty mentioned above, of reconciling the omnipotence, omniscience, and benevolence of God with the existence of evil. How does St. Paul deal with that? By what simile does he illustrate God's dealings with men?

Pupil.—He asks whether the potter has not power to make some vessels for honour and others for dishonour.

Teacher.—But I do not see the force of that argument as you put it. The question is, not whether God has *power* to predestine men to sin, which all would admit, but whether it is *right* that it should be so. Give me the four terms of St. Paul's simile in the usual way.

Pupil.—As the potter has power to make some vessels to honour and others to dishonour, so God has power to make some men for righteousness and others for sinfulness.

Teacher.—Now, do you not see that this does not meet the objection of those who say, "Yes, we know God has the *power*, but is it *right*"?

Pupil.—I see; but I cannot explain it.

Teacher.—The argument we want is this: "The potter has the *right*," not "the *power*,"—is it not?

Pupil.—Yes.

Teacher.—Well, we shall find what we want in the original, if we look into it. The word translated "power" should be translated "right." It means authority, lawful power.[1] The potter has *right* and *au'hority* over the clay in virtue of his mental superiority. He knows what is best, the clay does not. Hence it would be absurd for the clay to remonstrate against the potter. Similarly, in wisdom, love, and power God is infinitely superior to men. He has *authority* over us in virtue of His infinite superiority; and it is absurd for those who believe in God to doubt for a moment that we are being shaped by Him for the best possible end, whatever that end may be. St. Paul does not solve the problem. He cuts the knot by bidding us trust in the Supreme, who by His attributes claims our trust. Meanwhile, dismissing the attendant difficulties, St. Paul dwells emphatically on the fact that the righteousness of men is not the result of a transaction or bargain between God and man; it cannot be attained in the way of wages for works, or obedience to a "law." It is a gift, and the whole process of bestowal is a favour or "grace." God not merely foreknew His children, He also predestines; then He called, then He justified, and finally glorified. We are now brought naturally to the terms "justification" and "imputation of righteousness." God is said to reckon or impute righteousness to those who believe in Him—as, for instance, to Abraham. The simple act of faith in God's promise caused God to reckon Abraham righteous. Now,

[1] ἐξουσίαν

is it possible for God to reckon a man to be righteous when he is not?

Pupil.—No. But God may pardon a man's sin, and treat him as though he were sinless even though he be a sinner.

Teacher.—True. We considered that question in the chapter on Forgiveness, and we decided that all forgiveness is based on the belief that human nature is intended by God to be sinless, according to the pattern of Christ, and that a power is given by God to men of putting away one another's sins. There is no imposture or make-believe whatever in it. But to "reckon" a man righteous is more than to treat him in the same way as though he were righteous, it means to *esteem* him righteous. Now God cannot be mistaken in His estimation. It therefore follows that Abraham not only was esteemed righteous by God, but was righteous. If this be so, why does not St. Paul use the plain and straightforward phrase "Abraham was righteous"?

Pupil.—I do not know.

Teacher.—What did the Jews mean exactly by "righteousness"? What is the meaning of the Greek word for it?

Pupil.—It means justice.

Teacher.—Yes, and justice meant "conformity with the law." A "just" man was one who "walked in all the commandments and ordinances of the Lord blameless."[1] The Jews technically considered justice or "righteousness" to be a state attainable by obedience to the Mosaic law—by "the works of the law," as St. Paul says. Now St. Paul wishes to point out that perfect righteousness cannot be thus obtained. No one has ever perfectly fulfilled the law. The law reveals righteousness, and makes men who deviate from its enactments conscious of sin, but it does not take away sin or make men righteous. No man can ever obtain the sense of sinlessness by his own actions. True righteousness has another source. What source?

Pupil.—God.

[1] St. Luke i. 6.

Teacher.—Yes. All righteousness proceeds from God, and is accepted by men as a free gift from God through the instrumentality of faith. Every one who has ever been really righteous must have accepted his righteousness in this way. Abraham, for example, lived before the law, could not therefore fulfil its enactments, and was therefore unable to obtain "righteousness" in the strict Jewish sense of the term. But he had faith in God, and faith is the germ of righteousness; and God, who sees the tree in the germ, reckoned the faith of Abraham to be equivalent to the fulfilment of the works of the law, *i.e.* "righteousness." God reckoned it to be so, because it was so. He imputed righteousness because righteousness was there in the germ, not indeed visible to men, who require the fruit of works before they can distinguish the living from dead faith, but perfectly visible to God, who forecasts the spiritual processes which will develop faith into action, and in whose eyes a thousand years are as one day. A good deal of the difficulty arises from a double meaning of the word "righteousness." If the word means "fulfilment of the Mosaic law," then the reckoning of righteousness to Abraham was, in the bare literal sense, a fiction, because Abraham had not fulfilled the law in the letter, though he had in the spirit. But if the word means the "fulfilment of the law of God," then there is no fiction at all.

In close connection with "righteousness" and "the reckoning of righteousness" comes "justification." It is unfortunate that the connection has not been better preserved in our translation. Instead of "justify," "make righteous" would better explain the meaning. We found "righteous" an ambiguous word, and the dependent word "justify" or "make *righteous*" must necessarily partake in these ambiguities. It may mean, to endow a person with "righteousness" according to the moral law of God, or to endow a person with righteousness in the technical Jewish sense, *i.e.* obedience to the Mosaic ordinances. In the latter sense, taken literally, God does not "justify" men. He cannot endow them with obedience to ordinances that they have not obeyed. But He can, and does, without any fiction, endow them with "righteousness" according to the spirit of the Mosaic law, according to the law of God. By faith in God we are raised up into communion with Him; we feel that we are His children, and are at one with Him. This state of communion with God is righteousness; it expresses itself in actions—in love, mercy, truthfulness, and peace; but these outward actions are not the causes which induce God to love us; they are the results of His love. If we hoped to buy God's favour by love and mercy, love and mercy would become "works," and we should be under "a law," and not under "grace."

The great means by which God excites our faith is the Gospel of Christ, and, above all, the tidings of the death of Christ, which is the culminating expression of Christ's sacrifice. By faith in Christ we recognize God as a Father; we are not merely brought by Christ to God, we are made one with Christ, partakers of His life, death, sufferings, and resurrection. We lose ourselves in Him. We cease from hoping to obtain God's favour by our own righteousness or sacrifices; Christ's righteousness is imparted to us, and Christ's sacrifice becomes ours through faith. As the sacrifices of the law were offered for the purification, not merely of the single person who offered up the sacrifice, but of all who were sprinkled with the blood of the animal, in token of participation, so we, who believe in Christ, are sprinkled with the blood of His sacrifice, and His sacrifice purifies us.

It should be noticed that here, as elsewhere, St. Paul does not treat of the individual so much as the collective body of mankind, who have a continuous history, and whose apparent retrogression in one age can be compensated by progress in another. The branch of Israel that is lopped from off the olive-tree of the Church can be regrafted a thousand years hence. The sin of Adam is more than compensated by the righteousness of Christ. The law caused sin to abound, but the abundance of sin prepared the way of grace. The Apostle does not try to deny or explain that apparent waste of spiritual life in particular cases, which accompanies the general development of humanity. He leaves that question unsolved, almost untouched, contenting himself with tracing the progress of the race as a whole. The incarnation and death of Christ is the central fact of the history of the world which is to answer all doubts and mental difficulties. It is a sufficient justification for any event to say that it prepared the way for the coming of Christ and the proclamation of the Gospel to the Gentiles. The sin of Adam, the fall of man, the introduction of death, the rigidity of the imperfect law, the consequent disobedience of Israel, the captivity or destruction of the chosen people, the demoralization of the survivors, the "conclusion of the whole world in unbelief," the rejection of Christ—all these are so many stages in the glorious opening of the revelation of God to the whole world. If the Apostle admits that God "hath concluded all in unbelief," he adds that God did this in order "that he might have mercy on all;" and a review of the history of mankind, with all its sins and imperfections, leads the Apostle to this exclamation as his most natural conclusion: "O the depth of the riches both of the wisdom and knowledge of God! How unsearchable are his judgments, and his ways past finding out!"

CHAPTER XII.

CHRISTIAN CASUISTRY, OR THE APPLICATION OF CHRIST'S TEACHING TO MODERN TIMES.

Teacher.—It has been urged as an objection against Christ's teaching that, considered as a law, it is not only scanty but also often inapplicable to modern times. What part of the Gospels most resembles a law, a collection of precepts?

Pupil.—The Sermon on the Mount.

Teacher.—And in the Sermon on the Mount, what precept occurs about giving?

Pupil.—"Give to every man that asketh of thee."[1]

Teacher.—Is that applicable to modern times?

Pupil.—People do not, at all events, put it in practice.

Teacher.—No; and those who know most about the poor say that we ought not to put it in practice. Indiscriminate almsgiving, giving "to every man that asks," is said to be the cause of infinite misery and crime in our great cities. In sparsely inhabited districts, where industry and self-respect abound, the precept might still hold good; and in the particular circumstances, and for the particular persons to whom the precept was addressed by our Lord, it no doubt was good; but for us, in London, obedience to that precept is bad, and therefore contrary to the will of Christ. The literal obedience to this precept has been, I may almost say, the ruin of entire nations. The countries in which Christianity (in its traditional form and uncontrolled by any sort of use of reason) has been most influential—Spain, for instance,

[1] St. Luke vi. 30.

and Italy—have been economically ruined by almsgiving. It is therefore true that Christ's teaching is, as a law, sometimes inapplicable to modern circumstances. But we dealt with this objection above, and how did we meet it?

Pupil.—By saying that we are not under law, but under a Spirit. Christ's Spirit guides us, and tells us what we ought to do.

Teacher.—And the characteristic operation of Christ's Spirit is what?

Pupil.—Communion, concord, love.

Teacher.—It is obvious that, if a man loves his neighbour, he is sure to do him no wilful harm. Therefore, if we are under the guidance of the Spirit of love, however dull and stupid we may be, we are less likely to harm our neighbour than a very intelligent, selfish man. But we may do harm, for all that. A father may love his children, but do them irreparable injury, both bodily and mentally, and even morally, by ignorance or foolish indulgence. And we said above that indiscriminate almsgiving, though it may proceed from pure philanthropy, does much mischief. Hence, beside love, something else is wanted for Christian action. What is it?

Pupil.—Wisdom.

Teacher.—Yes; or in ordinary life perhaps common sense would be a better word. Now, as regards some duties which were required to be enforced with special emphasis during the times of the early Christians, we shall find the New Testament ample and minute. What duties are these?

Pupil.—Love, mercy, forgiveness, humility, sympathy, peace, patience, and purity.

Teacher.—What are the duties that are not so fully enforced?

Pupil.—Justice, firmness, bravery, and patriotism.

Teacher.—True. Industry is enjoined on one or two occasions by St. Paul, but not so often as some other virtues. Frugality, thoughtfulness, and prudence are not emphasized. Truthfulness is, perhaps, taken for granted. It is enjoined at least once, but not so emphatically as we enjoin it now. You see, then, the direction in which we must look most carefully when we try to sketch the duties of a Christian life. It is the social and political aspects of life that most require our attention. Let us briefly run through the duties of a Christian man,—and first his duty towards God.

Pupil.—His duty is to love and trust God.

Teacher.—Yes. The love which a child feels for its father is all that God asks from us; this, and the feelings and actions that naturally spring from it. Next towards ourselves. It is, of course, impossible to consider our duty towards ourselves apart from our duties towards others. But there are duties which we may be said to owe to ourselves as children of God. Our bodies, we are taught by St. Paul, are the temples of the Holy Spirit, and purity and temperance may be regarded as tributes due to the dignity of our redeemed nature. We have no right to degrade ourselves any more than to spoil God's other handiwork. Again, suppose a man has some faculty which he feels ought to be developed, and which calls him to a particular course of life. It may be that he has an aptitude for the study and practice of medicine, or painting, or music, or preaching, or acting. It is possible that his friends may desire him to adopt some more obvious and easy plan of life that will entirely ignore this talent. And there may be circumstances (as, for instance, the poverty or death of parents) which may make it right that he should earn money at once for himself by any lawful means, even at the cost of neglecting the path which God had apparently marked out for him. But this ought not to be done without due consideration. Every faculty given by God to man is a grace or gift. By the grace of God a man is, whatever he is as he ought to be, whether he be an acute lawyer, or a skilful physician, or a deep theologian, or an honest and energetic tradesman. A man ought to feel throughout his life that his vocation or "calling" is one to which he is called by God. To take a lucrative path in life, merely because it is lucrative, and in spite of definite faculties tending in another direction, is to disobey God's "calling" and to dislocate oneself, as it were, from one's fit place in the members of Christ's Body. Such an abuse of God's gifts cannot but give a lower tone to one's life, and is likely to end either in moral and intellectual degradation or else in lassitude and unavailing regret. It may be that tastes and inclinations are deceptive, and do not indicate any real power. Self-conceit and vanity often give a man an exaggerated notion of his power. A mistaken decision may be arrived at; but the attempt to decide ought to be made.

For the same reason a man is bound to have regard to his health and strength, and to avoid all habits that may unfit him for meeting the sudden claims that society may make upon him. Such considerations, beside others, will condemn gluttony, intoxication, whether private or public, and sensuality. They will also condemn (and this is a fact not sufficiently borne in mind) excessive work, whether bodily or mental. A man has no more right (exceptional circumstances being put out of consideration) to over-work his body or his brain than he has to over-eat or over-drink. His health is not his own, and he has no right to trifle with it.

This is also true, and more generally recognized, of a man's spiritual condition. There may be certain employments, amusements, or societies that may be innocent for others, but injurious for us. We are therefore bound to find out our peculiar dangers, and, where we may lawfully do so, we ought to avoid them. Watching as well as praying is inculcated by our Lord, and watchfulness ought to be accompanied by common sense. The law by which habit makes actions less impressive, but more easy, is a law of our human nature ordained by God. A man is not to be above taking advantage of the law, or too proud to trouble himself about the formation of habits. Habits of order, forethought, deliberation, and punctuality, often extend their influence into the moral side of action. For example, deliberation in those who are young and thoughtless may often prevent those hasty utterances which are more than exaggerations, and tend to become, in course of time, not much less than untruths. The same habit, joined with a rooted sense of the distinction between anger and fretfulness, prevents those bursts of bad temper which sometimes disgrace Christian men. The Christian should feel, as the Stoic felt, that no action is "indifferent;" it must be either useful or useless, good or bad. "Whatever is worth doing is worth doing well;" or, in the words of St. Paul, "whether we eat or drink, or whatever we do, we ought to do all to the glory of God."

We now pass to the duty toward society. Nature places a man in more than one society. The country, the neighbourhood, all have their claims upon us; but what is the society which encircles us closest, and presents the strongest claims?

Pupil.—The family.

Teacher.—First, then, comes the duty toward one's parents. This is so forcibly enjoined by nature that it ought not to need any special inculcation in a collection of Christian precepts. As a fact, it is often found that there is less respect and obedience paid to parental authority by Christians than by heathens. Where the duty toward one's neighbour is but faintly recognized, it is natural that the duty toward the parents should assume large and almost excessive proportions, as among the ancient Romans. There are some cases—for instance, marriage—where a son or daughter may feel it wrong to be entirely guided by parental authority. But in all cases, even where obedience cannot be paid, deference and respect ought not to be wanting; and respect ought to spring, not from a conventional feeling of the duty towards parents, but from genuine affection, and from reflecting how in one's old age one would like oneself to be treated by one's children. It is said that in England, as compared with other countries, the respect for parents is at a low ebb. Public opinion demands a considerable, sometimes an excessive, provision for children from parents, but does not demand in return that parents should be supported in their old age by their children. With the Greeks, on the other hand, it was so natural that aged parents should depend upon their children, that their language contained a word especially adapted, and almost appropriated, to express the "feeding of parents in their old age." Medea represents the feeling of all Greek mothers when she says—

> " Verily, I once had many hopes of you, my children,
> That you would *support me in my old age,*
> And, when I died, that you would lay out my corpse."

The reason for this change is perhaps partly that parents can now make provision for their old age which they could not then. The machinery for accumulating and for receiving the fruits of accumulation has been so improved that not many kind or prudent parents need, or would, throw themselves upon the affection and support of their children in old age. But perhaps this change of circumstances gives less development to the feeling of respect and tenderness which children should entertain for their parents. It is by no means uncommon among the poorer classes for children who are not in want, and a good way above want, to leave their parents to be supported, like paupers, by the State. A Greek heathen would have been ashamed to do this.

Then comes the duty of parents toward their children. On one point St. Paul is very emphatic here. "If any man," he says, "provide not for his own, he hath denied the faith, and is worse than an infidel." This duty is pretty well recognized, though even now a man who dies, after living in a state of comfort, and leaves his wife and children totally unprovided for, is not quite so severely reprobated as he should be. There are so many means—life insurance for one— by which a man can provide for those who are dependent upon him in the event of his death, that the neglect to make such provision is inexcusable. The spirit of St. Paul's precept also condemns those who enter into marriage without the means and prospects of supporting a family. But, besides providing for their bodily wants, the father is bound to see that his children are so educated that they shall be prepared for the work of life. The State itself would interfere, would it not, to prevent a father from bringing up his children in such a way that their senses—the sense of hearing, for instance, or the power of speaking—remained unexercised and undeveloped, so that they grew up dumb and deaf?

Pupil.—Yes.

Teacher.—Well, but reading is a second sense of hearing, and writing is a second power of speaking, each, though artificial, almost as necessary in these times as the natural sense of hearing and power of speech. Therefore a father is bound to see that his children have these powers, and all others necessary for the work of life, developed by education. This is one of the best instances to show that we must not limit our Christian activity to the circle of duties enumerated in the Old and New Testaments. The word "educate" is scarcely mentioned in the whole of the Bible, yet in modern times the diffusion of education is one of the most important duties that devolve upon us—more important than almsgiving, which is a duty recommended in almost every page of the Bible.

Now passing to the duty toward our country, we find very few precepts on this subject. It was the part of the Christians during the early ages of the Church tó hold aloof from public life. They could fill no public offices; for every magistracy required a recognition of false gods. They lived as a proscribed, but for the most part practically tolerated, sect. The danger was, that some of the Christian body, revolting at irregular oppression and sometimes systematic persecution, might join in plots and conspiracies for the overthrow of the established governments. The only precepts, therefore, relating to political life enjoin on the disciples the duty of remembering that the guardians of public order are ordained by God, and that the Christian must live in quiet subjection, paying taxes and rendering obedience according to law. But now that Government has become Christian, our duties have become much more numerous and complicated. There are not only negative duties, such as abstinence from sedition and turbulence, from all attempts to defraud the public authorities, and from corruption in the exercise of the franchise; there are also positive duties, the duty of voting in the best possible way, and therefore of forming our opinions on public subjects with the greatest possible accuracy; the duties of serving as jurors for the preservation of law and as soldiers for the safety of the country; and, generally, we lie under the obligation to contribute as far as in us lies, directly and indirectly, to the welfare of our native land.

Here, and in everything that relates to public morality, we are greatly inferior to the ancient Greeks and Romans in their noblest days. The duty of serving the State as jurors, or soldiers, or in other public capacities, is often either evaded or very imperfectly recognized. The State is regarded as an enemy when it interferes with private comfort. Taxes cannot be collected to the full amount unless every avenue to fraud is closed with the strictest vigilance. Public monuments are often wantonly defaced, and the public convenience is set aside on the slightest pretext of private inconvenience. The reason for this is no doubt thoughtlessness, the same feeling through which a child picks a flower in a park (though he would not do so in a private garden), because he thinks no one in particular is injured; whereas, if many children thought and acted as he did, the park would soon be despoiled, and the whole body of the people would have their pleasure diminished. A similar feeling in men induces them to put the public service after all other considerations. "Everybody's business," says the proverb, "is nobody's business." But when this pernicious principle has once pervaded the whole of a nation, and when private interests make themselves felt in the law-courts, the Government offices, and the governing body itself, then the life of the nation is poisoned, and there only wants some sudden crisis, as of war, to bring out the latent disease into a fatal prominence. War coming suddenly on such a nation will find fleets badly built and equipped, armies badly provisioned, arms ineffective, ammunition insufficient, soldiers ill-trained, and, in a word, everybody and everything inferior to what it professes to be; the whole nation becomes corrupted by selfishness, luxury, sloth, and suspicion, and must in the nature of things succumb to the superior patriotism of the first foreign assailant.

To explain this neglect of the claims of society, we must look to the undue respect which is felt for wealth. If a man is well off, and passes through life without doing much harm to his fellow-creatures, he is thought rather well of than otherwise. To be respectable is synonymous in many mouths with being rich. A "gentleman" is often explained to be one who "lives on his own means." This might be excusable in the feudal times, when the first in wealth and power were also first in the battle-field; or in the Greek cities, where the rich equipped ships and gave public exhibitions at their own expense and served in person in the ranks; but it is inexcusable now. Do-nothings have no place in a Christian nation. There is no room for a torpid member in the body of Christ. It is not necessary that all the members should have the same work. There is need of the brain and stomach as well as the hand and foot. But every member must do some work. Our servile and unreasonable worship of wealth is a perversion of Greek and Roman tradition, handed down from the times when trade and commerce were the tasks of slaves, and gymnastics and war the only fitting occupations for free men. It was a part of the heathen theory to exalt warlike wealth, and despise traffic and manual labour. The Christian theory is that every man, from the artisan to the king, has his calling from God, and is what he is by the grace of God, and that no one need be ashamed of his work, if his work is useful and he is an able workman.

There remains the duty toward one's neighbour individually, a subject full of difficulties, which cannot be treated of here for want of space. But the great maxim that we are to "do to others as we would that they should do to us" will guide us rightly, if we will but remember that the "as we would" must refer to the wish, not of a bad, but of a *good* man, placed in his neighbour's circumstances. Take a case. Suppose a murderer on the point of being hung, or consigned to long imprisonment, says to us, "If you were in my case you would not like hanging or imprisonment, therefore do not hang or imprison me." What are we to reply?

Pupil.—Society could not go on without punishment.

Teacher.—Well, but he appeals to the Christian rule, "do as you would be done by." We must reply to him, that were we in his position we should feel bound to make compensation to society for the mischief that we had done, and he ought to be ready to do the same. But, were we in his place, we should be glad of opportunity for reflection and repentance, books and friends, some alleviation of the wretchedness of imprisonment, at all events some charitable hope about us, and consequently this we will grant him, since we should ourselves wish to receive it from others.

The laws of a country often exercise a disturbing influence on Christian morality. They take little cognizance of motives, and mostly regard only the injury to society. Yet their influence is so great that the magnitude of a *sin* is often unconsciously measured by the legal penalty of a *crime*.[1] Thus the laws shape public opinion, and public opinion modifies the opinion of individuals about right and wrong. It is well to remind ourselves sometimes that God deals with motives, not with "works;" that in His eyes a theft, that may be severely punished by the law, is more excusable than the systematic cruelty of a husband towards his wife of which the law takes slight account; and that the crime of infanticide may be in many cases visited by God on those who have not committed, but have indirectly caused, the murder. It may not be, indeed it is not, possible, that a crime should be punished in proportion to its sinfulness; but an excessive disproportion between what God considers sin and what the State considers crime must tend to confuse and blunt the moral sense. There is also confusion in many minds as to the nature of resentment and forgiveness; but these we discussed above.

I should like to add one word on the duty toward animals. It has been stated, even by so great an authority as Bishop Butler, that those who take it for granted that there is no future existence in store for what are called irrational animals have not brought forward any sufficient grounds for their conclusion. But, whatever may be thought on this point, it is evident that the care which the Creator has bestowed upon the adornment and development of the animal world should of itself prevent us from wantonly wasting the life of animals, or causing them unnecessary pain. Such

---

[1] For the distinction between *sin* and *crime*, see Part I. p. 39.

waste and torture react upon the torturers, and degrade and brutalize humanity. Our duty toward animals might therefore be thought to spring out of our duty toward ourselves. But it has a nobler source in regard for animals themselves. The thoughtless cruelty with which animals are often treated in England, especially by the young, is a blot upon our nation. The young are perhaps peculiarly liable to this accusation, but not the young alone. All ages and all classes are involved in this disgrace. It is difficult to draw the line which shall distinguish where the pain of animals legitimately subserves the interests of men and where it ceases to do so. But a Christian must surely feel that he is treading on dangerous ground when he defends the infliction of pain upon animals on the plea that he is procuring healthy excitement for himself. Still less defensible is the torture which is commonly inflicted without any plea of utility or amusement, for the mere purposes of fastidious luxury. If God be Love, that man will be most like God who can approach closest, and best imitate, the all-comprehensive interest which He manifests in His creatures, and the duty toward the Creator will involve some reflected duty toward all created things :—

> " He prayeth best who loveth best
> Both man and bird and beast."

We have not time to enter further into this subject, though we have done little more than touch upon it. The instances given above may be of some use in showing the method by which we must adapt the working of the one unchanging Christian principle to the various circumstances of different times. As long as we live and work in reliance upon the Holy Spirit, our work will be in harmony with the working of the world. For the Spirit will keep us in perpetual dependence upon Christ the King, who is working all things according to His will, and will prevent us from creating an independent, lifeless, and unprogressive law. Surrounded by violence, ignorance, and vice, the Spirit can make a way triumphing over evil, attracting all that is good; then only hindered, if ever hindered, when we attempt to help and patronize. A falling Rome, and an empire inundated by barbarians, could not destroy the Church. The waters might rise above the highest peaks: philosophy and art might be submerged: but, rise as it might, the deluge only raised higher the floating Ark that contained the hopes of all the world. It is in endeavouring to help the operations and define the teaching of the Spirit by narrow rules that our real danger lies. By ignoring the ties of home and country, the researches of criticism, the results of social and political experience, and the discoveries of natural science, we are virtually saying to the Holy Spirit, "Thus far shalt thou breathe, and no farther." Too often, in the attempt to construct a temple made by human hands for the habitation of the Spirit, men have succeeded in making nothing but a tomb. The Spirit has refused to breathe the oppressive air shut in by hard rules and dogmas, and has wandered freely forth, inspiring the hearts of those in every nation and rank of life who think for themselves, and say nothing but what they mean. Let us thank God that it is so; for here we have a guarantee that the Spirit of Christ is quite independent of our imperfect forms of Christianity. The Churches of Rome and England may cease to exist as distinct institutions; but the Church of Christ will exist as long as two or three are gathered together living and working in the Christian spirit.

QUESTIONS.

Chapter I. Lesson 1.

1. What is meant by "knowing Jesus"? Why is it desirable that we should know something of the times of Christ? Illustrate the latter part of your answer by instances.

2. How was (*a*) the Jewish people, (*b*) the Roman empire, prepared for Christ's coming?

3. Who were the "Galileans"? Write an imaginary speech by Judas of Galilee, calling on his countrymen to take up arms against the Romans.

Chapter I. Lesson 2.

1. Show the incompleteness of the deliverances effected by all the patriots of Judæa or Israel before the time of our Lord.

2. What arguments might be alleged against the patriotic desire to take up arms for the expulsion of the Romans?

3. Who were the Essenes? Why did they exercise less influence than the Pharisees?

Chapter I. Lesson 3.

1. What motives led the Pharisees to multiply comments on the law, and the Sadducees to retain the law as it stood?

2. What is the testimony of Josephus to the virtues and to the faults of the Pharisees?

3. What difficulty is there in determining the date of many portions of Rabbinical literature, and, consequently, the influence which may have been exerted upon that literature by Christianity?

Chapter I. Lesson 4.

1. Mention facts which show the weakness and unspiritual indiscrimination perceptible in the Rabbinical teaching.

2. What was the "hypocrisy" of the Pharisees? Why was their sin greater than that of "the sinners"?

3. Show that none of the Jewish sects contained the elements sufficient to regenerate the Jewish people.

Chapter II. Lesson 1.

1. Show (*a*) that it was probable that Jesus would be regarded as a Prophet, (*b*) that He was so regarded when He first proclaimed the kingdom of God.

2. Illustrate from the ancient history of Israel the distinction between baptism by fire and baptism by water.

3. Compare the preaching of John the Baptist with that of Isaiah or any other Prophet of the Old Testament.

Chapter II. Lesson 2.

1. How far may we regard the temptations of Jesus as similar to ours; how far must we regard them as different?

2. Point out the connection between the Baptism and the Temptations.

3. Of what nature was the temptation to turn stones into bread?

Chapter II. Lesson 3.

1. Of what nature was the temptation to worship Satan?

2. Of what nature was the temptation to leap down from the pinnacle of the Temple?

3. (*a*) In what respects was Jesus like, and (*b*) in what respects was He unlike, the ancient Prophets in the manner in which He proclaimed the kingdom of God?

CHAPTER II. LESSON 4.

1. Of what nature was the kingdom of God, and what was the law which regulated the relations of subject to sovereign, and subject to subject?

2. Can you reconcile the precept, "Turn to him the other cheek also" with "And if he neglect to hear them, let him be unto thee as a heathen or a publican"?

3. By what means were the disciples of Jesus enabled to obey His precepts? How does this distinguish Jesus from the ancient Prophets?

CHAPTER II. LESSON 5.

1. Why did Jesus resort to the parabolic method of teaching? Give His own reason, and explain it.

2. What difference is observable between the subject-matter of the first and of the last Parables?

3. "What went ye out for to see?" Give the context, and explain it.

CHAPTER II. LESSON 6.

1. Account for the constant mention of the subject of divorce in the New Testament.

2. "He must be raised again the third day." Illustrate from these words the difference between Jesus and the ancient Prophets.

3. What allusions does Jesus make to the Gentiles in the first three Gospels?

CHAPTER II. LESSON 7.

1. Trace the metaphorical expressions which describe the punishment of the wicked in the New Testament back to the Old Testament.

2. What is the origin of the word Gehenna or Hell? Trace the meaning of the word to its origin.

3. Who were spoken of by Jesus as liable to Gehenna or Hell?

Chapter II. Lesson 8.

1. "Suppose ye that I am come to give peace on earth? I tell you, Nay: but rather division." Explain this. Illustrate it by the experience of life.

2. Show that Jesus did "send division."

3. Why is the "coming of the Son of Man" associated with the fall of Jerusalem?

Chapter II. Lesson 9.

1. "There be some standing here which shall not taste of death till they see the Son of man coming in his kingdom." Explain this fully.

2. What is the difficulty connected with "eternal punishment"? Explain in your answer the difference between torture and punishment.

3. Reconcile together "We have found the Messias" and "Flesh and blood hath not revealed it unto thee, but my Father which is in heaven."

Chapter II. Lesson 10.

1. Why did not Jesus tell people that He was the Christ?

2. Why did Jesus attach such great importance to the confession of St. Peter?

3. Give a brief review of the life and success of Jesus as it might have appeared on the evening of the Lord's Supper from a worldly point of view.

Chapter II. Lesson 11.

1. Give an account of the Lord's Supper regarded as a Testament or Will.

2. Illustrate the Agony of our Lord from the Epistle to the Hebrews. Why is it our duty to try to apprehend something of the meaning of His Agony?

3. Why must the Agony of Jesus have consisted of something more than the mere fear of humiliation or pain? What was this "something more"?

CHAPTER II. LESSON 12.

1. Is it correct to say that "God was angry with Jesus for our sakes"?

2. "My God, my God, why hast thou forsaken me?" Explain this as fully as you can, quoting the Psalm from which the words appear to be extracted.

3. How might the death and temporary absence of Jesus prepare His Apostles to understand Him?

CHAPTER II. LESSON 13.

1. Compare and contrast Jesus of Nazareth with any of the ancient Prophets, illustrating your answer by the Epistle to the Hebrews.

CHAPTER III. LESSON 1.

1. What is the word by which St. John expresses a "miracle"? What question is suggested by this word?

2. Are we to believe the truth of any teacher who can work miracles?

3. What connection is there between healing the body and the soul? Illustrate your answer by reference to the cure of the "sick of the palsy," and to the Books of the Old Testament, Deuteronomy for instance.

CHAPTER III. LESSON 2.

1. Of what were Christ's miracles signs?
2. Why did Christ work miracles?
3. "He *could* there do no mighty work." Explain this.

Chapter III. Lesson 3.

1. What prophecy connected the healing of the diseased with the kingdom of God? Show that our Lord, when He sent His Apostles on their mission, recognized this connection.

2. It has been objected against the truth of the narratives of "possession" in the first three Gospels, that no such narratives are found in the fourth Gospel. Meet this objection.

3. Why are miracles not worked now?

Chapter III. Lesson 4.

1. Why did not Jesus give the Jews a sign from heaven?

2. What do you mean by a "law of nature"?

3. How would you answer the objection that Christ's miracles are against the laws of nature?

4. In what sense may it be said that Christ's miracles were natural?

Chapter IV. Lesson 1.

1. Show that Christ's sacrifice was not confined to His death.

2. Show that Christ's life must have been a life of intense pain.

3. Show how Christ's sacrifice is an *atonement* for us.

Chapter IV. Lesson 2.

1. In what consisted the superiority of Christ's sacrifice above the sacrifice of any other man who ever devoted himself to live and die for his fellow-men? Illustrate by reference to historical acts of self-devotion.

Chapter V. Lesson 1.

1. Why may we love bad men in spite of their bad deeds, and yet we may not hate good men in spite of their good deeds?

2. In what sense of the word *nature* are men sinful by *nature?* In what sense is it the *nature* of men to be righteous? Illustrate carefully the double meaning of *nature*.

3. Did the heathen before the time of Christ ever do any good actions? In your answer, comment upon the words of St. Paul, "In ourselves, that is in our flesh, dwelleth no good thing."

Chapter V. Lesson 2.

1. Show that philanthropy is not only a fulfilment of Christ's precepts, but also a natural consequence of Christianity.
2. How ought we to feel towards Nero?
3. "He knew what was in men." Show from this passage, and from the ordinary experience of life, that every man has something in him worth loving.

Chapter VI. Lesson 1.

1. Show that the remission of a penalty does not necessarily imply forgiveness.
2. Why is remission of punishment often considered identical with forgiveness?
3. Mention some of the requisites for performing the operation of forgiveness.

Chapter VI. Lesson 2.

1. Point out the connection between forgiveness and the "imputation of righteousness."
2. Show that the "imputation of righteousness" between man and man is not based upon a fiction.
3. Can we forgive unrepentant offenders? What ought to be our feeling toward them?

Chapter VI. Lesson 3.

1. Distinguish between vindictiveness, anger, and resentment.
2. Is resentment consistent with forgiveness?
3. Under what conditions is it possible to forgive and punish at the same time?

Chapter VI. Lesson 4.

1. Show the connection between the law of forgiveness and the law of sacrifice, and hence show that Christ alone could forgive men perfectly.

2. Show that faith is necessary for him who desires to receive forgiveness from a fellow-man. Faith in what?

3. In what sense can our faith be called a *condition* of God's forgiveness?

4. Show the natural connection between forgiving and being forgiven.

Chapter VII. Lesson 1.

1. Point out the difference between (1) the faith of the heathen idolaters, (2) the faith of the men of Israel, (3) the Christian faith in Christ.

2. In what sense may it be said that all faith has tended to Christ, even the faith of those who were born before the Christian era?

3. Point out the real similarity between the faith of the Syro-Phœnician woman and the faith that we ought to have.

Chapter VII. Lesson 2.

1. Show the naturalness of the influence exerted on morality by faith in Christ, and show that faith in Christ is not a mere speculative theory.

2. How ought our faith in Christ to affect our faith in our fellow-men? Illustrate from Shakespeare's *Timon of Athens.*

3. How will faith in Christ influence our views of sin and death?

Chapter VII. Lesson 3.

1. Show that faith in Christ ought to produce firmness of mind and constancy in us.

2. Reconcile together St. Paul's dictum that we are "justified by faith without works" and St. James' that "faith without works is dead."

3. "If ye have faith as a grain of mustard-seed, ye shall say to this mountain, Be thou removed and cast into the midst of the sea, and it shall be done." Explain this.

4. What are the three sources of our belief in Christ? Show by reference to the words of Christ, and by other proof, that faith in Him is not a mere intellectual assent to the truth of the Gospel narrative.

CHAPTER VIII. LESSON 1.

1. What objection can be urged against the utility of prayer derived from the prescience of God? How would you meet the objection?

2. With what other precept did Christ connect the precept to pray? What inference do you draw from this as to the utility of prayer?

3. What rule may we infer concerning prayer to God from the analogy of a child's prayers to its human parent?

CHAPTER VIII. LESSON 2.

1. What difficulty attends the words "Whensoever two or three of you shall agree touching anything that ye shall pray for, it shall be done"? Explain it.

2. In what circumstances is a prayer for fair weather justifiable?

3. Is sincere prayer ever wasted?

CHAPTER VIII. LESSON 3.

1. Show that a prayer which may be right in one period and nation may be wrong in another.

2. What argument may those who believe in a good and all-powerful God draw in favour of the lawfulness of prayer, from its universality and its moral utility?

[CHAPTER IX. LESSON 1.]

[1. Why is not almsgiving a sacrament?]

[2. Distinguish between the case apparently alluded to by Christ in

His discourse to Nicodemus and the case of those who decline or defer baptism on conscientious grounds.]

[3. What arguments may be urged for and against infant baptism?[1]]

[CHAPTER IX. LESSON 2.]

[1. What common point of agreement is there in all Christian theories about the Sacrament of the Lord's Supper?]

[2. Who is a "worthy" communicant? Who "unworthy"?]

[3. What is implied by the name "Communion" applied to the Lord's Supper?]

CHAPTER X. LESSON 1.

1. When, and why, do we speak of the Spirit of God instead of God?

2. How do you reconcile the statement that the Holy Ghost or Spirit was not given till Jesus was glorified with the mention of the Spirit of God in the books of the Old Testament?

3. Why were the disciples unprepared to receive the Spirit till Christ was taken from them?

CHAPTER X. LESSON 2.

1. What difficulties attend that explanation of the Pentecostal gift of tongues which supposes that the tongues were the spoken languages of the time?

2. What was the spiritual meaning of the manifestation of the Holy Spirit on the day of Pentecost? Explain it fully.

3. Distinguish between this manifestation and the manifestation to Elijah.

CHAPTER X. LESSON 3.

1. What was the spiritual meaning of the imposition of hands?

2. What would be the advantages, and what the disadvantages, if we could find in the Bible the exact solution of every question that suggests itself in modern life?

3. How would you meet the objection that Christianity is a very imperfect scheme of morality?

[1] See Preface.

Chapter X. Lesson 4.

1. Is calamity in itself a purifying agent?
2. Show that the Holy Spirit often produces a painful feeling on our hearts. Why?
3. How has the Holy Spirit modified (*a*) our morality, (*b*) our thoughts about the visible world, (*c*) our knowledge of science?

Chapter XI. Lesson 1.

1. Give a brief sketch of the spiritual process of redemption, as described by St. Paul?
2. In what senses does St. Paul use the words *nature, flesh,* and *this world*?
3. Why was it important to show that Christ's Sacrifice was pre-ordained before the foundation of the world?

Chapter XI. Lesson 2.

1. "Hath not the potter power over the clay?" Give the context and explain the argument.
2. In what technical sense does St. Paul use the word "righteousness"?
3. Show by examples that St. Paul treats less of the individual than of the collective body of mankind. How does St. Paul meet such difficulties as the existence of sin?

Chapter XII. Lesson 1.

1. Show by instances that the precepts of the Sermon on the Mount are not to be obeyed as a *law*, and that we must not look for a *law* in the Gospel.
2. What duties are brought into prominence, and what are kept in the background, in the New Testament? Why?
3. What duty is implied by the word "calling" applied to a man's occupation?

Chapter XII. Lesson 2.

1. Why has a man no right to over-work himself?
2. What is "the law of habit"? What is our duty as regards habits?
3. Compare the Greek and Roman standard of duty towards parents with the English standard. Why is it natural that in warlike nations the duty towards the parent should assume almost excessive proportions?

Chapter XII. Lesson 3.

1. Show that the duty of parents to their children includes provision for their education.
2. Why is patriotism and public spirit not inculcated in the New Testament?
3. Illustrate our inferiority to the ancient Greeks and Romans in all that relates to public duties.

Chapter XII. Lesson 4.

1. Point out the evil consequences of a low standard of public duty.
2. What is the origin of our undue respect for wealth?
3. With what qualifications must we accept the precept "Do to others as ye would that they should do to you"?

Chapter XII. Lesson 5.

1. Show how the laws of a country may sometimes exercise a disturbing influence in Christian morality.
2. Show that we have a duty to perform toward animals.
3. In what danger are we placed of attempting to limit the operation of the Holy Spirit?

August, 1870.
16, BEDFORD STREET, COVENT GARDEN.
London.

MACMILLAN AND CO.'S
THEOLOGICAL WORKS.

Ainger.—Sermons preached in the Temple Church.
By the Rev. ALFRED AINGER, M.A., of Trinity Hall, Cambridge, Reader at the Temple Church. Extra fcap. 8vo. 6s.
> Twenty-four Sermons:—Our Views of Heaven; Rest in Christ the True Communion of Saints; the Resurrection a Fact of History; Culture and Temptation; the Religious Aspect of Wit and Humour; the Life of the Ascended Christ, etc., etc.

Bernard.—The Progress of Doctrine in the New Testament. In Eight Lectures preached before the University of Oxford. By THOMAS D. BERNARD, M.A., Rector of Walcot. *Second Edition.* 8vo. 8s. 6d.

Binney.—Sermons preached in the King's Weigh House Chapel, 1829—1869. By THOMAS BINNEY, D.D. *New and Cheaper Edition.* Extra fcap. 8vo. 4s. 6d.

Birks.—The Difficulties of Belief in connexion with the Creation and the Fall. By T. R. BIRKS, M.A., Perpetual Curate of Holy Trinity, Cambridge. Crown 8vo. 4s. 6d.

Book of Praise Hymnal, compiled and arranged by Sir ROUNDELL PALMER.
 A — Royal 32mo., limp cloth. 6d.
 B — Small 18mo., larger type, limp cloth. 1s.
 C — Same Edition on fine paper, 18mo., cloth. 1s. 6d.
Also an Edition with Music, selected, harmonized, and composed by JOHN HULLAH. Square 18mo., cloth. 3s. 6d.

Burgon.—A Treatise on the Pastoral Office.
Addressed chiefly to Candidates for Holy Orders, or to those who have recently undertaken the cure of souls. By the Rev. JOHN W. BURGON, M.A., Oxford. 8vo. 12s.

Butler (G).—Sermons preached in Cheltenham College Chapel. By the Rev. GEO. BUTLER, M.A., Principal of Liverpool College. Crown 8vo. 7s. 6d.

— Family Prayers. By the Rev. G. BUTLER, M.A. Crown 8vo. 5s.

Butler (H. M).—Sermons preached in the Chapel of Harrow School. By H. MONTAGUE BUTLER, Head Master. Crown 8vo. 7s. 6d.

— A Second Series. Crown 8vo. 7s. 6d.

Butler.—Works by the Rev. WM. ARCHER BUTLER, M.A., late Professor of Moral Philosophy in the University of Dublin:—

— Sermons, Doctrinal and Practical.
Edited, with a Memoir of the Author's Life, by T. WOODWARD, M.A., Dean of Down. With Portrait. *Eighth and Cheaper Edition.* 8vo. 8s.

— A Second Series of Sermons.
Edited by J. A. JEREMIE, D.D., Regius Professor of Divinity in the University of Cambridge. *Fifth and Cheaper Edition.* 8vo. 7s.

— Letters on Romanism, in Reply to Mr. Newman's Essay on Development. Edited by T. WOODWARD, M.A., Dean of Down. 8vo. 10s. 6d.

Calderwood.—Philosophy of the Infinite.
A Treatise on Man's Knowledge of the Infinite Being, in answer to Sir W. Hamilton and Dr. Mansel. By the Rev. HENRY CALDERWOOD, M.A. *Second Edition.* 8vo. 14s.
"A book of great ability...... written in a clear style and may be easily understood by even those who are not versed in such discussions."—*British Quarterly Review.*

Cambridge Lent Sermons.—Sermons preached during Lent, 1864, in Great St. Mary's Church, Cambridge. By the BISHOP of OXFORD, Rev. H. P. LIDDON, T. L. CLAUGHTON, J. R. WOODFORD, Dr. GOULBURN, J. W. BURGON, T. T. CARTER, Dr. PUSEY, DEAN HOOK, W. J. BUTLER, DEAN GOODWIN. Crown 8vo. 7s. 6d.

Campbell.—The Nature of the Atonement and its Relation to Remission of Sins and Eternal Life. By JOHN M'LEOD CAMPBELL. *Third Edition, revised.* 8vo. 10s. 6d.

— Thoughts on Revelation, with special reference to the Present Time. By JOHN M'LEOD CAMPBELL. Crown 8vo. 5s.

— Christ the Bread of Life. An Attempt to give a profitable direction to the present occupation of Thought with Romanism. By J. M'LEOD CAMPBELL, D.D. *Second Edition, much enlarged.* Crown 8vo. 4s. 6d.

Challis.—Creation in Plan and in Progress: being an Essay on the First Chapter of Genesis. By the Rev. JAMES CHALLIS, M.A., F.R.S., F.R.A.S. Cr. 8vo. 3s. 6d.

Choice Notes on the Gospels, drawn from Old and New Sources. 4 vols. crown 8vo. 4s. 6d. each. St. Matthew and St. Mark in one vol., price 9s.

Cheyne.—Notes and Criticisms on the Hebrew Text
of ISAIAH. By the Rev. T. K. CHEYNE, M.A., Fellow of
Balliol College, Oxford. 8vo. 2s. 6d.
A critical discussion of about 50 passages in Isaiah, some probably corrupt, and all more or less obscure, together with a re-examination of the ancient interpreters, and a few fresh illustrations from MSS. in the Bodleian Library.

— The Book of Isaiah Chronologically Arranged.
An Amended Version, with Historical and Critical Introductions
and Explanatory Notes. By T. K. CHEYNE, M.A., Fellow of
Balliol College, Oxford. Crown 8vo. 7s. 6d.
The object of this edition is simply to restore the probable meaning of Isaiah, so far as this can be expressed in modern English. The basis of the version is the revised translation of 1611, but no scruple has been felt in introducing alterations, wherever the true sense of the prophecies appeared to require it.

Chretien.—The Letter and the Spirit.
Six Sermons on the Inspiration of Holy Scripture. By
CHARLES P. CHRETIEN. Crown 8vo. 5s.

Church.—Sermons preached before the University
of Oxford. By R. W. CHURCH, M.A., late Fellow of Oriel
College, Rector of Whatley. *Second Edition.* Cr. 8vo. 4s. 6d.

Clark.—Four Sermons preached in the Chapel of
Trinity College, Cambridge. By W. G. CLARK, M.A., Public
Orator in the University of Cambridge. Fcap. 8vo. 2s. 6d.

Clay.—The Power of the Keys. Sermons preached
in Coventry. By the Rev. W. L. CLAY, M.A. Fcp. 8vo. 3s. 6d.

Clergyman's Self-Examination concerning the Apostles' Creed. Extra fcap. 8vo. 1s. 6d.

Colenso.—Works by the Right Rev. J. W. COLENSO,
D.D., Bishop of Natal:—

— Village Sermons. *Seventh Edition.* Fcap. 8vo. 2s. 6d.

— Companion to the Holy Communion.
Containing the Service, and Select Readings from the writings
of Mr. MAURICE. 18mo. 1s.

Cotton.—Works by the late GEORGE EDWARD LYNCH
COTTON, D.D., Bishop of Calcutta:—

— Sermons, chiefly connected with Public Events
of 1854. Fcap. 8vo. 3s.

— Expository Sermons on the Epistles for the
Sundays of the Christian Year. Two Vols. Crown 8vo. 15s.

— Sermons preached to English Congregations
in India. Crown 8vo. 7s. 6d.

— Sermons and Addresses delivered in Marlborough College during Six Years. Crown 8vo. 10s. 6d.

Cure.—The Seven Words of Christ on the Cross.
Sermons preached at St. George's, Bloomsbury. By E. CAPEL CURE, M.A. Fcap. 8vo. 3s. 6d.

Davies.—Works by the Rev. J. LL. DAVIES, M.A., Rector of Christ Church, St. Marylebone.

— The Work of Christ; or the World Reconciled to God. With a Preface on the Atonement Controversy. Fcp. 8vo. 6s.

— Sermons on the Manifestation of the Son of God. With a Preface addressed to Laymen on the present position of the Clergy of the Church of England; and an Appendix on the Testimony of Scripture and the Church as to the possibility of Pardon in the Future State. Fcap. 8vo. 6s. 6d.

— Baptism, Confirmation, and the Lord's Supper, as interpreted by their Outward Signs. Three Expository Addresses for Parochial use. Fcap. 8vo., limp cloth, 1s. 6d.

— The Epistles of St. Paul to the Ephesians, the Colossians, and Philemon. With Introductions and Notes, and an Essay on the Traces of Foreign Elements in the Theology of these Epistles. 8vo. 7s. 6d.

— Morality according to the Sacrament of the Lord's Supper. Crown 8vo. 3s. 6d.

— The Gospel and Modern Life. Sermons on some of the Difficulties of the Present Day, with a Preface on the Theology of "The Pall Mall Gazette." Extra Fcp. 8vo. 6s.

De Teissier.—Works by G. F. DE TEISSIER, B.D.:

— Village Sermons. Crown 8vo. 9s.

— Second Series. Crown 8vo. 8s. 6d.

— The House of Prayer; or, a Practical Exposition of the Order for Morning and Evening Prayer in the Church of England. 18mo. extra cloth, 4s. 6d.

Donaldson.—A Critical History of Christian Literature and Doctrine, from the Death of the Apostles to the Nicene Council. By JAMES DONALDSON, LL.D. 3 vols. 8vo. cloth, 31s. 6d.

Ecce Homo.—A Survey of the Life and Work of Jesus Christ. *Tenth Edition.* Crown 8vo. 6s.

Eastwood.—The Bible Word Book.
A Glossary of Old English Bible Words. By J. EASTWOOD, M.A., of St. John's College, and W. ALDIS WRIGHT, M.A., Trinity College, Cambridge. 18mo. 5s. 6d.

Farrar.—The Fall of Man, and other Sermons.
By the Rev. F. W. FARRAR, M.A., late Fellow of Trinity College, Cambridge. Fcap. 8vo. 6*s.*

Forbes.—Village Sermons by a Northamptonshire Rector. With a Preface on the Inspiration of Holy Scripture. Crown 8vo. 6*s.*

— The Voice of God in the Psalms. By GRANVILLE FORBES, Rector of Broughton. Crown 8vo. 6*s.* 6*d.*

Gifford.—The Glory of God in Man.
By E. H. GIFFORD, D.D. Fcap. 8vo. cloth, 3*s.* 6*d.*

Golden Treasury Psalter. *The Student's Edition.*
Being an Edition with Briefer Notes of "The Psalms Chronologically Arranged by Four Friends." 18mo. 3*s.* 6*d.*

In making this abridgement of "The Psalms Chronologically Arranged" the Editors have endeavoured to meet the requirements of readers of a different class from those for whom the larger edition was intended.
Some, who found the large book useful for private reading, have asked for an edition of a smaller size and at a lower price for family use, while at the same time some Teachers in Public Schools have suggested that it would be convenient to them to have a simpler book, which they could put into the hands of younger pupils.

Hardwick.—Works by the Ven. ARCHDEACON HARDWICK:—

— Christ and other Masters. A Historical Inquiry into some of the Chief Parallelisms and Contrasts between Christianity and the Religious Systems of the Ancient World. *New Edition,* revised, and a Prefatory Memoir by the Rev. FRANCIS PROCTER. Two vols. crown 8vo. 15*s.*

— A History of the Christian Church.
MIDDLE AGE. From Gregory the Great to the Excommunication of Luther. Edited by FRANCIS PROCTER, M.A. With Four Maps constructed for this work by A. KEITH JOHNSTON. *Second Edition.* Crown 8vo. 10*s.* 6*d.*

— A History of the Christian Church during the REFORMATION. Revised by FRANCIS PROCTER, M.A. *Second Edition.* Crown 8vo. 10*s.* 6*d.*

— Twenty Sermons for Town Congregations.
Crown 8vo. 6*s.* 6*d.*

Howard.—The Pentateuch; or, the Five Books of Moses. Translated into English from the Version of the LXX. With Notes on its Omissions and Insertions, and also on the Passages in which it differs from the Authorized Version. By the Hon. HENRY HOWARD, D.D., Dean of Lichfield. Crown 8vo. GENESIS, 1 vol. 8*s.* 6*d.*; EXODUS and LEVITICUS, 1 vol. 10*s.* 6*d.*; NUMBERS and DEUTERONOMY, 1 vol. 10*s.* 6*d.*

Hervey.—The Genealogies of our Lord and Saviour
Jesus Christ, as contained in the Gospels of St. Matthew and
St. Luke, reconciled with each other, and shown to be in harmony with the true Chronology of the Times. By Lord
ARTHUR HERVEY, M.A. 8vo. 10s. 6d.

Hymni Ecclesiæ.—Fcap. 8vo. cloth. 7s. 6d.

Jameson.—Works by the Rev. F. J. JAMESON, M.A.

— Life's Work, in Preparation and in Retrospect.
Sermons preached before the University of Cambridge. Fcap.
8vo. 1s. 6d.

— Brotherly Counsels to Students.
Sermons preached in the Chapel of St. Catharine's College,
Cambridge. Fcap. 8vo. 1s. 6d.

Jones.—The Church of England and Common
Sense. By HARRY JONES, M.A. Fcap. 8vo. cloth, 3s. 6d.

Kingsbury.—Spiritual Sacrifice and Holy Communion. By T. L. KINGSBURY, M.A. Seven Sermons,
with Notes. Fcap. 8vo. 3s. 6d.

Kingsley.—Works by the Rev. CHARLES KINGSLEY,
M.A., Rector of Eversley, and Canon of Chester.

— Good News of God. *Fourth Edition.* Fcap. 8vo. 4s. 6d.

— Village Sermons. *Seventh Edition.* Fcap. 8vo. 2s. 6d.

— The Gospel of the Pentateuch.
Second Edition. Fcap. 8vo. 4s. 6d.

— Sermons for the Times.
Third Edition. Fcap. 8vo. 3s. 6d.

— DAVID.   Four Sermons.
David's Weakness—David's Strength—David's Anger—David's
Deserts. Fcap. 8vo. 2s. 6d.

— Sermons on National Subjects.
First Series. *Second Edition.* Fcap. 8vo. 5s.

— Sermons on National Subjects.
Second Series. *Second Edition.* Fcap. 8vo. 5s.

— The Water of Life, and other Sermons.
Fcap. 8vo. 6s.

— Discipline, and other Sermons. Fcap. 8vo. 6s.

— Town and Country Sermons.
Second Edition. Extra Fcap. 8vo. 6s.

Lightfoot.—Works by J. B. LIGHTFOOT, D.D.,
Hulsean Professor of Divinity in the University of Cambridge:

— St. Paul's Epistle to the Galatians.
A Revised Text, with Notes and Dissertations. *Third Edition, revised.* 8vo. cloth, 12s.

— St. Paul's Epistle to the Philippians.
A Revised Text, with Notes and Dissertations. 8vo. 12s. *Second Edition.*

— S. Clement of Rome. The Two Epistles to the Corinthians. With Introduction and Notes. 8vo. 8s. 6d.

Luckock.—The Tables of Stone. Sermons preached in All Saints' Church, Cambridge, by H. M. LUCKOCK, M.A., Vicar. Fcap. 8vo. 3s. 6d.

Maclaren.—Sermons preached at Manchester.
By ALEXANDER MACLAREN. *Third Edition.* Fcp. 8vo. 4s. 6d.

— A Second Series of Sermons. Fcap. 8vo. 4s. 6d.

Mackenzie.—The Christian Clergy of the First Ten Centuries, and their Influence on European Civilization. By HENRY MACKENZIE, B.A., Scholar of Trinity College, Cambridge. Crown 8vo. 6s. 6d.

M'Cosh.—Works by JAMES M'COSH, LL.D., Principal of Princeton College, New Jersey, U.S.:—

— The Method of the Divine Government, Physical and Moral. *Ninth Edition.* 8vo. 10s. 6d.

— The Supernatural in relation to the Natural.
Crown 8vo. 7s. 6d.

— The Intuitions of the Mind.
A New Edition. 8vo. cloth, 10s. 6d.

Maclear.—Works by G. F. MACLEAR, B.D., Head Master of King's College School, and Preacher at the Temple Church:—

— A History of Christian Missions during the Middle Ages. Crown 8vo. 10s. 6d.

— The Witness of the Eucharist; or, The Institution and Early Celebration of the Lord's Supper, considered as an Evidence of the Historical Truth of the Gospel Narrative and of the Atonement. Crown 8vo. 4s. 6d.

— A Class-Book of Old Testament History.
With Four Maps. *Fifth Edition.* 18mo. 4s. 6d.

Maclear (G. F.)—A Class-Book of New Testament History. Including the Connexion of the Old and New Testament. *Third Edition.* 18mo. 5s. 6d.

— A Class-Book of the Catechism of the Church of England. *Second Edition.* 18mo. cloth. 2s. 6d.

— A Shilling Book of Old Testament History. 18mo. cloth limp. 1s.

— A Shilling Book of New Testament History. 18mo. cloth limp. 1s.

— A First Class-Book of the Catechism of the Church of England, with Scripture Proofs for Junior Classes and Schools. 18mo. 6d.

— The Order of Confirmation. A Sequel to the Class-Book of the Church Catechism, with Notes, and suitable Devotions. 18mo. 3d.

Marriner.—Sermons preached at Lyme Regis. By E. T. MARRINER, Curate. Fcap. 8vo. 4s. 6d.

Maurice.—Works by the Rev. FREDERICK DENISON MAURICE, M.A., Professor of Casuistry and Moral Philosophy in the University of Cambridge:—

— The Claims of the Bible and of Science; a Correspondence on some questions respecting the Pentateuch. Crown 8vo. 4s. 6d.

— Dialogues on Family Worship. Crown 8vo. 6s.

— The Patriarchs and Lawgivers of the Old Testament. *Third and Cheaper Edition.* Crown 8vo. 5s.
This volume contains Discourses on the Pentateuch, Joshua, Judges, and the beginning of the First Book of Samuel.

— The Prophets and Kings of the Old Testament. *Second Edition.* Crown 8vo. 10s. 6d.
This volume contains Discourses on Samuel I. and II., Kings I. and II., Amos, Joel, Hosea, Isaiah, Micah, Nahum, Habakkuk, Jeremiah, and Ezekiel.

— The Gospel of the Kingdom of Heaven. A Series of Lectures on the Gospel of St. Luke. Crown 8vo. 9s.

— The Gospel of St. John: a Series of Discourses. *Third and Cheaper Edition.* Crown 8vo. 6s.

— The Epistles of St. John: a Series of Lectures on Christian Ethics. *Second and Cheaper Edition.* Cr. 8vo. 6s.

— The Commandments considered as Instruments of National Reformation. Crown 8vo. 4s. 6d.

Maurice.—Expository Sermons on the Prayer-Book. The Prayer-Book considered especially in reference to the Romish System. *Second Edition.* Fcap. 8vo. 5s. 6d.

— Lectures on the Apocalypse; or, Book of the Revelation of St. John the Divine. Crown 8vo. 10s. 6d.

— What is Revelation? A Series of Sermons on the Epiphany, to which are added Letters to a Theological Student on the Bampton Lectures of Mr. MANSEL. Cr. 8vo. 10s. 6d.

— Sequel to the Inquiry, "What is Revelation?" Letters in Reply to Mr. Mansel's Examination of "Strictures on the Bampton Lectures." Crown 8vo. 6s.

— Lectures on Ecclesiastical History. 8vo. 10s. 6d.

— Theological Essays. *Second Edition.* Cr. 8vo. 10s. 6d.

— The Doctrine of Sacrifice Deduced from the Scriptures. Crown 8vo. 7s. 6d.

— The Religions of the World, and their Relations to Christianity. *Fourth Edition.* Fcap. 8vo. 5s.

— On the Lord's Prayer. *4th Edition.* Fcp. 8vo. 2s. 6d.

— On the Sabbath Day: the Character of the Warrior; and on the Interpretation of History. Fcp. 8vo. 2s. 6d.

— Learning and Working. Six Lectures on the Foundation of Colleges for Working Men. Crown 8vo. 5s.

— The Ground and Object of Hope for Mankind. Four Sermons preached before the University of Cambridge. Crown 8vo. 3s. 6d.

— The Conscience. Lectures on Casuistry delivered before the University of Cambridge. 8vo. 8s. 6d.

— Social Morality. Twenty-one Lectures delivered in the University of Cambridge. 8vo. 14s.

Moorhouse.—Works by JAMES MOORHOUSE, M.A., Vicar of Paddington, Middlesex:—

— Some Modern Difficulties respecting the Facts of Nature and Revelation. Fcap. 8vo. 2s. 6d.

— Our Lord Jesus Christ the subject of Growth in Wisdom. Four Sermons (being the Hulsean Lectures for 1865) preached before the University of Cambridge; to which is added Three Sermons preached before the University of Cambridge in February 1864. Crown 8vo. 5s.

— Jacob. Three Sermons preached before the University of Cambridge in Lent, 1870. Fcap. 8vo. 3s. 6d.

Morse.—Working for God, and other Practical Sermons. By FRANCIS MORSE, M.A. *Second Edition.* Fcap. 8vo. 5s.

O'Brien.—Works by JAMES THOMAS O'BRIEN, D.D., Bishop of Ossory:—

— An Attempt to Explain and Establish the Doctrine of Justification by Faith only. *Third Edition.* 8vo. 12s.

— Charge delivered at the Visitation in 1863. *Second Edition.* 8vo. 2s.

— Vindication of the Irish Clergy. 8vo. 2s. 6d.

— Charge delivered in 1866. 8vo. 2s.

Plea for a New English Version of the Scriptures. By a LICENTIATE of the Church of Scotland. 8vo. 6s.

Potter.—A Voice from the Church in Australia: Sermons preached in Melbourne. By the Rev. ROBERT POTTER, M.A. Extra fcap. 8vo. 4s. 6d.

Prescott.—The Threefold Cord. Sermons preached before the University of Cambridge, by J. E. PRESCOTT, B.D. Fcap. 8vo. 3s. 6d.

Procter.—A History of the Book of Common Prayer: with a Rationale of its Offices. By FRANCIS PROCTER, M.A. *Eighth Edition*, revised and enlarged. Crn. 8vo. 10s. 6d.

> In the course of the last twenty years the whole question of liturgical knowledge has been reopened with great learning and accurate research, and it is mainly with the view of epitomizing their extensive publications, and correcting by their help the errors and misconceptions which had obtained currency, that the present volume has been put together.

Procter and Maclear.—An Elementary Introduction to the Book of Common Prayer. By FRANCIS PROCTER, M.A., and G. F. MACLEAR, B.D. *Fourth Edition*, rearranged and supplemented by an explanation of the Morning and Evening Prayer and the Litany. 18mo. 2s. 6d.

Psalms (The), Chronologically Arranged. An Amended Version, with Historical Introductions and Explanatory Notes. By FOUR FRIENDS. Cr. 8vo. 10s. 6d.

Pullen.—The Psalter and Canticles, Pointed for Chanting, with Marks of Expression, and a List of Appropriate Chants. By the Rev. H. PULLEN, M.A. 8vo. 5s.

Ramsay.—The Catechiser's Manual; or, the Church Catechism Illustrated and Explained, for the use of Clergymen, Schoolmasters, and Teachers. By ARTHUR RAMSAY, M.A. *Second Edition.* 18mo. 1s. 6d.

Reynolds.—Notes of the Christian Life.
A Selection of Sermons by HENRY ROBERT REYNOLDS, B.A., President of Cheshunt College, and Fellow of University College, London. Crown 8vo. 7s. 6d.

Roberts.—Discussions on the Gospels.
By the Rev. ALEXANDER ROBERTS, D.D. *Second Edition*, revised and enlarged. 8vo. 16s.

Robertson.—Pastoral Counsels. Being Chapters on Practical and Devotional Subjects. By the Rev. JOHN ROBERTSON, D.D. *Third Edition*, with a Preface by the Author of "The Recreations of a Country Parson." Extra fcap. 8vo. 6s.

Romanis.—Sermons preached at St. Mary's, Reading.
By WILLIAM ROMANIS, M.A. *First Series.* Fcap. 8vo. 6s.

— Second Series. Fcap. 8vo. 6s.

Scott.—Discourses. By ALEXANDER J. SCOTT, M.A., Professor of Logic in Owen's College, Manchester. Cr. 8vo. 7s. 6d.

Selwyn.—The Work of Christ in the World.
By G. A. SELWYN, D.D., Bishop of Lichfield. *Third Edition.* Crown 8vo. 2s.

— Verbal Analysis of the Bible. Folio. 14s.

Sergeant.—Sermons.
By the Rev. E. W. SERGEANT, M.A., Assistant Master at Winchester College. Fcap. 8vo. 2s. 6d.

Shirley.—ELIJAH; Four University Sermons.
I. Samaria.—II. Carmel.—III. Kishon.—IV. Horeb. By W. W. SHIRLEY, D.D., late Professor of Ecclesiastical History in the University of Oxford. Fcap. 8vo. 2s. 6d.

Simpson.—An Epitome of the History of the Christian Church. By WILLIAM SIMPSON, M.A. *Fourth Edition.* Fcap. 8vo. 3s. 6d.

Smith.—Obstacles to Missionary Success among the Heathen. By W. SAUMAREZ SMITH, M.A., Fellow of Trinity College, Cambridge. (The Maitland Prize Essay for 1867). Crown 8vo. 3s. 6d.

— Christian Faith. Sermons preached before the University of Cambridge. By W. SAUMAREZ SMITH, M.A., Principal of St. Aidan's College, Birkenhead. Fcap. 8vo. 3s. 6d.

Smith.—Prophecy a Preparation for Christ.
Lectures by R. PAYNE SMITH, D.D., Regius Professor of Divinity, and Canon of Christ Church, Oxford. Being the Bampton Lectures for 1869. 8vo. 12s.

Swainson.—Works by C. A. SWAINSON, D.D.,
Norrisian Professor of Divinity at Cambridge:—

— A Handbook to Butler's Analogy.
Crown 8vo. 1s. 6d.

— The Creeds of the Church in their Relations
to Holy Scripture and the Conscience of the Christian. 8vo. 9s.

— The Authority of the New Testament, and other
Lectures, delivered before the University of Cambridge. 8vo. 12s.

Taylor.—The Restoration of Belief.
New and Revised Edition. By ISAAC TAYLOR, Esq.
Crown 8vo. 8s. 6d.

Temple.—Sermons Preached in Rugby School
Chapel in 1858, 1859, 1860. By FREDERICK TEMPLE,
D.D., Chaplain in Ordinary to her Majesty, Head Master of
Rugby School, Chaplain to the Right Hon. the Earl of Denbigh.
Third and Cheaper Edition. Extra fcap. 8vo. 4s. 6d.

Thring.—Sermons delivered at Uppingham School.
By the Rev. E. THRING, M.A., Head Master. Crown 8vo. 5s.

Thrupp.—Works by the Rev. J. F. THRUPP:—

— Introduction to the Study and use of the
Psalms. 2 vols. 8vo. 21s.

— The Burden of Human Sin as borne by Christ.
Three Sermons preached before the University of Cambridge,
Lent 1865. Crown 8vo. 3s. 6d.

— The Song of Songs. A New Translation, with
a Commentary and an Introduction. Crown 8vo. 7s. 6d.

Todd.—The Books of the Vaudois.
The Waldensian Manuscripts preserved in the Library of Trinity
College, Dublin, with an Appendix by JAMES HENTHORN
TODD, D.D., Professor of Hebrew at Dublin University.
Crown 8vo. 6s.

Tracts for Priests and People. By Various Writers.
First and Second Series. Crown 8vo. 8s. each.

— Nos. one to fifteen, sewed. 1s. each.

Trench.—Brief Notes on the Greek of the New
Testament (for English Readers). By the Rev. FRANCIS
TRENCH, M.A. Crown 8vo. cloth. 6s.

"A very useful work, enabling the unlearned reader to see at once the places
in which our translation is not quite literal or defective in force."—*Spectator.*

THEOLOGICAL WORKS.

Trench.—Works by R. CHENEVIX TRENCH, D.D., Archbishop of Dublin:—

— Notes on the Parables of our Lord.
Tenth Edition. 8vo. 12s.

— Notes on the Miracles of our Lord.
Ninth Edition. 8vo. 12s.

— Sermons preached in Westminster Abbey.
Second Edition. 8vo. 10s. 6d.

— On the Authorized Version of the New Testament. *Second Edition.* 7s.

— Commentary on the Epistles to the Seven Churches in Asia. *Third Edition, revised.* 8s. 6d.

— Synonyms of the New Testament.
New Edition. 1 vol. 8vo. 10s. 6d.

— The Fitness of Holy Scripture for Unfolding the Spiritual Life of Man; Christ the Desire of all Nations; or the Unconscious Prophecies of Heathendom. Hulsean Lectures, Fcap. 8vo. *Fourth Edition.* 5s.

— Subjection of the Creature to Vanity, and other Sermons. Fcap. 8vo. 3s.

— Studies in the Gospels. *Second Edition.* 8vo. 10s. 6d.

— Shipwrecks of Faith: Three Sermons preached before the University of Cambridge, in May, 1867. Fcap. 8vo. 2s. 6d.

— The Sermon on the Mount. An Exposition drawn from the Writings of St. Augustine, with an Essay on his merits as an Interpreter of Holy Scripture. *Third Edition, enlarged.* 8vo. 10s. 6d.

— Primary Charge. 8vo. 2s.

— Charges delivered in 1866 and 1869.
8vo. 1s. each.

Tudor.—The Decalogue Viewed as the Christian's Law, with special reference to the Questions and Wants of the Times. By the Rev. RICHARD TUDOR, B.A. Crown 8vo. 10s. 6d.

Tulloch.—The Christ of the Gospels and the Christ of Modern Criticism. Lectures on M. RENAN's "Vie de Jésus." By JOHN TULLOCH, D.D., Principal of the College of St. Mary, in the University of St. Andrew. Extra fcap. 8vo. 4s. 6d.

Vaughan.—Works by CHARLES J. VAUGHAN, D.D., Master of the Temple:—

— **Christ Satisfying the Instincts of Humanity.** Eight Lectures delivered in the Temple Church. Extra fcap. 8vo. 3s. 6d.

Eight Discourses on Christ as satisfying the several instincts of Truth, Reverence, Perfection, Liberty, Courage, Sympathy, Sacrifice, and Unity.

— **Memorials of Harrow Sundays.** A Selection of Sermons preached in Harrow School Chapel. With a View of the Chapel. *Fourth Edition.* Crown 8vo. 10s. 6d.

— **St. Paul's Epistle to the Romans.** The Greek Text, with English Notes. *Third Edition, revised and enlarged.* Crown 8vo. 7s. 6d.

— **Twelve Discourses on Subjects connected with** the Liturgy and Worship of the Church of England. Fcap. 8vo. 6s.

— **Epiphany, Lent, and Easter.** A Selection of Expository Sermons. *New Edition.* Crown 8vo. 10s. 6d.

— **Foes of Faith: Unreality, Indolence, Irrever-** ence, Inconsistency. Sermons before the University of Cambridge, November, 1868. Fcap. 8vo. 3s. 6d.

— **Lectures on the Epistle to the Philippians.** *Second Edition.* Crown 8vo. 7s. 6d.

— **The Book and the Life: and other Sermons,** Preached before the University of Cambridge. *New Edition.* Fcap. 8vo. 4s. 6d.

— **Lectures on the Revelation of St. John.** *Third and Cheaper Edition.* 2 vols. extra fcap. 8vo. 9s.

— **Life's Work and God's Discipline.** Three Sermons before the University of Cambridge in April and May, 1865. Fcap. 8vo. 2s. 6d.

— **Words from the Gospels.** A Second Selection of Sermons preached in the Parish Church of Doncaster. *Second Edition.* Fcap. 8vo. 4s. 6d.

— **Lessons of Life and Godliness.** A Selection of Sermons preached in the Parish Church of Doncaster. *Fourth and Cheaper Edition.* Extra fcap. 8vo. 3s. 6d.

— **Lessons of the Cross and Passion.** Six Lectures delivered in Hereford Cathedral during the Week before Easter, 1869. Fcap. 8vo. 2s. 6d.

Vaughan (C. J).—The Epistles of St. Paul.
For English Readers. Part I. containing the First Epistle to the Thessalonians. *Second Edition.* 8vo. 1s. 6d. (Each Epistle will be published separately.)

— The Church of the First Days:
Series I. The Church of Jerusalem. *Second Edition.*
  " II. The Church of the Gentiles. *Second Edition.*
  " III. The Church of the World. *Second Edition.*
Fcap. 8vo. 4s. 6d. each.

— The Wholesome Words of Jesus Christ.
Four Sermons preached before the University of Cambridge, in November, 1866. *Second Edition.* Fcap. 8vo. 3s. 6d.

Vaughan.—Works by DAVID J. VAUGHAN, M.A., Vicar of St. Martin's, Leicester:—

— Sermons preached in St. John's Church, Leicester, during the Years 1855 and 1856. Crown 8vo. 5s. 6d.

— Sermons on the Resurrection. With a Preface.
Fcap. 8vo. 3s.

— Christian Evidences and the Bible.
New Edition, revised and enlarged. Fcap. 8vo. cloth, 5s. 6d.

— Sermons on Sacrifice and Propitiation.
Fcap. 8vo. 2s. 6d.

Venn.—On Some of the Characteristics of Belief,
Scientific and Religious. Being the Hulsean Lectures for 1869. By J. VENN, M.A., Fellow and Lecturer of Gonville and Caius College, Cambridge. 8vo. 6s. 6d.

Warington.—The Week of Creation; or, The Cosmogony of Genesis considered in its Relation to Modern Science. By GEORGE WARINGTON, Author of "The Historic Character of the Pentateuch Vindicated." Crown 8vo. 4s. 6d.

Westcott.—Works by BROOKE FOSS WESTCOTT, B.D., Assistant Master in Harrow School:—

— A General Survey of the History of the Canon
of the New Testament during the First Four Centuries. Crown 8vo. *Third Edition in the Press.*

— Characteristics of the Gospel Miracles.
Sermons preached before the University of Cambridge. *With Notes.* Crown 8vo. 4s. 6d.

— Introduction to the Study of the Four Gospels.
Third Edition. Crown 8vo. 10s. 6d.

Westcott.—The Bible in the Church.
A Popular Account of the Collection and Reception of the Holy Scriptures in the Christian Churches. *Second Edition.* 18mo. 4s. 6d.

— The Gospel of the Resurrection:
Thoughts on its Relation to Reason and History. *New Edition.* Fcap. 8vo. 4s. 6d.

— A General View of the History of the English Bible. Crown 8vo. 10s. 6d.

— Christian Life Manifold and One. Six Sermons preached in Peterborough Cathedral. Crown 8vo. 2s. 6d.

Wilkins.—The Light of the World. An Essay.
By A. S. WILKINS, M.A., Professor of Latin in Owen's College, Manchester. Crown 8vo. 3s. 6d. *Second Edition.*

Wilson.—An English Hebrew and Chaldee Lexicon
and Concordance to the more correct understanding of the English Translation of the Old Testament, by reference to the Original Hebrew. By WILLIAM WILSON, D.D., Canon of Winchester, late Fellow of Queens' College, Oxford. *Second Edition*, carefully revised. 4to. cloth, 25s.

Wilton.—The Negeb; or, "South Country" of
Scripture. By the Rev. EDWARD WILTON, M.A., Oxon. With a Map. Crown 8vo. 7s. 6d.

Woodford.—Christian Sanctity.
By J. RUSSELL WOODFORD, M.A. Fcap. 8vo. cloth. 3s.

Woodward.—Works by the Rev. HENRY WOODWARD, M.A. Edited by his Son, THOMAS WOODWARD, M.A., Dean of Down:—

— The Shunammite.
Second Edition. Crown 8vo. cloth. 10s. 6d.

— Sermons. *Fifth Edition.* Crown 8vo. 10s. 6d.

Worship (The) of God and Fellowship among Men.
Sermons on Public Worship. By Professor MAURICE and Others. Fcap. 8vo. cloth. 3s. 6d.

Worsley.—Christian Drift of Cambridge Work.
Eight Lectures recently delivered on the Christian Bearings of Classics, Mathematics, Medicine, and Law Studies prescribed in its Charter to Downing College. By T. WORSLEY, D.D., Master of Downing College. Crown 8vo. cloth. 6s.

www.ingramcontent.com/pod-product-compliance
Lightning Source LLC
Chambersburg PA
CBHW032058220426
43664CB00008B/1055